Eureka!

The Entrepreneurial Inventor's Guide to

DEVELOPING, PROTECTING, AND PROFITING FROM YOUR IDEAS

ROBERT J. GOLD

PRENTICE HALL
Englewood Cliffs, New Jersey 07632

Prentice-Hall International (UK) Limited, *London*
Prentice-Hall of Australia Pty. Limited, *Sydney*
Prentice-Hall Canada, Inc., *Toronto*
Prentice-Hall Hispanoamericana, S.A., *Mexico*
Prentice-Hall of India Private Limited, *New Delhi*
Prentice-Hall of Japan, Inc., *Tokyo*
Simon & Schuster Asia Pte. Ltd., *Singapore*
Editora Prentice-Hall do Brasil, Ltda., *Rio de Janeiro*

10 9 8 7 6 5 4 3 2 1

Library of Congress Cataloging-in-Publication Data
Gold, Robert J.
  Eureka! : the entrepreneurial inventor's guide to developing,
protecting, and profiting from your ideas / Robert J. Gold.
    p.   cm.
  Includes index.
  ISBN 0-13-011735-8
    1. Inventions—Handbooks, manuals, etc.   2. Inventions—Marketing—
Handbooks, manuals, etc.   I. Title
T339.G64   1994
608.73—dc20   94-5540
                                                                       CIP

ISBN 0-13-011735-8

PRENTICE HALL
Career and Personal Development
Englewood Cliffs, NJ 07632

Simon & Schuster, A Paramount Communications Company

Printed in the United States of America

This book is dedicated to my parents,
Frank and Etta Gold,
who taught me that the glass is
always half full, never half empty.

Acknowledgements

I would like to acknowledge the guidance, love, support, backing, caring, expert advice, and general help of the following people throughout the years, without which this book would not have been possible:

Frank and Etta Gold, Susan A. Gold, K.D. Gold, Jerry "Yoda" Koszut, Darci R. Bedell, Mona Zimmerman, Ray Bard, Dr. Floyd Gusack, Ben DiVenti, Gary Whitten, Sgt. Wayne Corcoran, Francis and Floyd Langner, David Langner, Deby K. Bell, Meg Tynan, Dr. Robert J. Champer, Donna McKennon, Gary Shafto, Nora Comstock, James Burke, Tom Ashmore, Capt. Robert Lindsey, Capt. Robert Scanlon, Don Wynnyczok, Fred Hammer, Dan Jennings, Dr. Thad Gillespie, Bob Pearsall, Vince Anthony, Maury Benkoil, Tracy Carlson, "The Burke," Susan Bland, the many students who have taken my course at the University of Texas at Austin and become my close friends, and, of course, the fine people at the University of Texas Informal Classes.

Thank you!

Eccentricity has always abounded when and where strength of character has abounded; and the amount of eccentricity in a society has generally been proportional to the amount of genius, mental vigor, and moral courage which it contained.

John Stuart Mill

Introduction: What This Book Will Do for You

 This book has been written for the inventor who must do more than come up with a good idea. Today's inventor also must be a promoter, a technician, a project manager, and—most of all—a leader. The term I have coined for this type of individual is "entrepreneurial inventor." I use this term extensively throughout this book, because it sums up the type of inventors who will lead us into the twenty-first century: those who can survive and thrive in a highly competitive, rapidly changing product marketplace.

Our ideas are our greatest source of wealth. People with ideas—those, of course, who really want to *do* something with those ideas—need only to know the right system of protocols and paperwork to be able to succeed in entrepreneurial inventing. Helping you understand the protocols and paperwork of inventing is one of the major aims of this book.

Icons visually representing major topics in each chapter outlined below are shown next to respective chapter paragraphs discussed, and are to be found in the Table of Icons on pages xiii–xix.

The book's chapters and what they cover are:

Chapter 1, "Inventor and Entrepreneur: Life in the Creative Fast Lane," looks at the many challenges inventors face in today's increasingly global, increasingly interconnected economy.

Chapter 2, "The Ups and Downs of Entrepreneurial Inventing," examines the pleasures and stresses of being an inventor and entrepreneur, and how these factors affect all parts of your life.

Chapter 3, "From Brainstorm to Project: Using the Mental Tools of Invention," presents some of my techniques for generating ideas, moving them forward as well-organized, viable projects, seizing opportunities, fending off dangers, and minimizing the risks from an "idea crash."

Chapter 4, "Patents and Patent Attorneys," discusses the most important form of protection for an invention and how you should go about hiring a patent attorney to secure a patent for your product.

The focus of Chapter 5 is "Copyrights, Trademarks, and Other Protections" that can help you both in the domestic and international marketplaces.

Chapter 6, "Starting the Design Process," shows you how to establish the design parameters of your project, as well as how to get started with vital artwork.

Chapter 7, "Building and Testing Your Ideas," examines the different forms of prototypes and how to test them for durability and safety. Also examined are sources of parts for prototypes and how to gather the right tools.

Chapter 8, "The Delicate Art of Raising Funds," explores the inventor's side of the sometimes-intimidating, but vitally important money equation. It shows how to get support for a project without losing control of it.

In Chapter 9, the focus is on "Getting Help When You Need It: Key Sources of Information and Support." This is a look at important data resources and data acquisition techniques, as well as how to find the agencies, organizations, and individuals who can help you turn your ideas into projects—and profits.

Chapter 10 shows you the best ways for "Building and Maintaining Your Network"—your contacts with people who can help you make your products and career a success.

Chapter 11, "Establishing Your Credentials as an Entrepreneurial Inventor," presents valuable tips for establishing your credentials and enhancing them with letters of reference and recommendation.

In Chapter 12, the focus is on "Creating and Building Your Images." The entrepreneurial inventor actually must project three separate images to the public: a company image, a product image, and an inventor image.

Chapter 13, "Marketing Your Invention and You All the Way to the Bank," shows you how to capitalize on the powers of publicity, promotion, and marketing and how to create multiple opportunities for your products.

Appendix I contains valuable and helpful information on "Government Agencies, Inventor Associations, and University Resources" that can assist the entrepreneurial inventor in many different ways.

In these chapters, scores of topics are covered that can help any entrepreneurial inventor, from novice to expert, succeed.

Inventing: A Road Less Traveled

Each year, thousands of would-be entrepreneurs come up against a seemingly insurmountable wall of unexpected problems and challenges. For inventors, that wall stands twice as high. Yet, with rare exceptions, the obstacles thrown up by that wall can be negotiated, especially when you understand the techniques and strategies of entrepreneurial inventing.

The art of inventing itself must be cultivated, encouraged, and even humored at times. Inventing has long been a calling without guidance or formal training. Courses on how to be an inventor are rare. Today, many great ideas are born in large industrial research laboratories. But the independent inventor is still the soul of inventing. His or her spirit is extolled in every product that comforts our lives and gives peace and fun to our daily existence.

I have been inventing since I was a child, but it was not until many years later that I began calling myself an inventor. I thought that inventing was something great minds did for the benefit of mankind. How could *I* be an inventor? Actually, many of us are inventive souls; we simply lack the skills, tools, and drive necessary to take inventive thoughts to productive outcomes.

This book is my contribution toward helping my fellow inventors learn these skills, gather the right tools, and develop the necessary drive, so they can avoid many of the pitfalls of the inventor's life.

Invention, it can be argued, is the ultimate stab at immortality. Some inventions are short-lived, like shooting stars. Others are steps leading upward from one level of civilization to the next, or dots on a timeline, or signposts on the eternal highway from cave to condo.

The moment of invention is the ultimate high! But the ability to follow through on your idea can become a heavy burden to carry. Inventors know who they are and appreciate the raw genius and courage of other inventors, because they know the path that must be followed. Inventors see the reality of their product as their brainchild, and they want it to become reality just as they want any child to grow to adulthood.

The road of entrepreneurial inventing will seem to twist and branch off every time you think it can be traveled without fear of losing your way. And you must understand that your little piece of immortality may become a foreign knock-off just hours after it has appeared at its first trade show. But these matters can't stop the true entrepreneurial inventors of the world. It shouldn't matter if you are working in the top-secret laboratories of major industry or in a moldy basement workshop—the bond is there. It takes its own kind of "right stuff" to travel this path of uncertain gain and certain frustration.

Good luck, and never give up your dreams!

Robert J. Gold

Icon Table
of Contents

DOCUMENTATION

This Icon represents the written documentation of an idea, prototype or design. It will also appear when documentation is needed to carry out an inventor function.

MASTER FORM:

Copy 1st DON'T WRITE ON THIS FORM

This Icon means this form is a master document and should only be used for copying. Retain original and use the copies as worksheets.

TELEPHONE SKILLS

This Icon means that telephone work will be needed to complete this inventor function. It may involve communications for research, networking or raising capital.

SELF PROMOTION

This Icon means this inventor function involves publicity and promotion efforts on the part of the inventor.

PRESENTATION ARTWORK

This Icon means that the inventor function will involve the creation or use of professional presentation art and materials.

DESIGN / PROTOTYPE TOOLS

This Icon means this information concerns design and/or prototype tools. These tools are the physical instruments used to develop, design or construct prototypes.

DESIGN CRITERIA

This Icon means this information is part of the design criteria for an invention. This information relates to the basic development of the invention parameters.

BRAINSTORMING

This Icon represents inventor brainstorming functions and abilities and will appear when brainstorming functions are needed by an inventor.

CONTRACTS AND AGREEMENTS

This Icon means this information either concerns agreements and contracts, or is an agreement or contract sample.

U.S. PATENT AND LEGAL SYSTEM

This Icon means this information involves patents and the patent system; or legal matters involving the inventor or the invention.

PRESS COVERAGE

This Icon means this inventor function involves newspaper or other written media coverage. This may be spontaneous media attention or generated by an inventor's efforts.

CHECKLIST

This Icon means that this page contains an inventor checklist. Checklists are important inventor tools for establishing basic criteria for many phases of an invention.

PROTOTYPES

This Icon means this information concerns a phase of the prototype process.

RAISING CAPITAL

This Icon means this information concerns the process for raising capital for an invention.

CORRESPONDENCE

This Icon means this information concerns various types of correspondence that inventors must use to accomplish invention related goals.

MARKETING

This Icon means this information concerns marketing and/or attaining a market niche for an invention.

SECRECY

This Icon represents inventor secrecy functions & responsibilities. This Icon will appear when secrecy paperwork will be needed by the inventor to progress in a given area.

BASICS OF INVENTING

This Icon is the universal symbol for an "idea." It represents information that contains the author's personal views on being an inventor and the basic mindset of inventing.

WRITING SKILLS

This Icon represents the various writing skills that an inventor needs to accomplish a given task. Writing skills are one type of "Stepping-Stone Technique" for inventors.

SYSTEM ORGANIZATION

This Icon means this information relates to the way the "Entrepreneurial Inventing System" is organized for use by the inventor.

ESTIMATES & PROJECTIONS

This Icon means this information is about estimates and projections that an inventor will need to use during the development of an invention.

INVENTOR MINDSET

This Icon represents the way an inventor is "plugged" into the world. This information reflects the way an inventor sees the world and the way the world sees the inventor.

PEOPLE SKILLS

This icon means that this information pertains to interpersonal "people skills" needed by an inventor .

MANUFACTURERS

This Icon means this information is about vendors and suppliers of goods and services that are important to an inventor. It also represents avenues of marketing via manufacturers.

NEW TECHNOLOGIES

This Icon means this information concerns new technologies and the way they are used, viewed or exploited by an inventor.

STEPPING-STONE TECHNIQUES

This Icon means this information concerns one of several techniques an inventor can use to expand business and personal opportunities.

RESEARCH TOOLS

This Icon represents the research tools an inventor needs to accomplish a given task. Research tools can incluode physical tools, written material, computer skills and the mental attitude of the inventor.

HOME AND LIFE

This Icon means this information relates to an inventor's home life, using his home as his office and his interaction with his friends and family .

DATA ACQUISITION

This Icon means this information concerns ways an inventor may obtain and use any type of verbal, written, audio or video information.

CREDENTIALS

This Icon means this information relates to any activity that helpos an inventor generate letters of reference that establish him as an inventor, entrepreneur or solid citizen.

T.V. & MOVIE PUBLICITY

This Icon means this information concerns ways an inventor may obtain or use any type of Radio, TV or movie publicity or promotion.

IMAGE

This Icon means this information concerns the image generated by an inventor, his company or his product.

THE GOVERNMENT

This Icon means this information concerns ways the government interacts with inventors, their products and their patents.

MUST BE DONE IN PERSON!

This Icon means this information concerns an item which must be taken care of in person by the inventor or his appointed representative.

Contents

Chapter 1

Life in the Creative Fast Lane

**Whatever you can do, or dream you can, begin it.
Boldness has genius, power, and magic in it.**

—Goethe

  It's not easy to be an entrepreneur or an inventor in today's fast-changing, increasingly global business arena. If you are the type of person who seeks calm predictability, you shouldn't even be considering a field that combines both of these career challenges: entrepreneurial inventing.

As an entrepreneurial inventor, you must live by your wits, your creativity, your contacts, your organizational and fundraising skills, and your leadership. Much of your success also depends on how well you understand the processes and protocols that stand between your dreams and that rewarding day when a unique, new product—your idea—rolls off the assembly line and goes to market.

In this chapter, you will learn how to create the ultimate product and survive and prosper by juggling several projects at once. You will gain a clearer understanding of the markets for your inventions and the phases that virtually every project goes through as it advances from concept to completion. Also, you will see how three powerful forces—luck, serendipity and synergy—affect your ability to create new inventions. Understanding these forces can help you turn them to your advantage.

Creating the Ultimate Product

 It has often been said that every product must have three distinct attributes if it is to succeed in the marketplace for any length of time. The first of these

1

attributes is the price for which you can produce the product, versus the higher price for which you can sell it. The second attribute is the ability of the product to be sold in large quantities without saturating the market. The third attribute is the ability of the product to make the consumer want to purchase it more than once, thus maintaining its market.

The finest product has these three qualities honed to the finest edge. First, the ideal product can be—in the words of a familiar saying—"made for a penny and sold for a dollar." It is designed so it can be manufactured inexpensively enough for profitable mass production, yet it can be priced high enough to turn a profit while appealing to all buyers. Second, the ideal product is ultimately disposable. This forces the buyer to eventually have to purchase another unit. Otherwise, the market would become saturated with the product, and sales might be limited to one item per customer. Third, the ideal product is addictive. It is designed to make the buyer want to use it again and again. This creates a customer dependency—real, psychological, or imagined—that results in steady sales of the product.

Many products fulfill these goals and have the qualities of the ultimate product. This does not mean that the products ultimately are good or bad, only that they are great sellers. They boast large revenues and have created a niche in the world market. Within this definition, one of the closest things to an ultimate product is the cigarette. It is inexpensive to produce compared with its final street price, yet it is within the daily financial reach of almost every consumer who wishes to use one. Cigarettes burn up with each use, making them a perfectly disposable item. Finally, the nicotine addiction associated with cigarettes creates a physical and psychological need to use the product again and again.

Two other examples of almost ideal products—ironically linked to cigarettes—are matches and disposable lighters. They, too, are inexpensive to produce, they are used up after a relatively low number of applications, and they are directly linked to a physically additive product. Matches and disposable lighters, however, also have hundreds of other uses across all layers of society, so their continued use and sales are ensured.

Yet another example of the ideal product is the disposable razor: cheap to produce, thrown away after a few uses, and directly linked to a socially addictive behavior, being clean-shaven.

If you can get some or all of these characteristics into a safe product that has no detrimental effects on society, you have a great chance of success in the marketplace.

The Three Rules of Inventing

 The success of any inventor's project is linked to three basic rules of inventing. Understanding these rules can help you keep your entrepreneurial inventing efforts on track and use your resources in the most efficient way.

RULE #1: YOU DON'T HAVE TO KNOW EVERYTHING. You can find the people who have the information you need to succeed in your venture.

Surround yourself with expert advice from several sources. This will give you the best chance of not overlooking an important facet of your project. One of the easiest ways to find this expert advice is to consult the *Encyclopedia of Associations,* described in Chapter 6, "Key Sources of Information and Support." Every association is a major source of experts and data on the field in which they operate. Most are very helpful to inventors in search of information and advice.

RULE #2: REMEMBER THAT MARKET IS EVERYTHING.   Without a market, you are just creating a vanity invention for yourself. I believe in the basic Edison philosophy of making money with an invention. First, make sure your idea has a strong market base or a secure niche. This is done through basic research. Second, locate your sources of financing *before* starting any full-scale development.

RULE #3: DEVELOP THE CONCEPT AT YOUR OWN PACE.   Keep a project within the limits of your time and available resources. If you overextend yourself and your resources, your project may collapse under its own weight. Know your own limits and work right up to them, but don't kill yourself trying to exceed them. Always use whatever help you can find. Remember that the best entrepreneurial inventors are great project managers, as well.

The Three Markets for Inventions

As an entrepreneurial inventor, you have three markets for your products: consumer, industrial and governmental. You may sell your product in just one of these markets, in two, or in all three. Determining your primary and secondary markets can be of crucial importance to your success. Many inventors-turned-business persons often do not have the slightest idea where to sell or promote their concepts.

Always explore all possible market areas before ruling them out as potential money makers. Many simple household inventions have found major markets in industry and government use. Likewise, many industrial creations have become consumer household and sporting goods products, as well as items used by government agencies.

Use the brainstorming techniques described in the next chapter to try to develop additional market concepts for your product. Make use of the many resources in this book as you research various avenues for marketing your invention. And strive to have several projects going at the same time. As you do so, you must keep in mind that the inventing process will go through distinct phases.

The Twelve Phases of Invention

In my definition of the inventing process, there are twelve distinct phases in a product's developmental life cycle. The sequence in which the phases occur can vary, and will depend upon the invention, the inventor, and the particular circumstances of the idea. The successful entrepreneurial inventor, however, must understand these twelve phases and remain flexible, ready to move with the ebb and flow of an invention's life cycle.

PHASE 1: CONCEPT AND IDEA DEVELOPMENT.   This is when you get the basic idea, through stroke of genius, insight into a problem's solution, brainstorming, or other process. This phase also involves documenting the original idea, reviewing its feasibility, and developing subsequent improvements.

PHASE 2: INITIAL PATENT CONSIDERATIONS.   This phase involves the initial consultation with a patent attorney or doing a preliminary patent search at a library equipped with patent records.

PHASE 3: INITIAL FINANCIAL CONSIDERATIONS.   In this phase you start your research into two areas (1) initial funds to organize the project, and (2) the potential markets for your product, to ensure that it will be something more than a vanity invention.

PHASE 4: FIRST PROTOTYPE DEVELOPMENT.   This phase involves the physical and artistic development of a prototype, as well as the descriptive artwork for the product. The prototype is used to demonstrate or physically illustrate the product. The artwork is used to show the product's features and benefits to prospective investors.

PHASE 5: MARKET RESEARCH.   This is the "testing the waters" phase. It involves getting feedback from the industry in which the invention would be used and sold. The process includes doing statistical research and demonstrating the concept to manufacturers and end users for feedback that can be incorporated into the final product design.

PHASE 6: PUTTING ON THE "JAZZ."   In this phase you start putting a face on your company and product. This means creating an image for your invention. This image is used in the process of raising capital for various purposes, such as concept development, prototypes, production, and sales and marketing. Putting on the jazz is a cross between two familiar concepts: "the art of the deal" and "putting on a dog-and-pony show." The entrepreneurial inventor can use dog-and-pony shows to get the attention of investors, manufacturers, and the media (see page 148).

PHASE 7: LEGAL CONSIDERATIONS.   In the legal phase of the invention process, you must consider patents, copyrights, and trademarks. And you must develop a long-range view of how the invention may interact with, or clash with, existing laws concerning product safety and sales restrictions.

PHASE 8: GETTING FULL-SCALE BACKERS.   This phase involves using your networking contacts to find the best possible deals in every other phase of the invention process. Some inventions require large-scale investment to get off the ground, while others can become successful on a shoestring. In any case, getting backers is often essential for a particular invention to become a successful product.

PHASE 9: DOING THE PRE-PRODUCTION WORK.   Now it's time to turn the prototype into a salable product. This phase may require people with specialized skills to help you design and package the product, as well as set up manufacturing and marketing. Networking skills also are important in this phase.

PHASE 10: PRODUCTION.   In this phase, you must decide whether to manufacture your product in-house or let another company produce it. Many financial considerations may come into play during this phase, along with considerations over market demand and pricing.

PHASE 11: MARKETING.   The marketing phase involves networking to get the widest possible recognition and acceptance of the invention. The market is the strongest determining factor for the length of the invention sales factor.

PHASE 12: SALES.   The sales phase should be the ultimate goal of the entrepreneurial inventor. Without this phase, no invention will last long, regardless of its merit. The sales phase is a direct function of the product's developmental characteristics and market. If the product has been developed successfully, so that it is unique, functional, appealing, and needed, then the marketing efforts should succeed in selling the product to the end user.

The Three Not-So-Mystical Forces of Inventing

 People in the general public tend to look upon inventing as some sort of magic process. Certainly, the changes brought about today by new products and new technology happen so fast that the casual observer often attaches a mystical air to the process. It is *not* magic, of course. Three not-so-mystical forces play key roles in the success or failure of a project. They are luck, serendipity, and synergy.

LUCK: WHEN OPPORTUNITY MEETS PREPAREDNESS.   Many people feel that they can succeed only if they can catch "a lucky break." They fail to realize that we can make our lucky breaks by being prepared to take advantage of an opportunity. How many times has an opportunity passed you by, because you were not in a position to capitalize on it? Being prepared means more than being in the right place at the right time, although that *does* help. What it really means is that you must have a vision of your goals and a plan to get you from where you are right now to where you want to be. General George Patton, who didn't believe in waiting around for luck to strike, once said, "Better a plan today than a perfect plan tomorrow." Make your plans now, and you can create your own luck!

SERENDIPITY: THE ART OF BEING ABLE TO PROFIT FROM THE UNEXPECTED.   Serendipity simply means allowing yourself new ways to look at resources and situations. By examining everything from different perspectives, you can create new ways to use almost anything that crosses your path.

SYNERGY: MIXING UNRELATED FORCES TO CREATE A NEW DIRECTION FOR ACTION.   A synergy is a totally new, but acceptable and comfortable, direction for action. Synergies are powerful inventing tools that have worked since the dawn of time. They are the true essence of creative adventurism. A synergy can be important not only in product development but in business relationships, as well.

Charting Your Progress: A Guide to the Invention Process

 The figures that follow illustrate the invention process and provide a blank worksheet that you can photocopy and use as a guide when organizing and measuring your own efforts. Each time you move into and through the twelve phases for a new product, remember these words from the nineteenth century German philosopher Johann Wolfgang von Goethe: "Daring ideas are like chessmen moved forward; they may be beaten, but they may start a winning game."

Many people who come up with very good ideas feel that merely having the thoughts are work enough and that someone now should make them rich for being so clever. Entrepreneurial inventing, however, is the intellectual and commercial doppelganger of explorer or adventurer. There are enough risks to make even the strongest individual think twice. Yet, there also are enough potential rewards to satiate even the most jaded among us.

Here is the bottom line in entrepreneurial inventing. Nothing will ever be accomplished if you don't try, or if fear of failure or uncertainty about the future are paramount in your mind. Take your ideas and your dreams and forge ahead. Be an explorer and an adventurer. Just do it!

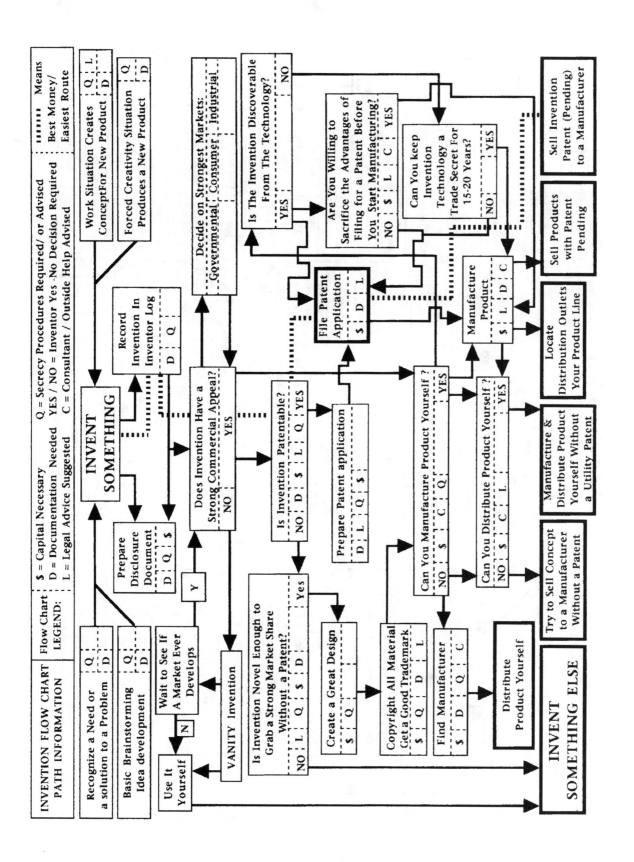

INVENTION FLOW CHART PATH INFORMATION | Flow Chart LEGEND:

$ = Capital Necessary   Q = Secrecy Procedures Required/ or Advised
D = Documentation Needed   YES / NO = Inventor Yes -No Decision Required
L = Legal Advice Suggested   C = Consultant / Outside Help Advised
······ Means Best Money/ Easiest Route

- Work Situation Creates Concept For New Product | Q L D
- Forced Creativity Situation Produces a New Product | Q D
- Recognize a Need or a solution to a Problem | Q D
- Basic Brainstorming Idea development | Q D

INVENT SOMETHING

- Record Invention In Inventor Log | D Q
- Prepare Disclosure Document | D Q $
- Wait to See If A Market Ever Develops — Y / N
- Use It Yourself
- VANITY Invention

Does Invention Have a Strong Commercial Appeal? — NO / YES

Is Invention Novel Enough to Grab a Strong Market Share Without a Patent? | NO L Q $ D — Yes

Decide on Strongest Markets: Governmental, Consumer, Industrial

Is The Invention Discoverable From The Technology? — YES / NO

Is Invention Patentable? | NO D $ L Q — YES

Prepare Patent application | D L Q $

Prepare Patent application

File Patent Application | $ D L

Are You Willing to Sacrifice the Advantages of Filing for a Patent Before You Start Manufacturing? | NO $ L C — YES

Can You keep Invention Technology a Trade Secret For 15-20 Years? | NO — YES

Create a Great Design | $ Q

Copyright All Material Get a Good Trademark | $ Q D L

Find Manufacturer | $ D Q C

Distribute Product Yourself

Can You Manufacture Product Yourself ? | NO $ C Q — YES

Can You Distribute Product Yourself ? | NO $ C L — YES

Manufacture Product | $ L D C

Try to Sell Concept to a Manufacturer Without a Patent

Manufacture & Distribute Product Yourself Without a Utility Patent

Locate Distribution Outlets Your Product Line

Sell Products with Patent Pending

Sell Invention Patent (Pending) to a Manufacturer

INVENT SOMETHING ELSE

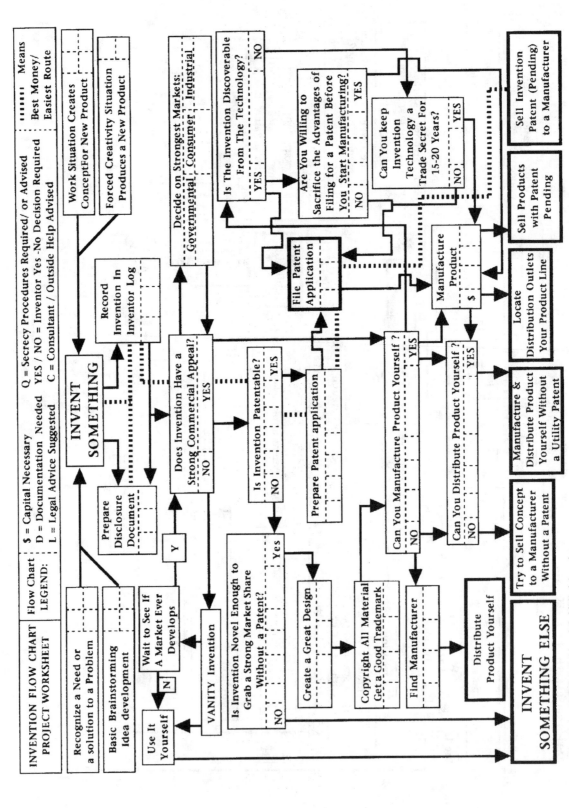

INVENTION FLOW CHART

Copyright 1992 R.J. Gold and GoldMind Associates

Chapter 2

The Ups and Downs of Entrepreneurial Inventing

Whatever you do, you need courage.
Whatever course you decide upon,
There will always be someone to tell you
You are wrong.

Ralph Waldo Emerson

 Whatever your reasons for inventing and pushing your creations into the marketplace, you will be subject to the many elations and stresses that come with the territory. These ups and downs affect entrepreneurial inventors in several distinct areas of their lives. These areas include finances, family, job, emotional state, friends, and the future. I call these ups and downs the "3P psychology" of the entrepreneurial inventor's life. On the upside are these 3Ps: pride, power, and potential. On the downside, the 3Ps are: paranoias, plateaus, and pitfalls. Let's look briefly at how each can affect your efforts as an inventor and entrepreneur.

The Upside: Pride, Power, and Potential

 These constitute the upside, the lighter side, of the 3P psychology. A great sense of pride, power, and potential can come from being an inventor—and those same senses can be heightened when you succeed as an entrepreneur, as well. This good side of entrepreneurial inventing has, throughout the ages, helped inventors hold onto their dreams. The positive feelings of accomplishment and satisfaction can be almost overwhelming at times.

9

Pride

The feeling of accomplishment. Inventors do something that most people never do: They create their own little piece of immortality. Some of these pieces of immortality are little more than small signposts on the eternal highway of history. But others take us into new fields of existence for humanity as a whole. Most inventors feel a basic sense of accomplishment at taking an idea and turning it into a reality. Most people never really know that feeling, because it does not easily exist in the lives of the general public. Granted, everyone feels a sense of accomplishment at doing something. But inventors know a very special type of accomplishment that is both real and mystical. Inventing is a primal creative process that links back to ancient man's first glimmer of thought and will link to the limits of man's achievements on distant planets in the far future. Knowing you are an inventor and that your idea may somehow change history can be a powerful ego booster and source of extreme pride.

If you are charged with energy about your concept, an aura of positive energy can envelop your project. Inventing generates excitement within the inventor and the people he or she touches with the project. If an invention doesn't stir this type of response, you may need to rethink it or how it is being presented. A good idea will be full of positive energy. People will feel the excitement of its potential for making money or changing a small part of the world—or both.

Inventing can make you feel more positive about yourself and your abilities. Most people grow up with many different insecurities about who they are and what they can contribute to the world. Inventing is one of the few endeavors where you can utilize every creative fiber of your being. Being able to do this generates a positive mental attitude about who you are and where your life can lead. If you have the ability to come up with one good idea, you probably have dozens of more ideas inside your head, just waiting to be unleashed. That's a good feeling!

Power

You're in the driver's seat—it's your project! Very few occupations or projects that you can take on in your lifetime can give you the unbridled authority and decision-making power of inventing something. It's your baby, your concept, your decision on what to do, how to do it, and in what direction to run with it. This alone can be an overwhelmingly good feeling for many people. It's a little scary. But you can turn that uneasy feeling into positive energy by realizing that it's your decision on how fast to launch a concept—If you want to start from scratch and do every phase of development right through marketing the idea, you can. But if you only want to create the concept and then try to sell it (after taking the proper steps to protect the idea), you can do this, too. The only limits are the ones you impose on yourself.

Your intellectual property has real worth if the idea is sound. Inventors are among the few who can start with absolutely nothing except an image in the mind's eye. That little piece of "intellectual property," as the patent office calls it, is as real and valuable as real estate or cash in the bank, if the idea is viable and the inventor has the ambition to pursue it to its logical conclusion. This is one of the greatest aspects of inventing, but it is also the great equalizer. You don't have to be born with money or position in society to attain great wealth or status as an inventor. You need only think up the next great invention in any particular field.

You can have a sense of actually creating your own destiny. Almost any person who has ever taken the leap into inventing can tell you that it is the quickest way to grab hold of your future and start directing your destiny, instead of just letting it happen to you. Your life can be altered by the people you meet and the events you create. And it can happen as soon as you try to do anything about your concept. W.H. Murray of the Scottish Himalayan Expedition said it best: "Until one is committed, there is always the chance to draw back, always ineffectiveness. Concerning all acts of initiative there is one elementary truth, the ignorance of which kills countless ideas and splendid plans: That the moment one definitely commits oneself, then providence moves, too. All sorts of things occur to help one that would never otherwise have occurred. A whole stream of events issues from the decision, raising in one's favor all manner of unforeseen incidents and meetings and material assistance, which no man could have dreamed would have come his way."

Being an inventor places you in powerful company. Edison, Bell, Marconi, Watt—the list of great inventors is almost endless. Yet many people still ridicule those who try to use their creative gift to invent. Know that the profession of inventing, whether full-time or part-time, places you in powerful company in the eyes of history. Use this knowledge as a cloak to deflect some of the cold rhetoric of your detractors. Only history will tell if you leave your mark. But rest assured you are traveling a path that has lead others to power, fame, and fortune. Most inventors don't invent for those reasons. Still, you should never lose sight of the fact that they are real and could come your way.

Potential

Inventing is one of the few occupations that has vast potential recognized by all. Most career choices have strict limits on what can be attained or earned. Inventing has no such limitations. You can invent one or thousands of products during your career, and any one or all of them could bring lasting fame and fortune. The potential of inventing is so great that the governments of all civilized countries have to run entire bureaucratic agencies (their patent offices) just to keep the ownership of intellectual property in an orderly fashion. No other single occupation is given this time, energy, and effort by all the major governments.

Talents and connections acquired along the path of inventing can help you step up to bigger and better things in life. Opportunities opened up by inventing can lead to job offers, writing careers, consulting contracts, speaking engagements, and many other unforeseen paths that you may choose to travel.

Serendipity is the inventor's best friend and sometimes can increase the potential of a project far beyond original expectations. The unexpected can happen on a regular basis when you are creating a new technology. Good inventors learn to take advantage of the effects of serendipity to multiply the opportunities of the moment. This often leads to increases in the potential of a project. It may be interlinked with other opportunities, and additional paths for diversification suddenly may be opened.

The Downside: Paranoias, Plateaus, and Pitfalls

 Even when things seem to be rolling along without a hitch, you can start worrying about the many things that can go wrong. Or, suddenly, you may discover that there's no longer any need to worry: Things *have* gone wrong, and you have to fix them in a hurry. To succeed in entrepreneurial inventing, you have to be able to understand and fight your paranoias, push past the plateaus that stop many people, and constantly be wary of the pitfalls that can swallow up inventions—and inventors.

Paranoias

These are fears that can be thrust upon you by circumstances and the people around you. Some examples of these fears are as follows:

Other people's fears projected onto you. Many people cannot see themselves succeeding at a given task. Thus, they cannot see how you can do it, either. So they will try to persuade you to turn back before it is too late. Don't believe them—it's their fear, not yours. If you have confidence in your idea, forge ahead until you either succeed or you come to your own conclusion (based upon knowledge, not fear) that the project no longer is worth your time and effort.

Your own fear of failure. This can be the hardest stumbling block for any inventor to get over. But Henry Ford once noted: "Failure is the opportunity to start over again...more intelligently." Some of the greatest successes in many fields have come only after many failures. As an inventor, you must learn to take failure as a learning experience. Thomas A. Edison had more than 6,000 failures before he finally succeeded in creating a light bulb. When asked about those many failures, he replied: "I now know 6,000 ways *not* to make a light bulb."

Fear of being unable to live up to the potential of your own idea. Every good idea seems to have the potential for changing some part of the world in which we live. Not every idea has to do this, however. Nor does every idea have to succeed at every moment. If you cannot make an idea live up to its potential, this does not mean that you have failed as an inventor. It only means that time or circumstances or both may not have been right for that particular idea.

The fear of financial failure. This is a very real fear for most inventors. Invention often can be a money-consuming occupation with few financial returns until a project's ultimate fruition. You should try to minimize the financial risks of entrepreneurial inventing by maintaining a full-time job or spreading the capital investment in an idea over several investors. These two techniques can help you survive the financial roller coaster ride most inventors must endure with their creations.

Don't quit your job unless you are absolutely sure you have enough financial resources to see you through the invention process. Many great inventors with major, money-making products got to their positions by inventing part-time. Inventing can be the world's greatest hobby...until the opportunity comes along to make it your occupation.

Fear of the future. Some people think that destiny is something to be awaited. Wrong! Destiny is something to be created, just like an invention. The future is what you make of it. As an inventor, you should look at the future as an asset to be exploited. The future is the inventor's ballpark, and your chances of hitting a grand slam can be just as good as your chances of striking out. Only the future will tell, and only your willingness to take a chance on that future will let you see if you are going to be a success.

The fear of being ridiculed. Throughout history, many great minds have been ridiculed by the mindless hordes who can't comprehend what it means to have an original idea. Inventors are almost always in the position of having to "put up or shut up" about their ideas. But remember this: Once your invention is created and accepted, you will have entered the long, proud tradition of inventors who have shaped this planet's history since the beginning of time. Inventions are an important part of society's ability to advance in every field. So let friends, family, co-workers, or others have their say, even if you don't like what you hear. Just keep in mind the importance of what you are trying to accomplish.

The fear of not being perceived as you want to be. Okay, every inventor wants to be seen as the next Edison or Bell, but that may not happen to you. But do have confidence in two things. One, you may indeed be the next Edison or Bell. Or, two, if your invention is not earthshaking and does not make you rich and famous, you still will have the satisfaction of being an inventor. Either way, you can create an "inventor's image" for yourself and be perceived as you want to be perceived.

Plateaus

Plateaus are the levels that every invention must pass to accomplish the ultimate goals of market acceptance, sales, and making money for the inventor. Some people fear that hitting certain plateaus can break the momentum of a project. But in the product development process, plateaus can offer some important opportunities to the inventor and his or her invention. The following are some of the major plateaus that you may encounter while pursuing ideas and products as an entrepreneurial inventor.

The original concept and the decision to go on. This is the first and most important plateau in the life cycle of an invention. This is when you make the decision to go on with an idea, to commit resources, time, and energy to try to turn a mere thought into a physical reality. Without the commitment to this plateau, the idea is doomed. Many people who give up at this plateau later see ideas they have had come out as other people's successful inventions. Of course, they then kick themselves mentally for having not proceeded with the concept.

The first converts: true believers with money or services. You reach this plateau the moment to get another person to commit money or resources of any type to your idea. This is a small plateau, but it is an important one, because it is proof positive that your idea is not just a wild daydream exclusive to your little part of the Twilight Zone. As more people comit time, resources or help of any sort to your project, the momentum will grow. This momentum, in turn, will give you a running start toward reaching the next plateau.

Proving your idea works. Some ideas don't even have this plateau; it is self-evident that they work. Other projects, however, need prototypes, market research, and hands-on testing to prove the validity of a concept. Proving your idea works can be the hardest, yet most satisfying plateau for an inventor to reach. Regardless of market acceptance, popular acceptance, or peer acceptance, just proving that your brainchild works is an awesome reality with incredible satisfaction for the inventor.

The downside to this plateau, however, is just as powerful, since the entire project can come to a crashing halt if the product concept cannot be proven valid. At this point, the series of other plateaus may vanish, and the inventor may drop into personal and financial oblivion. You should carefully think through a concept before trying to attempt the entire project. Be certain that the product technology does not depend upon wishful speculation. Almost all of the best inventions are based upon sound technology that hasn't been used before in a particular way.

Proving you have a market. Remember, market is everything. Proving that you have a market is a plateau that can be reached easily if you gather the right data from the industry for which your invention is intended. If similar products exist, you should use this data to prove that your idea is better and will capture part of the existing market. If your product is radically new, then you should use the data to prove that a need exists that is not being filled by any other product. Once you can prove you have a market, your idea will gain credibility, and you can more easily raise capital, if needed.

First manufactured product. This plateau can be reached only by accomplishing almost all of the items on the invention flow chart. By the time this occurs, it often means that you have gotten extensive support in production from an established manufacturer, and the risks and problems have been spread out to a better comfort level for all concerned. Of course, if you are producing your invention in-house, then the risks and other problems may continue to be a source of worry until substantial sales have been made.

First media attention. This a very important plateau for any entrepreneurial inventor. It can be very satisfying, because the media attention can give major credence to a concept. But it also can be a dangerous plateau. Inventors and their products can be ruined by untimely media hype, or if the attention takes an angle that is inappropriate for the inventor's purpose. As an entrepreneurial inventor, you should look to publicize yourself first, then your inventions. Publicity that focuses primarily on you can be used many times to help create your "public" face as an inventor. Your public image then can be used for raising capital and for getting other publicity about your products. But be aware: if a particular invention gains too much publicity before it is ready to be marketed, that publicity, to a certain extent, can hamper the product's ability to get publicity later, when it is needed to spur sales.

Pitfalls

Pitfalls are all of the things that can go wrong or must be resolved before you can attain any real measure of success with your invention. The following are some of the major pitfalls you may confront as an entrepreneurial inventor—and issues you must confront within those pitfalls.

PITFALL #1: CAN YOU PROVE AN IDEA IS YOUR ORIGINAL CONCEPT?
This can become an extremely important point for any inventor, and it is the reason why proper documentation is so important. If you cannot prove an idea or "intellectual property" is yours, then you may face a wide range of difficulties in even starting to develop the project. *Always* do your homework. And focus on the following three questions.

Is this an old idea that I have just never heard of? If you don't research your concept thoroughly, you may discover later that the idea already has been tried and abandoned by others. This is the basic reason for talking to people in the field where you feel your invention or concept might be sold or used. Here is an example of this pitfall. A friend of mine came up with an idea for a give-away "Single Band Radio" and started a business around this concept. It seemed like a great idea: Give away an AM or FM radio able to receive only one station. Sell radio stations on the concept of promoting their programming this way and ensuring advertisers a captive audience. Unfortunately, the legality of the concept is highly dubious. It violates all of the other local stations' First Amendment free-speech rights. And it had been tried by another entrepreneur in the early days of portable "pocket" radios and quickly slapped down by the Federal Communications Commission. My friend didn't do his homework on the concept and ended up investing a lot of time and money to get it going. He was temporarily crushed, both financially and spiritually, when he finally was confronted with the truth. (Luckily, he recovered by rerouting his energies into another business idea.) The moral of this story is that a little basic research on any concept is the best foundation for a successful venture.

Have you done a preliminary patent search? Doing a preliminary patent search is not as hard as it sounds. Most large libraries have facilities for doing this, and a librarian can give you instructions on how to use the computer. The information you can glean from this search often will be enough to help you justify or alter your game plan for the development of your concept. Once you are satisfied that your concept can be patented, you may still want to hire a professional patent-search firm to do a more extensive, cross-referenced search before you file a patent application.

Have you done a library search for similar ideas? Libraries are one of the entrepreneurial inventor's best resources. Use them to search through trade journals and other literature pertaining to the invention's field. The search will give you insights into such things as the market for your invention, the sophistication level of comparable products, and problems that your product might address. Many good libraries have computer-search facilities for magazine articles and book topics. One good article search often can give you many leads for additional information and reference sources.

PITFALL #2: ARE YOU CAPABLE OF DEVELOPING YOUR IDEA?   Just because you have an idea does not mean you can do something with it. This may sound cruel, but it is the truth in some instances. Before trying to proceed, every inventor should ask himself or herself the following questions regarding development.

1. Do you know the right technical questions to ask?

Avoid trying to invent in a field so alien to your education and abilities that you do not know the right questions to ask. Wishing for a new product and having a firm grasp on what the invention would do are two different things. If you cannot write a fairly cohesive, detailed description of how a product will work, then your chances of getting the project off the ground are slim.

2. Do you have the time and money to chase your dream?

You must be capable of taking on a project that may significantly alter your lifestyle in terms of free time and available money. Are you willing to devote the effort necessary to track down what you will need to complete the task? If not, then you may be fooling yourself by even starting the invention process. If you already have invented something, you still have to face the marketing and production hurdles.

3. Can you withstand the emotional tidal waves of being an entrepreneurial inventor?

This is often the hardest factor. All of the pressures of daily life are compounded by the ordeals of inventing. Even the strongest individuals sometimes have difficulty bearing up to the financial roller coaster combined with the ever-present peer pressures and family pressures. If you have supportive family and friends, however, you may have the winning edge that will help sustain you throughout the inventing process. If your family and friends are *not* supportive, then be prepared for a rough time.

4. Do you have the skills and resources?

Okay, you have a great idea, but you need a prototype to prove it's a worthwhile product. Can you develop even a minimal prototype if you can't get help? If you have a great inventive mind, but you are "Mr. All Thumbs" when it comes to building anything, you will need to hire the services of a model maker or a prototype machine shop. Before you go that far, however, you must have the right drawings to give to the model builder or machine shop. Those drawings will cost money, if you can't do them yourself. In all of the different phases of inventing, you will find that you either must use your own skills to bypass expenses or spend money on making the idea come to fruition. If your skills and finances are not up to the task, rethink the entire process. Plan out the development so it becomes part of your scheduled and budgeted expenses each month. Don't let the invention process ruin you financially.

5. How complicated is your idea?

Even the simplest invention sometimes may require complicated manufacturing techniques for production. It may require expensive molds just to get it off the ground in its simplest form. When planning the invention pathway from idea to production, consider letting others take on some of the more complicated aspects of the development, in return for a piece of the action. This can offset the financial burden for many small inventors. Another avenue you can take is to alter your design or process so the same goal can be accomplished with less financial preparation and commitment.

6. Can you sustain your lifestyle during a business startup?

Business startups are the most demanding of all business ventures. But invention startups can be even harder. They can affect every phase of your lifestyle and emotional state. There is no easy advice that can prepare you for the dual challenges of being an inventor and entrepreneur. Just try to take every problem as it comes and try to keep your perspective. Remember, you *wanted* to do this, so don't let it become a burden. Try to keep looking at it as an adventure. This will help you keep a better mental outlook on the entire project.

PITFALL #3: CAN YOU PROTECT YOUR IDEA?   Protecting your idea is one of the most important preliminary aspects of inventing. If you can't keep an idea secret, then you have very little chance of succeeding in this world of stolen secrets and pirated ideas. An inventor's ideas are like a carpenter's tools. Without them, you can't build your career. Remember, loose lips do more than sink ships. They also sink inventors.

Do you know how to protect your idea? Not everyone understands the procedures for maintaining secrecy while still circulating information to those who need to know. You must learn how to handle secrecy agreements and disclosure documents. These legal forms and the procedures for implementing security procedures are not complicated. They are explained later in this book. But they are tricks of the trade that every inventor should learn.

Can you trust the people around you? Here is a simple rule: Don't trust anyone who may have even the slightest motive for harming you or your business aspirations. Picking those who are not to be trusted can seem like an easy process, but it may turn out to be the hardest judgment call you'll ever make. In my own efforts, I make it policy that everyone has to sign a secrecy agreement *before* they get to see a new idea. I mean *everyone*! And this is how I get around the possibility of hurting someone's feelings: I explain to them that if my idea becomes involved in a court case, I might lose if the other side can show that someone who had *not* signed the secrecy agreement also knew about my invention. Signing the secrecy agreement also can help certain people, such as close friends and family, feel like they are part of the secret and part of your secret world of inventing.

When you must deal with people you don't know, it is serious business to have all meetings documented and have all parties sign the appropriate agreements. Anyone who wants to do business on a legitimate level will have no trouble signing a secrecy agreement. However, beware of people who balk at such agreements. They almost always have ulterior motives.

Are you documenting your idea in realistic ways? Jotting down an idea and showing it around as your concept is a fast way to look like an amateur in the invention game. Ideas should be documented in a fashion that reflects a level of professionalism. The original idea may have been written on a cocktail napkin, and it should be kept in a safe place for evidence of conception. But the idea that the inventor shows the world is a reflection of his or her ability and should be of high quality. Document the conception of an idea with the signature of a witness and the date. Always remember that inventors' ideas can be—and frequently are—challenged by others. Keep all data confidential and on a need-to-know basis.

Can you stand up to legal challenges? An idea may be so good that it threatens other people's products or livelihoods. This can lead to legal challenges, injunctions, and lawsuits. Consequently, every inventor needs good legal counsel. Even people who try to help you or get on your bandwagon can pose serious legal hassles with contracts. Some of them may jockey for control of your concept's future and the profits that come with it.

If you invent a new type of weapon or tool, can you live with its use or misuse? An inventor never knows what connection to the future his or her invention will have. Are you ready for the social implications if your invention changes something that is good into something that is bad? Even an innocent invention that seemingly has no social significance can alter the fragile balance of a society in one way or another. History is full of instances where inventions developed for one purpose have been used for another, very different purpose.

Balancing the Upside and Downside

 "Chance always favors the prepared mind," said Louis Pasteur. The upside and downside of entrepreneurial inventing are intermixed on a daily basis. You must be prepared for a real roller coaster ride through life. If you crave an existence that is calm and mundane, *don't* be an inventor, especially an entrepreneurial inventor. Inventors are driven, not by a desire for fame and fortune but by a vision of their creation. One of the world's most famous inventors said it best: "The hope of wealth or the desire for fame will never make an inventor...you may give him wealth or take from him everything he has; and he will still go on inventing. He can no more help inventing than he can help thinking or breathing. Inventors are born, not made."

That last line is true about the person but not about the skills you must have or the ones you must learn to be a successful entrepreneurial inventor in the 1990s and beyond. If Alexander Graham Bell were alive and inventing today, he would say, "Inventors are born *and* made."

Chapter 3

From Brainstorm to Project: Using the Mental Tools of Invention

Thinking is an experiment dealing with small amounts of energy, just as a general moves miniature figures over a map before setting his troops in action.
Sigmund Freud

 Few things happen in this world until someone gets an idea and acts upon it. Great ideas almost always seem to come from an interaction of the subconscious mind working with the conscious mind to overcome some personal or business hurdle.

Many people consider creativity a talent or gift that is unavailable to the average person. But I believe this is a fallacy perpetuated by the lack of real "brain training" in our school system.

One of the great things about being an entrepreneurial inventor is that you constantly get to use the most valuable asset you have: your mind. Not only do you get to exercise your brain in the pursuit of prosperity and happiness, you also have the chance to create your own destiny through what I consider the ultimate mind adventure, *brainstorming*.

The Power of Brainstorming

 Brainstorming is the art and science of creating ideas through a combination of sustained random and radical thinking. To me, brainstorming also is one of the most enjoyable methods of creative thinking, as well as one of the key tools of inventing. It can lead to unexpected lines of thought and open new vistas for the imagination.

There are many ways to brainstorm. It can be done individually or in groups. Most important to remember is that there are no hard-and-fast rules. I have relied upon several brainstorming techniques to get my own creative juices flowing and to get a project or product moving into high gear. Some of these techniques, described later in this chapter, include role-playing, mind mapping, and forced creativity. However, one form of brainstorming I use often is a concept that I call the "Fields of the Future Cross-Referencing," or FCR.

Using FCR to Create New Products

 I developed FCR to help entrepreneurial inventors look at new product fields which do not currently exist. The FCR process allows an individual or group to start with a new product market and evaluate the parameters for products that could serve that market. These parameters serve to create an "envelope" in which the new products exist. By defining the envelope, you can see the possible applications for the products. FCR can be a great first step for product concept development, because it creates entirely new industries and fields of endeavors for the future. At the same time, it is a simple yet powerful technique. The following exercise shows how it works.

FCR Brainstorming Exercise. To use FCR, start with a list of twelve to twenty-four product fields that exist today, then cross-reference them to make entirely new fields of endeavor. Each combination of fields can suggest products that will serve the needs of that new field or interest. The following list is only a sample of the types of fields that can be used. I have provided eighteen fields. You can add another six of your own choosing for your first try at FCR.

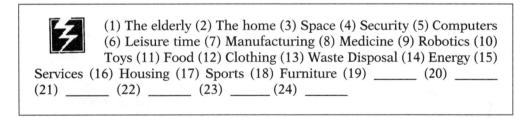

(1) The elderly (2) The home (3) Space (4) Security (5) Computers (6) Leisure time (7) Manufacturing (8) Medicine (9) Robotics (10) Toys (11) Food (12) Clothing (13) Waste Disposal (14) Energy (15) Services (16) Housing (17) Sports (18) Furniture (19) _____ (20) _____ (21) _____ (22) _____ (23) _____ (24) _____

To use FCR, simply try different combinations of topics. Choose 10 and 1, for example, and you get "toys for the elderly." This is a new field to consider for future products. With much of the world population getting older and living longer, more productive lives, toys for the elderly could become a profitable field for inventions. Now that you have selected a field to consider, the next step is to list common elements, or parameters, for the product line that you would offer to that market. For example, toys for the elderly might require parameters such as: *large lettering,* for those with failing eyesight; *large and easy-to-use controls,* to compensate for senior citizens' diminished manual dexterity; and *variable-complexity operation,* so that persons of all levels of mental alertness can enjoy the toy. These parameters create the "operational envelope" within which the product must exist, so it will meet the needs of its target audience. The operational envelope should contain the following information: The product's maximums and minimums (in categories such as size, shape, weight, and controls); and the possible features and benefits of the product for its selected market (for example, exercise, therapy, stress relief, and social interaction).

FCR Exercise Sheet. Here is an exercise sheet that can help you create your own Fields of the Future product category and select the operational envelope. To use the sheet, first select two numbers from the above list and place them in the first two spaces after "FCR." Then enter the new product field on the line to the right of the "=" sign. At "A" enter the product's minimums and maximums. At "B" enter the possible features and benefits for the product.

      Fields of the Future Cross-Reference _____

FCR: _____ + _____ = _____

_____

A. _____

_____

B. _____

Once you have tried FCR, you may find that it is a valuable tool for brainstorming—and one that you will use often. Other types of brainstorming, however, may prove helpful. And sometimes, you may find it valuable to use more than one technique.

Role Playing

To use this technique, you manipulate the paths that your thoughts travel, by asking yourself a series of questions and writing down your answers. The questions below can help you get started. You can add others that may even become your favorites as you start applying this technique to the inventing process.

1. Turn the idea inside out and what do you get? In other words, what is the reverse of this idea? How does the idea operate backwards?
2. How would a child see this problem? Make a list of the ways a child could use this idea.
3. How would an alien (from another country or another planet) tackle this idea?

4. What do you see when you make fun of this idea? How many jokes can you think of that use this idea?

5. How many different materials could be used to change the idea into a product? Now, try to imagine the product being made from materials that are wrong for the idea. How would that change the concept?

6. If you had a wish machine, how would you program it to accomplish the task at hand?

7. If you were a wizard, how would you create the product?

8. If you were president of a giant corporation, how would you proceed with the task?

9. If you had unlimited funds to make the idea into a product, how would that change the idea? How would it be changed if you had to make it from reusable materials only?

10. If you were a crazy inventor, how would you solve the problem at hand?

The role-playing technique can lead you to many different and wild ideas. One way to expand upon these ideas is to use another brainstorming technique, mind mapping.

Mind Mapping

 This technique uses associations to create an ever-expanding network of related ideas. Mind mapping is useful for getting an overview of a concept's

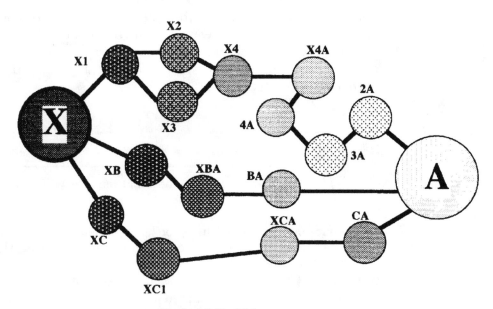

Project Mind Map
Sample Progression of Tasks
from Point "X" to Point "A"

operational envelope and the path you must take to accomplish your goal. It lacks the vast potential of other techniques to create entirely new products. But mind mapping is a good way to continue a brainstorming session into its next phase: project planning. The basic idea of mind mapping is to have a goal and work out the smallest possible steps backward from that goal to your current position in the project. In the generic example, the goal is "A" and the "now" starting point is "X." Each bubble represents a task between you and your goal.

Forced Creativity

 In the course of my career, I have often been forced to be very resourceful when dealing with the many complexities of a new product's development. Many times, the right parts or the right resources have not been available to complete a given task in the proper manner. But when I am forced to decide between giving up or finding a novel solution, I always opt for the latter.

Out of these experiences, I have developed a way to brainstorm that I call "forced creativity." When you are in a forced creativity situation, you must think your way to success. Most people don't realize that we are placed into forced creativity circumstances on a regular basis in our personal and business lives. Unfortunately, most people also don't excel at overcoming the obstacles involved with these circumstances unless their personal fortunes are on the line.

The forced creativity exercise that follows has been used successfully in my entrepreneurial inventing classes at the University of Texas at Austin. It sets up circumstances that usually bring out very creative solutions. Before doing the exercise, you need to gather two or more common objects that you ordinarily would throw away at home or in your office. These can be such objects as paper towel tubes, empty soda bottles, used deodorant containers, and so forth. Almost any discarded items can present the challenge needed to make the exercise work.

 Forced Creativity Scenario

Here is the situation that requires you to do some fast—and—creative thinking:

1. Your multimillionare Uncle Joe has just died and left you a large part of his estate, provided you can meet the conditions of his will. (This is the incentive part of the deal.)

2. He has left behind a warehouse full of parts like the ones you have in your hand. (These are the discarded items selected by you for the exercise. In my class, I give out a short piece of rubber tubing from a bicycle inner tube and

two vinyl caps about the size of a shotgun shell.) Uncle Joe has left five million of each part at your disposal.

3. Your task, if you want to be able to inherit some of his millions, is to fashion a product from these parts. If you can come up with something that uses the parts in the same ratio that they are present in your hands (one of each), you will have enough to produce five million products. Your Uncle Joe's estate then will pay you the "perceived value" of the product, whatever it is. If you create something worth five cents, you will get $250,000 as your inheritance. If you create something with a marketable value of $3, you will get $15,000,000.

4. If you have to use more of the available parts per product, your ability to produce the final number will go down in direct proportion from five million. If you have to use any outside materials, besides items such as glues, staples, pop rivets, or thread, the value of the product will go down in direct relation to the cost of the additional materials. Otherwise, you can cut, shred, spindle, or manipulate the materials in any way you see fit to produce your product.

5. The final product prototype does not have be the store-ready product. It can be rude and crude, but it must be as close to functionally real as possible. In other words, a person looking at the product should not have to use his imagination to see its use or value.

I presented this exercise to every class I taught over a three-year period. The prototypes that emerged showed me just how imaginative people can be when faced with a forced creativity situation. Although not all of the students successfully created a product, more than 150 prototypes were turned in. Out of these, there were only five cases where ideas were duplicated. That's real creativity at work!

Asking the Right Questions and Organizing Your Ideas

 To succeed as an entrepreneurial inventor, you must know how to ask yourself and others the right questions about a concept, so you can determine whether or not it truly is worth developing into a product. You must also be able to organize your ideas into projects, tasks, and sub-tasks that can be tracked and managed from conception to completion.

To help you, I have developed four techniques. Other entrepreneurial inventors have used these techniques to organize and manage their ideas and projects to successful outcomes. These techniques are:

- The Basic Idea Research and Development Sheet
- The Idea Development Checklist
- The Basic Idea Development Sheet
- The Danger/Opportunities List

REALLY USE YOUR BRAIN

The Brain as seen from the front

RIGHT	LEFT
DAYDREAMING	WORDS
IMAGINATION	NUMBERS
RHYTHM	LISTS
COLOR	LOGIC
CONCEIVE IDEAS IN MULTIPLE DIMENSIONS AS WELL AS IN TIME	ORDER ANALYSIS SYSTEMS

INVENTOR FUNCTIONS

* Original Inventive Ideas Via Brainstorming
* Ability to See Product Needed To Solve Problem
* Concept Development Skills
* New Marketing Ideas
* Prototype Production Skills
* Writing And Image Creation Skills for The Invention

* Creating Projections & Estimates for Sales, Marketing & Production
* Writing Business Plans
* Raising Capital Through Personal Presentations
* Organizing Resources for Prototypes And Production
* Creating Realistic R&D Plans

FOR IDEAS TO EQUAL INCOME

Inventors need both sides of their brain to function in harmony in order for the invention process to function at maximum efficiency. The modern inventor needs more than simple ideas to compete in today's competitive environment. He needs to be able to integrate various business skills with creativity to take his invention from an idea to the world marketplace.

Every Idea Is for the Birds

One way to start asking the right questions at the right time is to use my Basic Idea Research and Development Sheet (BIRDS) method. This checklist can give you a good idea where you stand in relation to how well you have thought out the entire project. It also acts as a guide to the basic questions you should be asking yourself. These questions should be the basis of your business plan and your ability to put your plan into action. If you don't have answers to most, if not all, of the BIRDS questions, then you are not really ready to do much more than continue thinking about the idea. Napolean once said, "'How' and 'Why' are words so important that they cannot be used too often." The BIRDS checklist builds upon Napolean's views and expands it to include the basics of a good report: why, who, what, when, where, and how. You can feel confident that you are on the road to success only when these six queries can be answered fully and understood in relation to your project.

The BIRDS checklist that follows is a master form that you can copy and use in different projects. You may want to start a BIRDS checklist on each idea as it comes to you. Completing all of the information on any single idea may take considerable time. But when you have completed the checklist, you can feel secure that you know what you want to do, why you are doing it, who will be part of the project, how you will proceed, where it will happen, and when. This knowledge is essential to the success of any entrepreneurial inventing endeavor.

BIRDS

Basic Idea Research & Development Sheet
Initial Concept Evaluation Data

CONFIDENTIAL DISCLOSURE INFORMATION
Copyright 1992 GoldMind Associates & R.J. Gold

INVENTOR _____ **DATE:** _____
CONCEPT NAME _____
_____

(I) WHY

(1) Why are you attempting this particular project?
_____
_____
_____
_____

(2) Why now?
_____
_____
_____
_____
_____

(3) Why do you feel it will succeed?
_____
_____
_____

(4) Why should others have confidence in this idea and / or your ability
to make it work?
_____
_____
_____
_____

(II) WHO

(1) Who is my market?
_____
_____
_____
_____

(2) Who will be my biggest enduser?

_____
_____
_____

(3) Who do I absolutely need (besides myself) to make this project a success?

_____
_____
_____

(4) Who are my suppliers?

_____
_____
_____
_____
_____

(5) Who will support the project?

_____
_____
_____
_____
_____

(6) Who will oppose the project?

_____
_____
_____
_____

(III) WHAT

(1) What is the basic concept?

_____
_____
_____
_____

(2) What makes it different from other concepts in the same field?

_____
_____
_____
_____
_____
_____

(3) What are its features and benefits (FAB)?

_____
_____
_____
_____
_____

(4) What do you want to do with the concept / invention?

_____
_____
_____
_____

(5) What is the market for the concept / invention?

_____
_____
_____
_____

(6) What resources, capital and equipment is needed to make this concept / invention a success?

_____
_____
_____
_____
_____

(7) What are the obstacles to the success of this project?

_____
_____
_____
_____

(IV) WHEN

(1) When do you want to start this project?

_____
_____
_____
_____

(2) When will you start this project?

_____
_____

(3) When do you want to finish this project?

_____
_____

(4) When must you finish this project?

_____

_____

_____

(V) WHERE

(1) Where is your market?

_____

_____

_____

_____

(2) Where is your best source of investment?

_____

_____

_____

(3) Where are your best suppliers?

_____

_____

_____

_____

(4) Where will you produce your product?

_____

_____

_____

(5) Where will you operate this business?

_____

_____

_____

(6) Where (geographically) will you find your largest customer base?

_____

_____

_____

_____

_____

(7) Where will you penetrate your first markets?

_____

_____

_____

_____

_____

(VI) HOW

(1) How will you find your customers?

_____
_____
_____
_____

(2) How will you contact your customers?

_____
_____
_____
_____
_____

(3) How will you sell your customers?

_____
_____
_____
_____

(4) How will you find backing / capital for the project?

_____
_____
_____
_____

(5) How will you support yourself while working on this project?

_____
_____

(6) How will you convince others to back your efforts in this project?

_____
_____
_____
_____

(7) How will you produce your first prototype?

_____
_____
_____
_____

(8) How will you market your efforts in this project?

_____
_____
_____
_____

(9) How will you profit from this project?

_____
_____
_____
_____

(10) How will your backers profit from this project?

_____
_____
_____
_____

NOTES ON THIS PROJECT:

_____
_____
_____
_____
_____
_____
_____
_____
_____
_____
_____
_____
_____
_____
_____
_____
_____
_____
_____
_____
_____
_____
_____
_____
_____
_____
_____
_____
_____

The Idea Development Checklist

Once I have completed the BIRDS, I use my Idea Development Checklist (IDC) as the next element in my efforts to organize and document a new concept. Before you detail your idea in a formal disclosure document (described later in this book), you should evaluate your concept to see if it is worth pursuing on a commercial scale. You can use the Idea Development Checklist to make this evaluation, by determining how each of the 24 categories on the IDC pertain to your invention. If an overwhelming number (roughly 90% or more) are positive, then the project has commercial potential. If too many areas show insurmountable obstacles or pose problems such as environmental concerns or poor financial returns, then the invention may not be worthy of the time, effort, and money necessary to develop it. If, after using the IDC, you consider the idea viable, then you should file a formal disclosure document with the Disclosure Document Program of the Patent and Trademark Office.

The most important thing to remember when filling out the Idea Development Checklist is to be absolutely honest with yourself about the answers. Lying to yourself will only defeat the IDC's purpose.

To successfully complete the twenty-four items, you must devote a great deal of thought to your concept, and you must write down a great deal of information. When the IDC is properly and honestly filled out, however, it can help start you on the basic research path that your concept will need to succeed. The data you assemble can be used to create estimates, projections, and prototype designs. The IDC also can become a cornerstone of an invention's development patent work.

NOTE: On the IDC form that follows, you will see entries labeled, "Ref. BIDS Sheet." These are cross-references to another checklist introduced later in this chapter, the Basic Idea Development Sheet.

Documenting an Idea as It Develops

The Basic Idea Development Sheet (BIDS) (pp. 42–44) is an essential tool that every inventor should have in abundance. The BIDS allows an idea to be developed in bits and pieces, while retaining all of the proper witness documentation and cross-referencing necessary to let the development process flow smoothly. The concept behind the BIDS system is simple: When an idea is conceived and documented in a bound book, it can become difficult for you to write down in that same book all other information and developments pertaining to the idea.

The BIDS system consists of three sheets. BIDS #1 is the Project Coordination Sheet. BIDS #2 is the Graphics Sheet. BIDS #3 is the Data Sheet.

The Project Coordination Sheet is used as a cover sheet for each group of other BIDS forms. The Project Coordination Sheet records the purpose and scope of the work being done. It acts as the start and finish point for each

IDEA DEVELOPMENT CHECKLIST

IDEA NAME: _____

INVENTOR'S NAME: _____ DATE: _____

CONCEPT DESCRIPTION: _____

_____

_____

(1) POTENTIAL MARKET: Ref. BID Sheet: _____

_____ Very small, specialized or market is restricted by unchangeable factors.

_____ Small, regional or semi-specialized market.

_____ Market size if unknown (until extensive research is completed).

_____ Medium market size; crosses industry, social, age or other limiting boundaries.

Notes on potential market: ( ) Industrial ( ) Household ( ) Governmental

_____

_____

_____

(2) PRODUCT LIFECYCLE: Ref. BIDS Sheet: _____

_____ Very short; product wears out or is disposable after 1 use.

_____ Short; product is a temporary purchase for specific application (2-10 uses).

_____ Medium; product can be used multiple times but is expected to wear out.

_____ Medium-long; product may last a long time depending upon wear & tear.

_____ Long; product is expected to last several years in good operating condition.

_____ Unknown; product lifecycle performance has no background for comparison.

Notes on lifecycle:

_____

_____

_____

(3) LEGALITY: Ref. BIDS Sheet: _____

_____ Current laws prohibit manufacture ( ) and sale ( ) in some ( ) /all ( ) states.

_____ Current laws demand licensing of this type product for consumer use.

_____ Legality of product is unknown (until extensive research is completed).

_____ Current laws at state level effect this type product in some way.

_____ Current laws at federal level effect this type product in some way.

_____ No current laws effect the manufacturer ( ) / sale ( ) of this type product.

Notes on product legality:

_____

_____

_____

(4) PRODUCT SAFETY: Ref. BIDS Sheets: _____

_____ Construction, function or design makes it unsafe for most of general public.

_____ Construction, function or design makes it unsafe for most people.

_____ Product needs safety warnings or special training to operate.

_____ Safety factors are unknown (until extensive research is completed).

_____ Similar products are generally safe with proper user orientation.

_____ Similar products have good safety record.

_____ Construction, function or design makes it safe for most of general public.

_____ Product needs no safety warnings or special training to operate.

Notes on product safety: ( ) Industrial use ( ) Household use ( ) Governmental use

_____

_____

_____

(5) PRODUCT DURABILITY: Ref. BIDS Sheet: _____

_____ Low grade components; expected to break under stressful use.

_____ Product is designed to withstand some mis-handling before damage occurs.

_____ Medium grade components; will last normal lifecycle with rough handling.

_____ High grade components; will exceed normal lifecycle with rough handling.

_____ Super tough components; expected to perform without damage under stress.

Unknown; product durability has no background for comparison.

Notes on product durability:

(6) USAGE LEARNING CURVE: Ref. BIDS Sheet: _____

_____ Long learning curve with low ( ) medium ( ) high ( ) retention.

_____ Medium learning curve with low ( ) medium ( ) high ( ) retention.

_____ Fast learning curve with low ( ) medium ( ) high ( ) retention.

_____ Easy learning curve due to little or no procedures.

_____ Medium tough learning curve due to mild procedures.

_____ Tough learning due to complicated procedures.

_____ Unknown; product learning curve has no background for comparison.

Notes on product learning curve: Projected Learning Curve Timeframe:

_____

_____

_____

(7) PRODUCT SERVICEABILITY: Ref. BIDS Sheet: _____

_____ Easy serviceability; due to modular design or other user friendly design features.

_____ Medium serviceability; due to design or easy customer part replacement.

_____ Hard serviceability; due to complicated assembly or permanently assembled parts.

_____ Customer can service this product; product requires periodic service by owner.

_____ Customer cannot service this product; product must be factory serviced.

_____ No service ever needed for this product due to design.

_____ Unknown; product service has no background for comparison.

Notes on product serviceability:

_____

_____

_____

(8) ENVIRONMENTAL IMPACT: Ref. BIDS Sheet: _____

_____ None; product has no production / use waste or detrimental byproducts.

_____ Marginal; product's production ( ) / use ( ) has slight E.I. side effects.

_____ Considerable; product's production ( ) / use ( ) has large E.I. side effects.

_____ Unquestionable; product's production ( ) / use ( ) has large E.I. side effects.

_____ Severe; product's production ( ) / use ( ) has long term E.I. side effects.

_____ Product's existence has positive E.I. on community.

_____ Unknown; product E.I. has no background for comparison.

Notes on environmental impact:

_____

_____

_____

(9) DEVELOPMENTAL CURVE: Ref. BIDS Sheet: _____

_____ Long developmental curve using low ( ) medium ( ) high ( ) research rate.
_____ Medium developmental curve with low ( ) medium ( ) high ( ) research rate.
_____ Fast curve with low ( ) medium ( ) high ( ) research rate.
_____ Medium tough developmental curve due to more intensive research needed.
_____ Tough developmental due to complicated research needed.
_____ Easy prototype development due to simple design ( ) and materials ( ).
_____ Medium prototype development due to advanced design ( ) and materials ( ).
_____ Tough prototype development due to complex design ( ) and materials ( ).
_____ Unknown; product developmental curve has no background for comparison.

Notes on product development curve; A Projected Development Timeframe:

_____
_____
_____

(10) PROJECT INVESTMENT COSTS: Ref. BIDS Sheet: _____

_____ No external investment; project can be funded by inventor out of his own pocket
_____ Low external costs; due to simple construction ( ) and manufacture ( ).
_____ Low; due to simple promotion ( ) and marketing techniques ( ).
_____ Medium; due to more advanced construction ( ) and manufacturers ( ).
_____ Medium; due to more advanced promotion ( ) and marketing techniques ( ).
_____ High external costs; due to complex construction ( ) and manufacture ( ).
_____ High; due to complex promotion ( ) and marketing techniques ( ).
_____ Unknown; product investment has no background for comparison.

Notes on project investment: Projected Total Costs:

_____
_____
_____

(11) CURRENT DEMAND: Ref. BIDS Sheet: _____

_____ Very small and unstable market demand; couldn't support project effort.
_____ Small and stable market demand; could support project effort w/o competition.
_____ Medium market demand; could support project effort with light competition.
_____ Medium-Large market; could support project effort with some competition.
_____ Large market; could support project effort with major competition.
_____ Current Demand is unknown (until extensive research is completed).

Notes on current demand: ( ) Industrial ( ) Household ( ) Governmental

_____
_____
_____

(12) FUTURE DEMAND: Ref. BIDS Sheet: _____

_____ Very small and unstable market demand; market probably won't last long.
_____ Small and stable market demand; could support future sales w/o competition.
_____ Medium market demand; could support future sales with light competition.
_____ Medium-Large market; could support future sales with some competition.
_____ Large market; could support future sales with major competition.
_____ Future Demand is unknown (until extensive research is completed).

Notes on future demand: ( ) Industrial ( ) Household ( ) Governmental

_____
_____
_____

(13) PROMOTION REQUIREMENTS: Ref. BIDS Sheet:_____
_____ Low promotional costs; due to self promoting nature of product.
_____ Easy promotion effect due to unique nature of product.
_____ Medium promotional costs; due to basic advertising and promotion required.
_____ Medium promotion effort; due to public's unfamiliarity with product concept.
_____ High promotional costs; due to complex market and six of potential market.
_____ Major promotional effort required; due to need to educate public from scratch.
_____ Unknown; promotional requirements have no background for comparison.
Notes on promotional requirements: Projected Totals: Costs: _____ Time: _____

_____
_____
_____

(14) MANUFACTURING COSTS: Ref. BIDS Sheet: _____
_____ No tooling investment; project can be manufactured from stock items.
_____ Low manufacturing costs; due to simple construction ( ) and design ( ).
_____ Medium manufacturing costs; due to more advanced construction ( ) and design ( ).
_____ High manufacturing costs; due to complex construction ( ) and design ( ).
_____ Unknown; manufacturing cost projection has no background for comparison.
Notes on manufacturing costs: Projected Total Costs:

_____
_____
_____

(15) PROFITABILIYY: Ref. BIDS Sheet: _____
_____ Low profitability; due to complex promotion ( ), design ( ) and manufacture ( ).
_____ Medium profitability; due to simpler promotion ( ), design ( ) and manufacture ( ).
_____ High profitability; due to simplest promotion ( ), design ( ) and manufacture ( ).
_____ Unknown; profitability projection has no background for comparison.
Notes on profitability: Projected Total Profits:_____ Timeframe: _____

_____
_____
_____

(16) STABILITY OF DEMAND: Ref. BIDS Sheet: _____
_____ Very unstable market demand; Fad type market probably won't last long.
_____ Stable market demand; strong consumer ( ), industrial ( ), gov't ( ) base.
_____ Very stable; necessity of life type product with strong yearly demand.
_____ Stability of demand is unknown (until extensive research is completed).
Notes on stability of demand: ( ) Industrial ( ) Household ( ) Government

_____
_____
_____

(17) PATENTABILITY: Ref. BIDS Sheet: _____
_____ Patent search underway or already conducted.

_____ Patent application underway or application accepted/serial number issued.
_____ No patent sought; product can be manufactured and sold without protection.
_____ Low chance of patentability; due to large number of other similar patents.
_____ Medium chance of patentability; due to lower number of other similar patents.
_____ High chance of patentability; due to small number of other similar patents.
_____ Unknown; no patent search done yet.
Notes on patentability: Projected Total Patent Costs: _____ Timeframe: _____
_____
_____
_____

(18) PROTECTIBILITY: Ref. BIDS Sheet: _____
_____ No patent sought; product can be manufactured and sold without protection.
_____ Patent sought; product cannot be manufactured and sold without protection.
_____ Low chance of protectibility; due to no trade secrets ( ) or no patent protection ( ).
_____ Medium chance of protectibility; due to a trade secret ( ) or patent pending ( ).
_____ High chance of protectibility; due to patent issued ( ) or multiple trade secrets ( ).
_____ Unknown; project has no background for comparison.
Notes on protectibility:
_____
_____
_____

(19) FEATURES AND BENEFITS (FAB): Ref. BIDS Sheet: _____
_____ None; product is a rehash of other products dressed up to get in on a market.
_____ Small; product is only slight improvement over existing products in field.
_____ Medium; product has time ( ) and labor ( ) saving aspects over existing products.
_____ Large; product has may time ( ) and labor ( ) saving aspects over existing products.
_____ Major; product is unique in field with many new and important features.
_____ Unknown; project has no background for comparison.
Notes on features and benefits:
_____
_____
_____

(20) COMPETITION (NEW AND EXISTING): Ref. BIDS Sheet:_____
_____ None; product is currently alone in the field and little is expected upon intro.
_____ None but it is expected upon intro to field; competitor will have short lead time.
_____ None but it is expected upon intro to field; competitor will have longer lead time.
_____ Small; product has existing competition but it is limited in scope; expected to stay static.
_____ Medium; existing market is stable but there is plenty of room for all products.
_____ Large; product has many competitors and will have a hard time penetrating market.
_____ Major; product may be unable to penetrate market due to huge established competitors.
_____ Unknown; product competition has no background for comparison.
Notes on new and existing competition:
_____
_____
_____
_____

(21) DEVELOPMENTAL EXPENSES: Ref. BIDS Sheet:_____
_____ None; product is a currently fully developed and ready to market.
_____ Small; product design is simple and costs for pre-production are limited.
_____ Medium; product requires some molds or other developmental expenditures.
_____ Large; product has many developmental expenses including molds and testing.
_____ Unknown; product development has no background for comparison.
Notes on developmental expenses:

_____
_____
_____
_____

(22) FUNCTIONAL FEASIBILITY: Ref. BIDS Sheet: _____
_____ None; product already proven unfeasible in present paper ( ) / physical ( ) design.
_____ Functional prototype has ( ) / has not ( ) already been produced ( ) and tested ( ).
_____ Small; product design needs revision prior to prototyping and testing.
_____ Moderate; product design appears to function OK under most circumstances.
_____ Major product has proven itself under severe paper ( ) / physical ( ) test circumstances.
_____ Unknown; functional feasibility has no background for comparison.
Notes on functional feasibility:

_____
_____
_____
_____

(23) PRODUCTION FEASIBILITY: Ref. BIDS Sheet: _____
_____ None; product already proven unmanufacturable in present design.
_____ Production prototype has ( ) / has not ( ) already been produced ( ) and tested ( ).
_____ Small; product design needs revisions prior to production tooling or set up.
_____ Moderate; product design appears to be manufacturable by planned methods.
_____ Major; product is designed for assembly and production methods are simple & clear.
_____ Unknown; production feasibility has no background for comparison.
Notes on production feasibility:

_____
_____
_____
_____

(24) USER COMPATIBILITY: Ref. BIDS Sheet:_____
_____ None; product already proven user "unfriendly" in present design.
_____ Small; product design needs ergonomic revision prior to prototyping.
_____ Moderate; product design appears to be user friendly under most circumstances.
_____ Major; product has proven itself user compatible under sever user test circumstances.
_____ Unknown; user compatibility has no background for comparison.
Notes on user compatibility

_____
_____
_____
_____

part of a project's progress. It also correlates the BIDS work to the Danger/Opportunities (D/O) List described later in this chapter.

The Graphics Sheet is used to record drawings and other graphics, as well as important information associated with these visual materials.

The BIDS Data Sheet serves as the basic notation sheet in the development of a project. The Data Sheet should be used in any part of the invention project that requires a written description or documentation of such information as idea parameters and contacts.

Note that each BIDS in the example contains spaces for recording references to what I call a D/O List, or Dangers/Opportunities List. This is yet another valuable tool for organizing your ideas and asking the right questions that can lead to a successful and marketable invention. (See "Using the D/O List on page 45.)

In Chinese, the character for "crisis"　危机

comes from "danger"　危

plus "opportunity".　机

Dangers Versus Opportunities

The Chinese ideogram that represents "crisis" is made from the ideogram symbols for two other words: "danger" and "opportunity." Every task an inventor faces on the long path toward an invention's completion is either a danger to be dealt with or an opportunity to be explored. Thus, my D/O List was born. Over the years, I have found that taking on a project such as the creation of a new piece of technology can be an awesome, complicated task, particularly if it is not approached in the right way. The D/O List is a management system that can help you evaluate a project and organize it into manageable segments that create a flow.

Each project an entrepreneurial inventor undertakes can be seen as a series of tasks, and each one of these tasks can be broken down into a series of things to do. Ordinary "to-do" lists are okay for typical daily projects. Inventing, however, requires more intensive organizational skills. Inventing is a series of crisis management and project management activities that culminates in a completed concept. These are the elements of an invention project:

1. The *invention idea,* or overall concept.
2. The *project,* which is just one of many parts of the concept that must be accomplished.
3. *Tasks,* each of which are just one part of one project that must be completed.

BIDS # 1: PROJECT COORDINATION SHEET   PAGE CODE _____ SHEET ____OF _____
INVENTOR'S NAME:_____ **DATE:**_____
PROJECT NAME: _____
FIELD OF IDEA: _____
SPIN OFF IDEA FROM: _____
REFERENCE TO D/O™LIST ITEM: PAGE NO._____ **CODE:**_____ **LINE NO.**____
ORIGINAL IDEA [ ] IDEA UPDATE WORKSHEET [ ] OTHER [ ]_____
ORIGINAL IDEA PAPERWORK LOCATED AT: _____

THIS WORK IS IN REFERENCE TO ACCOMPLISHING THE FOLLOWING GOAL:

NOTES ON THIS WORK: (CHECK ALL THAT APPLY)
BASIC RESEARCH [ ]   CONCEPT FEASIBILITY [ ]   PROTOTYPE CONSTRUCTION [ ]
MANUFACTURER / VENDOR SELECTION [ ]   PUBLICITY & PROMOTION [ ]
MARKETING [ ]   NETWORKING [ ]   PATENT INFORMATION [ ] LEGAL INFO [ ]
PROJECT MANAGEMENT [ ]   ARTWORK [ ]   CORRESPONDENCE [ ]   RESOURCES [ ]

DATE THIS WORK STARTED:_____ **DATE THIS WORK FINISHED**_____
IS THIS WORK COMPLETE ? : YES [ ] NO [ ]
IF "YES": DOES IT FINISH THE D/O™ LIST ITEM AT TOP OF PAGE: YES [ ] NO [ ]

ADDITIONAL WORKED NEEDED TO BE DONE TO COMPLETE THIS ITEM:

I, _____, do hereby declare that the inventor named at the top of this page showed me this_____ page invention disclosure document on _____19_____. I have reviewed the information and fully understand the invention's operation, function and purpose. I have signed my name below as witness to the creation of this information.

Signed_____ Date_____

BIDS # 2: GRAPHICS SHEET GRAPHIC NO.:__________ SHEET ________ OF ________
INVENTOR'S NAME:____________________________________DATE:____________________
PROJECT NAME: ____
FIELD OF IDEA:____
SPIN OFF IDEA FROM: ____
REFERENCE TO D/O™LIST ITEM: PAGE NO.________ CODE:____________ LINE NO.______
ORIGINAL IDEA [ ] IDEA UPDATE WORKSHEET [ ] OTHER [ ]______________________
ORIGINAL IDEA GRAPHIC LOCATED AT: ____

GRAPHIC NAME:____
SCALE:____________________ MATERIAL(S):_______________________________________

I, _______________________________, do hereby declare that the inventor named at the top of this page showed me this______page invention disclosure document on _______________19______. I have reviewed the information and fully understand the invention's operation, function and purpose. I have signed my name below as witness to the creation of this information

Signed____Date__________________

Basic Idea Developemnt Sheets (BIDS)
Idea Documentation System By GoldMind™ Associates

BIDS # 3: DATA SHEET   PAGE CODE _____   SHEET ____OF _____

INVENTOR'S NAME:_____ DATE:_____

PROJECT NAME: _____

FIELD OF IDEA:_____

SPIN OFF IDEA FROM: _____

REFERENCE TO D/O™LIST ITEM: PAGE NO._____ CODE:_____ LINE NO._____

ORIGINAL IDEA [ ] IDEA UPDATE WORKSHEET [ ] OTHER [ ]_____

ORIGINAL IDEA PAPERWORK LOCATED AT: _____

I, _____, do hereby declare that the inventor named at the top of this page showed me this_____page invention disclosure document on _____19_____. I have reviewed the information and fully under-stand the invention's operation, function and purpose. I have signed my name below as witness to the creation of this information

Signed_____ Date_____

4. *Sub-tasks,* each which are one part of a task that must be completed.

5. *Do-items,* each of which are individual actions that must be taken to accomplish part of a sub-task.

These also are the hierarchical levels of the D/O List project management technique, explained later in this chapter.

Dealing with Dangers

Dangers are threats to a project and usually should be handled first. A danger is any task, sub-task, or item that can create additional work or set back the project if it is not taken care of in a certain manner or by a certain time. Dangers often are time-sensitive operations (TSO) such as deadlines for applications or payments. A time-sensitive operation is any item that has a start or finish date that will affect the overall project. A time-sensitive operation also can be a task-spinoff item. A task-spinoff item is any item that, if not completed, will keep an entirely separate part of the project from starting or completing. Time-sensitive operations and task-spinoff items, as you will see later, should be noted on the D/O List, so you can stay aware of matters that are hinge points for another item in the project.

If a task can be postponed without affecting the planned project outcome or keeping another part of the project from happening, then it is *not* a danger.

Seizing Opportunities

When you recognize opportunities and take advantage of them, your project often can be speeded up or completed with less difficulty. Opportunities are tasks that open pathways to making the project more fruitful. Opportunities can expand the horizon of an invention to include more profit potential or more possibilities for enhancing your career. Certain opportunities may also slow down the completion of a task, but they will not jeopardize the project outcome. You may even choose to pass up certain opportunities, and use your time and budget to deal more effectively with certain dangers.

Using the D/O List

When you fill out a D/O List, you define the parameters of the work to be accomplished, for every part of the project, and you flag the dangers and opportunities, as well.

D/O List Example. The following example illustrates the structure of the D/O List and shows how to use it.

Filling Out a D/O List. To use copies of the D/O List, fill out the blanks as follows:

Inventor: Place your name on this line, on each sheet.

Concept Name: Put the name of the invention idea on this line, on each sheet.

Inventor: _____ Date: _____ Page No. ____ of ____ Code: ____

Concept Name: _____ Specific Concept Sub-Part: _____

D/O™ Level: _____ From Page No.: _____ Line No.: _____

Master Item Name For This Sheet: _____

Line No.	D	O	TSO	Delegate	Item Description	Est. $	Act.	Due Date	Follow Up Status

Notes on this D/O™ List Sheet:

Generic D/O List™
Sample Format

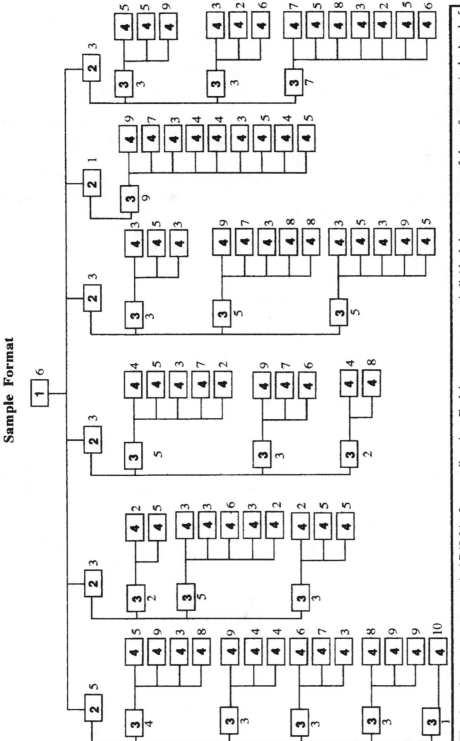

The chart above represents a typical D/O List for a small project. Each box represents an individual sheet or group of sheets for a particular level of the D/O List. The numbers in the boxes represent the level of the list at that point: 1 = Project Level; 2 = Task Level; 3 = Sub-Task Level; 4 = Do Items. The numbers outside the boxes represent the number of items on that particular sheet. Numbers outside the #4 boxes are the number of Do List items on those sheets. In this generic example there are a total of 366 individual Do Items on sheets #4 to satisfy the requirements of the original project sheet with six items. Each sheet of a D/O List may contain one or more specific items at that level. Each line item becomes a seperate sheet at the next lowest level. This allows you, the entrepreneurial inventor, to break down any Project into discrete Tasks; each Task into discrete Sub Tasks and those Sub-Tasks into discrete Do Items. You work from the bottom (Do Items) up to compete entire sheets (number 4) in order to check off one item on the list above it (number 3). When all the #4 sheets of a particular #3 sheet are finished, then you can check off the #3 item on the #2 sheet it is listed on. This allows you to review any project at any time to see the status of the entire Project in terms of individual Tasks, Sub-Tasks and Do Items needed to be completed to finalize the project.

47

D/O Level: On this line, place the level of classification that this sheet defines. The level is one of the following: Project, Task, Sub-Task, or Do-Item.

Page No. / Code: These spaces allow you to number and code each project sheet in any fashion you desire. This can help you use the D/O List sheets more productively. The Code space can be used to indicate an order of work, a secrecy level, a certain contractor, or a special service that must be used for items on the sheet.

From No.: This space is used to record an item number from another list. For example, if this sheet is D/O Level: Sub-Task, then its master item is from a Task sheet.

From Page: In this space, place the page number and code from the master item page where this item originated. This information can help you quickly backtrack to the source list.

Date: In this space, record the date that you start this particular sheet. This will give you a reference to compare against the dates listed later under the "Due Date" column.

Master Item Name: This is the same name the item is given as it appears on the sheet from which this Project, Task or Sub-Task is taken.

Once you have filled in the information at the top of the D/O List sheet, continue with the columns, as follows:

No.: Give each item on this page a separate number, starting with one. More than one line of space may be required to fill in the Item Description, so skip the lines you need before numbering the next item.

"D" or "O" Box: Place a checkmark in one box or the other, to indicate if this item is a Danger or an Opportunity. Always review all D/O Lists for checked "D" boxes and their corresponding "Due Date" boxes, to be sure that enough time is allocated to complete the items without endangering the project.

TSO: In this box place a date to start an item, if it has been determined to be a "Time Sensitive Operation" or "Task Spin Off." Remember that these can hold up the start or finish of another section of the overall project. All TSOs are considered Dangers. Check the dates in the TSO boxes regularly. If any of these TSOs are approaching a start or finish deadline, put them high on the priority list.

Delegate: Use this space to record who has responsibility for completing this item. It may be you, another person, or a particular company. Filling in this space is extremely important when you are working with a team or with various companies. It allows you to see at a glance who is working on what.

Item Description: In this space, write a description of what must be done. If you need more space, use the next line down under the same heading. Use as many lines as needed, but be sure you describe only one item to be done.

$ (Expenses): Enter a dollar amount that estimates the cost of this item or activity in the "EST." Box and the actual amount spent in the "ACT" Box. This lets you make cost estimates for sections of the project. The actual figures let you keep track of actual costs over the life of a project.

Due Date: Put the date that this activity must be completed, if it is a Danger. If it is an Opportunity, place the date that this activity must be completed to take advantage of this item. Leave the due-date blank if this item has no time sensitivity.

Follow Up: If additional follow-up is needed, place a "Yes" in this box to remind you to place this item on the appropriate new list or farther down the same list. A page and item number can be inserted in this box to indicate the path of the follow-up to the new location on the D/O List. When no further follow-up is needed, this particular item is finished. Indicate this by writing "DONE" in the box.

When all of the boxes on a particular sheet are completed, it is time to check off that item on the master sheet for the next highest level where the "Master Item Name" is a single line of that list.

Using the D/O List technique can become second nature within a short time. You will find that your productivity and sense of completing a given task will increase, because there no longer will be loose ends that can delay or destroy a project. The D/O List can simplify project management for single or multiple inventions. It can also be used to manage many other parts of your day-to-day life, so that you can better handle the dangers and opportunities that are always present in entrepreneurial inventing.

The Multiple Avenues Personal Survival System

Once you have mastered the art of managing one project and reached the marketplace, you are ready to tackle the challenges of juggling multiple projects. The problem for the entrepreneurial inventor is that one success may not provide long-term financial security. One success likely will not satisfy your creative desires, either. Instead, you will find yourself wanting to do more, perhaps develop several products at once.

The Multiple Avenues Personal Survival System (MAPS) is my own, personal system for surviving in the world of entrepreneurial inventing. It has helped others, and it can help you succeed, too. MAPS simply means that you should give yourself multiple avenues, or options, by always running more than one project at once. This may seem like an easy way to get overworked, but juggling several projects at once actually is the best way to invent. The reason why MAPS works is twofold and simple.

First, invention projects happen in phases that are spurts of creative energy. These phases require you to work diligently toward one or more areas of a project's completion. However, the completion of a phase usually will require waiting for other people, companies, or the government to take some sort of action. This can include, among other things, waiting for: a patent pending number or other information from the patent office; quotation requests from manufacturers and machine shops; and parts or artwork to be fabricated by various contractors. During these waiting periods, an entrepreneurial inventor can become restless or discouraged with a project. By having a another project going simultaneously, however, the waiting periods can become the starting points for the second project's phases. This jockeying back and forth between projects also helps keep the interest level high in both efforts, because your mind is not always thinking about the same problems. There is another benefit, as well. While you are working on the second project, you give your mind a brief rest from the first project's complexities. Yet you allow your subconscious to keep working on problems in the first project, and it sometimes will come up with solutions during this down time away from the initial project.

The second, and most important, reason for using the MAPS is that it is a simple mental and emotional survival system. It can keep you from going off the entrepreneurial inventor's deep end. By having two—or more—projects going simultaneously, you will never suffer the agony of an "idea crash." An idea crash occurs when a project comes to a sudden, and often unexpected, end. Sometimes, the end of an idea for an invention may occur because you have run out of money—yours or investors' capital. Other times, an idea crash may occur because somebody else's idea hits the market first and takes away the market or need for your invention. An idea crash can also happen because you have failed to do the proper initial research and suddenly discover that your idea already is patented or exists elsewhere. Whatever the reason, an idea crash can be devastating to the entrepreneurial inventor who only works on one idea at a time. It can seem like the whole world has come to a stop, and he or she must start all over again.

When an idea crash occurs while using the Multiple Avenues Personal Survival System, you can walk away from the wreckage without much emotional turmoil, because it was only one of a group of ideas that you had under development. You will know that you have other opportunities to immediately pursue.

This is how I use the MAPS: I like to keep several ideas in a sort of holding pattern. I have done some preliminary work on them, but I haven't committed too much in the way of time or cash to their development. However, I can see opportunities to sell at least one of the projects or push its development into high gear. When I have an idea crash on a current project, I only need to pull one of the other projects out of the holding pattern and make it one of the projects that receives my daily or weekly attention.

I developed the Multiple Avenues Personal Survival System from my real-world experiences on the rollercoaster lifestyle of entrepreneurial inventing. Once, my personal life and business life were almost destroyed, because of shortsighted planning while working on an invention. I put all of my eggs in one basket, and the idea crashed. By using the MAPS, you can set a variety of goals, keep sight of roadways to different opportunities, and never let an idea crash stop your forward movement in the fast lane of entrepreneurial inventing.

Chapter 4

Patents and Patent Attorneys

**Why and How are words so important
That they cannot be used too often.**
Napoleon Bonaparte

A patent for an invention is a grant of certain rights by the federal government to the inventor, through the Patent and Trademark Office. The rights conferred by the patent extend throughout the United States and its territories and possessions. Depending on the type of patent, it may be granted for fourteen (design patent) or seventeen (utility patent) years and is not renewable. The right conferred by the patent grant is, in the language of the statute and of the grant itself, "the right to exclude others from making, using, or selling" the invention. Note that what is granted is not the right to make, use, or sell, but the right to *exclude* others from making, using, or selling the invention. The person entitled to receive the patent grant is the inventor or his or her heirs or assigns.

Is There a Patent in Your Future?

Patents are an important part of the history of inventing, and almost every famous inventor has several patents to his or her name. But don't be fooled. Not every great invention needs a patent to be a success for the inventor. A patent is useless if there is no market for the patented invention. In other words, a patent can be just an ego gratification and a very expensive piece of paper if you don't figure out ways to make money from your creativity.

On the other hand, a patent also can be essential for the protection of your invention. You should refer any questions on patent law and procedures to a qualified patent agent or patent attorney. You also can consult the Patent and Trademark Office.

WHY YOU SHOULD NOT TRY TO BE YOUR OWN PATENT ATTORNEY.   As an entrepreneurial inventor, you must wear many hats. But one hat you should never wear is that of patent attorney—unless that is your chosen profession. Patent law is complex, and the procedures for attaining a patent are strict. Understanding the laws and procedures is a full-time job best left to the professionals. Obtaining a patent can be an indispensable part of your foundation for making deals and raising money. But attempting it as an amateur in the field could end up undermining all of your other efforts. Later in this chapter, I show you how to interview and retain a patent attorney.

You should, however, learn how to do preliminary patent searches and library searches. You must do this basic invention research to fill out tools such as the Idea Development Checklist described earlier in this book.

Patents Versus Trade Secrets

Many great inventions that have made money and lasted for many years are not patented. They rely on the protection of a *trade secret*. The best-known trade secret story is how the formula for Coca-Cola has been protected for many decades. Coke has never patented its unique formula, because the formula then would become public knowledge, an easy target for a competitor to try to duplicate without actually infringing upon the original.

If your technology—physical or chemical—is protected in such a way that you can keep it secret for fifteen or twenty years, then there may be no advantages in patenting your idea. Similarly, if your idea really needs to hit the market quickly (you have a Pet Rock-type novelty item, for example) there may not be time to consider the protection of a patent. (Author's note: There are several patents on Pet Rock-type items, so getting a patent on a quick-market novelty may still be a consideration.) Your long-term goals for an invention will contribute greatly to your decision on whether or not you need a patent.

The Three Types of Patents

As an inventor, you can apply for three types of patents: *utility*, *design*, and *plant*. Each of these patents serves a different role.

Utility Patent

The *utility patent* is the most common type of patent. It is what most people think of when they use the term "patent." A utility patent is based upon claims of how a machine operates. The actual function of the device is the only consideration of this patent. The wording of the utility patent describes the function of each individual part of the machine and how each part relates to every other part. A utility patent details the *how* and *why* of each component to show the overall workings of the device. It may also describe various applications of the technology.

A utility patent contains four distinct parts: the abstract; the specifications; the claims; and the drawings. The *abstract* is a short, very concise explanation of the overall workings of the patented invention. The *specifications* are very detailed wording that describes the physical or chemical construction and interaction of the parts of the device. This explanation may be worded to include various ways the same goal can be accomplished within the structure of the device. The specifications are linked with numbers associated with the patent drawings, so anyone may see the nature of the invention. The *claims* are the heart of the invention and the only section of the patent that really matters when it comes to actual legal protection. A patent can contain one claim—or it can have dozens. The claims are just that, claims to areas of protection under that particular patent. The more claims a patent has, the stronger the patent protection. The drawings, of course, illustrate the invention in great detail.

Design Patent

A *design patent* is a patent on the appearance of a device. A design patent is fairly easy to circumvent if the design is not totally conducive to the function of the device. Some inventors apply for a design patent in conjunction with a utility patent. They do this to cover a unique product both from the appearance and functional standpoints. No single claim can appear in both patents, however. The design patent has a life of fourteen years.

Plant Patent

A *plant patent* is a patent on a newly developed, asexually reproducible plant life form. Plant patents are part of a group of patents that include newly engineered life forms. The laws governing these patents are subject to changes, because of the advanced nature of the applicable sciences. The latest details on plant patents should be obtained from the U.S. Patent Office.

What Can Be Patented

The patent law specifies (1) the general field of subject matter that can be patented and (2) the conditions under which a patent may be obtained. In the language of the statute, any person who "invents or discovers any new and useful process, machine, manufacture, or composition of matter, or any new and useful improvements thereof, may obtain a patent," subject to the conditions and requirements of the law. The term *process*, as used in the definition, means that a process or method, and new processes, primarily industrial or technical, may be patented. The term *machine*, as it is used in the statute, needs no explanation. The term *manufacture* refers to articles that are made and includes all manufactured articles. The term *composition of matter* relates to chemical compositions and may include mixtures of ingredients as well as new chemical compounds. The classes of subject matter taken together include practically everything that is made by man, as well as the processes for making them.

There are some interesting exceptions, however. For example, the Atomic Energy Act of 1954 excludes patenting a device or process if the invention is useful solely in the utilization of special nuclear materials or atomic energy for atomic weapons.

The patent statute specifies that the subject matter must be "useful." The term *useful* in this connection refers to the condition that the subject matter has a useful purpose and also includes the ability to operate. In other words, a machine that will not operate to perform the intended purpose would not be considered useful.

Interpretations of the patent statute by the courts have defined the limits of subject matter that can be patented. For example, methods of doing business and printed matter are types of subject matter that cannot be patented. In the case of mixtures of ingredients, such as medicines, a patent cannot be granted unless there is more to the mixture than the effect of its components. So-called "patent medicines" ordinarily are *not* patented.

A patent *cannot* be obtained upon a mere idea or suggestion. The patent, instead, is granted for the actual new machine, manufacture, or composition of matter. A complete description of the actual machine or other subject matter to be patented is required, but the actual machine itself does not need to be fabricated before a patent can be granted. In rare cases where the patent office has extreme doubts about the workability of a machine, it may ask for a working model to validate the concept.

Keep in mind that an actual device does *not* have to be made to get a patent. This allows inventors to dream of concepts that are fantastic in scope but have their roots in reality. A perfect example of this type of inventing is a design for a new type of space station. You would not have to build it to get a patent from the Patent and Trademark Office.

Patent Pending

The words "Patent Pending" or "Pat. Pend." indicate that a patent has been applied for on a particular device. It does not mean that the manufacturer has patent rights, nor does it indicate that the device eventually will get a patent. The "Patent Pending" mark is used by confident and not-so-confident inventors and manufacturers to tell the world that they have established a paper trail of documentation that ends with a patent application. It means they are seeking protection and have filed the appropriate paperwork to get a patent. Only those people who have actually applied for a patent can put "Patent Pending" on a product. If you do so without filing the proper papers with the Patent Office, you are in violation of federal laws and are subject both to fines and imprisonment. Once a patent is issued the manufacturer is obligated to place the patent number on the device. The protection afforded by the patent law is considerably lowered if the patent number is not placed in plain sight on the device.

International Patents

An "international" patent that is valid in all countries simply does not exist. Every nation has its own patent laws governing how an inventor's rights are protected. Thanks to increased international cooperation, however, several groups of countries now have a common patenting process that is tied to one application. The best-known of these is the European Economic Community (EEC) or Common Market patent application. When you are accepted for a patent in one member country, you can get a simultaneous patent right in the other member countries. Each country still must issue its own separate patent, however, and the patents granted by each country have their own lifespans. One of the most recent additions to the international patent application process is an agreement, The Patent Cooperation Treaty (PCT), that has been signed by more than fifty countries, including Russia, Japan, Australia, Brazil and most of western Europe. For more information on international patents, contact the Patent and Trademark Office, Department of Commerce, Box PCT, Washington, DC 20231 or call (703) 557-2003.

How to Select a Patent Attorney

Finding a good patent attorney is an important step for any entrepreneurial inventor. But it is not a simple process. You must be able to evaluate the attorney and decide if you trust him or her to guard the concepts that you hope to develop into money-making products. To help simplify the evaluation and selection process, I have developed a checklist that is presented at the end of this chapter. Before you use the checklist, however, you should consider the following issues and questions associated with the search for counsel.

1. APPROACH THE PROCESS THE SAME WAY YOU DO WHEN SEEKING A DOCTOR.   The patent attorney is going to handle the "birth" of your idea, from conception to government grant of a patent. You must have a bond of trust and understanding, or the process will be very hard and frustrating. If you can't get along with your patent attorney on a personal level, think twice before entrusting him or her with your patent application.

Also consider where the patent attorney is located. Can you get an appointment and get there without a major hassle? Is the office staff cooperative? Both the location and the staff can play major roles in how well you get along with your patent attorney.

2. Check out some of the attorney's patent work.   Ask to see information about other patents, such as issued patent numbers, or names of inventions where he or she was the attorney of record. Examine the patents for obvious flaws in logic, coverage, and execution. Also consider the complexity of the patents the attorney has handled, versus the complexity of the work you want handled.

3. Talk with other inventors who have used the attorney.
Ask them about their working relationship. Is the attorney easy to work with? Does he or she waste a lot of money on time-consuming errors in procedures and work? Can you get the attorney on the telephone when you need to talk? Be cautious if the attorney is uneasy about you talking to some of his or her clients. This could indicate a problem. Ask the inventors how they were referred to the attorney. Try to speak with people who found the attorney through referrals from another attorney or through the Chamber of Commerce.

4. Ask the attorney for at least three types of references:
   a. Personal references. These are the least-believable, since some may be the attorney's best friends simply putting out the good word. But you can still get some colorful information about the attorney as a person.
   b. Inventor references. These are very important for sizing up the attorney's work.
   c. Business references. These will tell you how the attorney is seen in the business community. For the most truthful responses, try to get some business references from sources other than those suggested by the attorney.

5. Check with the state and local chambers of commerce.
Make sure that no complaints of professional misbehavior have been lodged against the attorney by inventors.

6. Check with the Better Business Bureau.   Make sure that no complaints have been lodged against the attorney's business practices.

7. Ask the attorney about his or her background.   Don't be afraid to ask questions. You will be entrusting this man or woman with your concepts, which you hope will make you money. Think of a patent attorney as the guardian of that trust, but don't take anything for granted. Find out everything you need to know to be comfortable with the attorney and his or her methodology and background. If you discover a difference of opinions about how things should be done, you may need to find another attorney. Specifically ask questions about the following issues:
   a. The number of years he or she has been in practice. Time and experience are almost one and the same in the legal profession, but

not always. A patent attorney may not have been handling patent applications throughout his or her legal career.

b. The number of patent applications the attorney has handled, and how many actually have become patents. This is not necessarily a reflection of the attorney's ability, but it can be a good indication of experience in filing patent applications and dealing with the patent office.

c. Does the attorney specialize in any certain field? Most patent attorneys have some specialized training in a technical field. Find out if the attorney's specialty or specialties coincide with your project. If they do not, and if your patent application is going to be very complex, you may want to go to another attorney who understands your field. If your patent application is fairly general in nature, the attorney's specialty may not be a real concern.

8. ASK THE ATTORNEY ABOUT HIS OR HER FEE SCHEDULE. How flexible is the payment schedule? How much money is expected up front? Most attorneys want a retainer that will cover their time and expenses through the actual patent application process. On average, this can range from $1,000 to $2,500 or so. Also ask about the estimated costs for your patent application. Most experienced attorneys can give you a ballpark estimate of what the entire process will cost.

9. ASK ABOUT TYPICAL TIME FRAMES AND ADDITIONAL COSTS.
Specifically:

a. Can the attorney give you a realistic estimate of how long it will take to write the application and get the artwork done? If the attorney is experienced at patents, he or she will be able to size up the work involved in filing your application.

b. How will the attorney's backlog of work affect your application? Find out if he or she has other major projects that will not allow actively starting on your application within a reasonable time.

c. Based upon your disclosures, does the attorney see any complications in the application or preparation of documentation, and will this cause delays or additional costs? For example, will an exceptional amount of patent drawings be required, or will there be unusual complexity in translating your idea to paper? A good patent attorney should be able to see problems after only a brief review of your idea.

10. ASK THE ATTORNEY FOR INFORMATION ABOUT HIS OR HER WORKING PARTNERS. Be sure to get answers to the following groups of questions about the other people in the attorney's circle of co-workers. These people will play an important part in the patent application process.

a. Who is the attorney's search firm, what kind of search firm are they, and how will they be paid? How long has the attorney worked with the search firm? Have they ever screwed up a search? How fast and accurate are they?

b. Does the attorney have a Washington, D.C., associate firm, or does he or she also do all of the patent office contact work? If the attorney does use an associate firm, how large is it and what is their track record?

c. Does the attorney work with other patent attorneys who can help you if he is sick, or disabled, or if he goes out of town or dies?

Once you are satisfied with the responses to your questions, you are ready to hire a patent attorney. Do not worry about revealing your idea to him or her. Patent attorneys have a "fiduciary responsibility" to keep a client's ideas confidential. The legal profession imposes strict penalties for violations of the attorney-client relationship. If you still feel uncomfortable about revealing your idea at a first meeting, ask the attorney to sign a secrecy or non-disclosure agreement. Most patent attorneys understand the inventor's strong need for secrecy and will have no problem with signing such an agreement. Some, however, may tell you that their professional ethics prohibit them from revealing ideas, and they will not want to sign the form. How you handle this situation is a matter of personal judgment.

Patent Attorney Checklist

The checklist on the next page contains the questions you should ask when you are ready to hire a patent attorney.

Special Resources for Inventors and Patents

Registered Patent Attorneys

For an official list of attorneys registered to practice before the Patent and Trademark Office contact: Office of Enrollment and Discipline, Patent and Trademark Office, Department of Commerce, Washington, DC 20231.

Patent Copies

Copies and specifications of any existing patent (not patents pending) are available from the Patent and Trademark Office for $1. Plant patents in color are $8. Contact: The Patent and Trademark Office, Department of Commerce, P.O. Box 9, Washington, DC 20231.

Patent Depository Libraries

At least thirty-one states have Patent Depository Libraries. These libraries have current issues of U.S. patents and most have an extensive collection of earlier issued patents. These collections vary from library to library. All of the

PATENT ATTORNEY CHECKLIST

ATTORNEY NAME: _____

ADDRESS: _____

CITY, STATE, ZIP: _____

TELEPHONE: _____ - _____

FAX:_____ DEDICATED LINE? _____

OFFICE HOURS: _____

DATE OF 1st INTERVIEW:_____ HIRE: YES_____ NO _____

1. Approach it like finding a doctor: Do you get a general feeling of trust from him/her?:
Yes _____ No _____ Other: _____
Comments: _____
_____

2. Where is he located? Can you get to see him without a major hassle?
Yes _____ No _____ Other: _____
Comments: _____
_____

3. Is his office staff cooperative?
Yes _____ No _____ Other: _____
Comments: _____
_____

4. Check out his other patent work: Ask to see information about other patents.
Done _____ Approved _____ Info given without problem: _____
Comments: _____
_____

5. Check with other inventors who have used him. Talk with them about their working relationship with the attorney. Is he easy to work with?
Yes _____ No _____ Other: _____
Comments: _____
_____

6. Does he waste a lot of money on time consuming errors in his procedures and work?
Yes _____ No _____ Other: _____
Comments: _____
_____

7. Can you get him on the phone when you need to talk to him?
Yes _____ No _____ Other: _____
Comments: _____
_____

8. Ask the inventors how they were referred to the attorney? (Make sure the inventors you're talking to aren't all close friends and relatives of the attorney; how were they referred to his office and by whom?.)
Done_____ Approved _____ Number of other contacts obtained:_____
Comments: _____
_____

9. Ask for references
a. Personal references:
Done_____ Approved _____ Number of other contacts obtained:_____

Comments: _____

_____

b. Inventor references:
Done _____ Approved _____ Number of other contacts obtained: _____

Comments: _____

_____

c. Business references:
Done _____ Approved _____ Number of other contacts obtained: _____

Comments: _____

_____

10. Check with the State & Local Chambers of Commerce
Done _____ Approved _____ State: _____ Approved: _____ Local: _____

Comments: _____

_____

11. Check with the Better Business Bureau:
Done _____ Approved _____ Number of other contacts obtained: _____

Comments: _____

_____

12. Questions to ask a prospective patent attorney
a. His background
I. The number of years he has been in practice: _____

II. Number of patents he has worked on: _____

Types of Patents: _____

III. Number of Successful Patents vs. Number Applied For: _____ vs. _____

IV. Does he specialize in any certain field? _____

13. His fee schedule: How flexible is he in working with you on the payment side of the picture? How much money up front?: _____

Basic Fee Schedule: $ _____ Down _____ Per visit $: _____

Terms _____

Comments: _____

_____

14. Estimated costs for your patent application.
Terms _____

Comments: _____

_____

15. Typical time frames and additional costs
a. Typical time frame for basic patent application
Time frame _____

Comments: _____

_____

b. Any backlog of work that will effect your application:
Terms _____

Comments: _____

_____

c. Based upon your disclosure to him, does he see any complications in the application or the preparation of the documentation that will cause any delays or extra costs:
Opinion _____

Comments: _____

_____

16. Who are his working partners:
Done _____ Approved _____ Number of other partners _____
Comments: _____
_____

17. His search firm:
Contact Number:_____
a. Their fees: _____
b. What are they?: _____
c. How will they be paid? _____
d. How long has he worked with them? _____
e. Have they ever screwed up a search?_____
Yes _____ No _____ Other: _____
Comments: _____
_____

f. How fast and accurate are they? _____
Comments: _____
_____

18. His Washington, D.C. associate firm:
a. Does he have one or does he do all the contact work with the patent office by himself?
Comments: _____
_____

b. If he does use a firm in D.C., how large a firm is he associated with and what is their track record?
Name:_____
Contact info:_____
Done _____ Approved _____
Comments: _____
_____

19. Does he have another attorney in his office that can help you if he is sick, disabled, out of town or dies?
Done _____ Approved _____ Number of other contacts obtained:_____
Comments: _____
_____
_____
_____

Misc. Notes:
_____
_____
_____
_____
_____
_____
_____
_____
_____
_____
_____
_____

libraries have CASSIS, the Classification and Search Support Information System, which enables interested parties to get on-line data assistance concerning patents directly from the data banks of the Patent and Trademark Office. For information on your nearest Patent Depository Library or more information on the system and services available, call 1-800-368-2532.

The Patent Gazette

The Patent Gazette is the official weekly publication of the Patent and Trademark Office. *The Patent Gazette* describes each new patent as it is issued and includes illustrations, when available. The Gazette is available by subscription for $250 a year via Fourth Class Mail and $360 a year via First Class Mail. Contact: the Superintendent of Documents, U.S. Printing Office, Washington, DC 20402 or call 202-783-3238 for more information.

Military and Government Agencies

The following military and government agencies are good sources of information related to patents in certain fields.

Department of Defense

The Department of Defense grants licenses under government law PL 96517. It also administers government-owned patents on a partial, non-exclusive, revocable, royalty and royalty-free, nontransferable basis to any American citizen or business entity capable of introducing the invention into commercial use. This provides good opportunities for an entrepreneurial inventor to take a piece of government-researched technology and team it with his ideas to create a new market.

For Navy patents, contact: Director, Navy Patent Program, Patent Counsel for the Navy, Department of Defense, 800 North Quincy Street, Arlington, VA 22217.

For Army patents, contact: Patents, Copyrights and Trademarks Division, U.S. Army, Legal Services Agency, 5611 Columbia Pike, Room 332A, Falls Church, VA 22041-5013.

Department of Energy

The Department of Energy is another important federal focal point for inventions and patents. For more information, contact: Energy Related Inventions Program, Office of Inventions and Small-Scale Technology, Conservation and Renewable Energy, Department of Energy, 1000 Independence Avenue S.W., M5C-24, Washington, D.C. 20585.

Department of Agriculture

The Department of Agriculture has patents available for license. These patents are the result of discoveries made by that agency's researchers. The Department of Agriculture's patents are available to any U.S. citizen or company without any license fee. For information about the available patents and complete information on the license program, contact: Acquisition and Assistance, Department of Agriculture, Room 528A, 6505 Belcrest Road, Hyattsville, MD 20782.

National Aeronautics and Space Administration (NASA)

The National Aeronautics and Space Administration has patents developed during the course of the space program. Abstracts on the patents that are available are published semi-annually in *NASA Patent Abstracts Bibliography*. This publication must be purchased from the National Technical Information Service (see address under NTIS). For more information on NASA patents, contact: Patent Matters, Office of General Counsel, NASA, 400 Maryland Avenue SW, Room F7037, Washington, DC 20546.

Department of Justice

The U.S. Justice Department can provide information to inventors seeking advice about government patent policy. The Justice Department also can advise inventors on various laws and legal matters concerning patents, trademarks and copyrights. For more information, contact: Intellectual Property Section, Anti-Trust Division, Department of Justice, 512 12th Street, N.W., Room 704, Washington, DC 20530.

National Technical Information Service (NTIS)

The National Technical Information Service (NTIS) publishes a newsletter entitled *Government Inventions for Licensing*. This publication describes miscellaneous patents available for licensing from the federal government. It is available by subscription for $205 per year. Contact the NTIS, Department of Commerce, 5285 Port Royal Road, Springfield, VA 22161.

National Inventors Conference and Exposition

A National Inventors Conference and Exposition is sponsored annually by the Patents and Trademarks Office and the Bureau of National Affairs. This major conference is held in Washington, D.C., each February, close to Thomas A. Edison's birthday. The events include speakers who address issues close to the hearts of inventors. There also are demonstrations by inventors and corporations. For more information, contact: Office of Public Affairs, Patent and Trademark Office, Department of Commerce, 2021 Jefferson Davis Highway, Room 1A05, Arlington, VA 22202.

Small Business Administration (SBA)

The U.S. Small Business Administration offers a free publication entitled *Can You Make Money With Your Idea or Invention?* This publication can help you identify if your idea has potential and tells what you can do to exploit it. Contact: SBA, 1441 L Street NW, Washington, DC 20416.

Chapter 5

Copyrights, Trademarks, Secrecy Agreements, and Other Protections

It is a matter of regret that many low, mean suspicions turn out to be very well founded.

Edgar Watson Howe

 At all stages of development, from initial concept to final product, you must be concerned with guarding your secrets and keeping your works out of the hands of competitors and opportunists. You also must be concerned with protecting your rights, as well as those of your family and heirs, to benefit to the fullest from the fruits of your creations.

Patents, examined in the previous chapter, are one of the most important protections available. This chapter explains other major types of protections that can be used by the entrepreneurial inventor and answers these questions:

1. How can copyrights and trademarks help protect your ideas and products?
2. When and how should you use an inventor's basic license/assignment agreement?
3. What documentation should you keep as you develop an idea into a product?
4. How and when should you use secrecy agreements and meeting forms?

Copyrights and Trademarks

 Copyrights and trademarks are two very important forms of intellectual property protection available to entrepreneurial inventors. They serve two different functions and can be used in conjunction with patents.

Copyrights

A copyright protects the writings of an author against copying. Literary, dramatic, musical, and artistic works are included within the protection of the copyright law, which, in some instances, also covers performing and recording rights. The copyright goes to the form of expression rather than to the subject matter of the writing. For inventors, copyrights only prevent others from copying the exact description of an idea as it is written. It does not prevent others from writing a description of their own or from making and using the machine described in the copyrighted materials. Copyrights must be registered in the Copyright Office of the Library of Congress. The Patent Office has nothing whatsoever to do with copyrights. To obtain more information on copyrights, write the Registrar of Copyrights, Library of Congress, Washington, D.C. 20540.

Trademarks

A trademark relates to any word, name, symbol or device that is used in trade with goods to indicate the source or origin of the goods and to distinguish them from the goods of others. Trademark rights may be employed to prevent others from using a confusingly similar mark. But trademark rights may not be used to prevent others from making the same goods or selling them under a nonconfusing mark. Similar rights may be acquired for *service marks,* which are marks used in the sale or advertising of services. Trademarks and service marks that are used in interstate or foreign commerce may be registered with the Patent Office.

General information about trademarks and the procedures for registering them are contained in a pamphlet, *General Information Concerning Trademarks.* The pamphlet may be obtained from the Patent Office, or by writing the Superintendent of Documents, U.S. Government Printing Office, Washington, DC 20402, or by calling (703) 783-3238.

To find out if another company is using a trademark or service mark similar to the one you intend to use, contact the Trademark Search Room at the Patent Trademark Office, Department of Commerce, 2011 Crystal Plaza Building #2, Arlington, VA 22202, (703) 557-3268. If you are unable to go to the office in person, your patent attorney or personnel at the Trademark Search Room should be able to recommend several persons or firms who can do the trademark search for you.

The Inventor's Basic License or Assignment Agreement

Licenses and *assignment agreements* are protective measures typically employed between an inventor and any party wishing to use the inventor's patent-protected concept. You should understand the differences between a license and an assignment agreement, particularly when you want to sell rights to a patent-pending or patented concept to a person, company, or corporation. You also should consult with your patent attorney *before* entering into such an agreement. The example form presented later in this chapter can be used to grant a *license* or an *assignment of rights*.

Here are the differences:

LICENSE.   A license grants the right to use a patent for a specific period of time. When the time expires, the license must be renewed if the licensee wants to continue using the patent. The license period allows the inventor to renegotiate the contract, when desired. A license can be revoked under various conditions set forth in the agreement by the inventor and the licensee. When a license is issued, the inventor still owns the patent application and the patent, when issued. The licensee's name does not appear on the patent.

ASSIGNMENT.   When you agree to an assignment, you hand over the basic ownership of your patent and all rights of that patent to the assignee. In most cases, an assignment is for the life of the patent. The assignment is registered with the patent office and becomes part of the patent records. If the assignment is done prior to the patent's issue, the assignee's name and address is listed on the patent above the inventor's name. This indicates that the assignee is the entity to contact for any discussion about acquiring rights for the patent. An assignment contract should be handled correctly the first time, because there may be no chance to renegotiate it. All patent agreements can include clauses that modify or amend the use or conditions that affect the patent. However, revoking an assignment usually only happens under extreme conditions that have been agreed to in advance.

A SAMPLE LICENSE AGREEMENT.   The form that follows on pages 68 and 69 is a sample license agreement. **WARNING:** Consult a patent attorney before using this or any other legal document in this book. Every inventor's situation is different. *The examples in this book are offered as guides only and should not be used without proper legal counsel.*

Here is a key to the blanks in the license agreement.

(1) Number of the day of the month
(2) Month
(3) Year
(4) Inventor's name
(5) Inventor's address
(6) Name of company or corporation

(7) State where agreement is made (usually your state if you sign it out of state)

(8) Company's address

(9) Patent number (NOTE: If you have a patent pending serial number instead of a patent, reveal this number only when the agreement is signed, not before.)

(10) Description of the technology

(11) Trade name, if any, of the technology

(12) Description of technology

(13) Trade name (if applicable)

(14) Name of state in which laws apply

(15) Inventor's address for mail

(16) Inventor's telephone number

(17) Company's address for mail

(18) Company's telephone number

(19) Inventor's signature

(20) Inventor's name printed under the line

(21) Signature of an officer of the company with authority to make a deal

(22) Officer's name printed below the line, with title

SOME NOTES ABOUT THIS SAMPLE AGREEMENT.   Section 1 grants worldwide rights to the licensee. Rights may be granted for any geographical area that the inventor negotiates with the *licensee*. By restricting the rights to within certain areas, you can make several deals with the same patent. Do not be quick to give up worldwide rights. Be sure the company seeking the license is capable of doing international sales and marketing.

Section 2 establishes a 5 percent royalty, which is good but not common. Inventors typically get royalties between 1 percent and 3 percent. Go for the highest royalty you can get. Ask for 10 percent at the start and let the potential licensee chew you down. Use the royalty issue as one of your bargaining points; something to be negotiated down, so you can retain more important parts of the contract in your favor.

Section 8 gives the other side of the agreement an "out" if your patent is not issued. I always include this section, so the other side feels protected. This section lets the contract continue indefinitely under the patent application process. As long as there is a patent pending, this agreement remains in effect. Patent applications often take years to complete.

Section 10, meanwhile, provides a very important "out" for the inventor. Always insist on this clause being in a final contract, because it can save you and your invention if the company gets into financial trouble or is sold to another company. In the event of bad financial troubles, you get the patent license back without it becoming endangered as part of the company's assets. If the company is sold to another company, you get the patent license back, if you want it, so you can negotiate for a better contract or for a new deal

(SAMPLE)

LICENSE AGREEMENT

Agreement effective this _____ 1 _____ day of _____ 2 _____ , 19 _____ 3 _____ , by and between _____ 4 _____ , whose address is _____ 5 _____ (hereinafter referred to as "Licensor" and _____ 6 _____ , a corporation organized under the laws of the State of _____ 7 _____ whose address is _____ 8 _____ (hereinafter referred to as "Licensee").

WITNESSETH

WHEREAS, Licensor is the owner of U.S. Patent application Serial No. _____ 9 _____ which covers a _____ 10 _____ and may develop, acquire and obtain patents in the United States and foreign countries from time to time relating to the construction of such devices (hereinafter called "Licensor's Patent Rights");

WHEREAS, Licensor has developed a body of technical and design information relating to the construction and operation of _____ 10 _____ (hereinafter called "Licensor's Technical and Design Rights");

WHEREAS, Licensor has now or shall develop certain proprietary rights in the name " _____ 11 _____ " (hereinafter called "Licensor's Name Rights"); and

WHEREAS, Licensee desires to obtain a license to manufacture and sell apparatus under Licensor's Patent Rights, Licensor's Technical and Design Rights and Licensor's Name Rights subject to the other terms and conditions of this agreement.

NOW, THEREFORE, in accordance with the premises and covenants herein contained, the parties hereto agree as follows:

1. Licensor hereby grants to Licensee an exclusive worldwide right and license under Licensor's Patent Rights and Licensor's Technical and Design Rights to Manufacture and sell _____ 12 _____ and to use Licensor's Name Rights in respect thereto.

2. In consideration for the aforesaid license under paragraph 1 I hereof, licensee hereby agrees to pay licensor a royalty of five percent (5%) based upon the gross sales price of any apparatus manufactured and sold which utilizes licensor's patent Rights, Technical and Design Information Rights and Name Rights.

3. Licensee shall have the right to extend sublicenses to others under the rights granted hereunder, including the use of the Licensor's Name Rights in motion pictures or publicity-oriented endeavors, so long as licensor shall receive from such sublicenses the royalty specified under paragraph 2 or, with respect to the use of the Licensor's Name Rights, an amount equal to five percent (5%) of the gross amount received from any sublicense.

4. Licensee agrees to maintain ordinary books of account covering all of its operations hereunder and to furnish to licensor on a quarterly calendar-year basis a report outlining all sales during the preceding quarter for which royalties are due hereunder, accompanying said report with the payment due for said quarter. Licensee agrees to make available at reasonable times and upon due notice said books of account for inspection by representatives of licensor.

5. Licensee agrees to mark all equipment produced under this license with the appropriate patent number or numbers as shall be required by licensor.

6. With respect to licensee's use of " _____ 13 _____ " as a trademark, licensor reserves the right to control the quality of all products bearing such trademark. Licensor may require the licensee, upon written notice, to stop production and sales of any device bearing the licensor's trademark, if in the opinion of the licensor the product is of a quality inferior to the quality agreed upon by the parties at the time of the start of manufacture. Licensee will require a written permission from the licensor to resume production.

7. Licensee agrees to hold licensor harmless with respect to any and all claims for damages, including reasonable attorney fees resulting from the manufacture, demonstration, marketing or sale of device licensed hereunder.

8. This agreement shall terminate pro tanto with respect to the license granted hereunder upon the expiration or termination of the patent included under Licensor's Patent Rights. The agreement shall, notwithstanding, continue (subject to any other termination provision hereof) for the life of any patent application or patent included in Licensor's Patent Rights.

9. This agreement may be terminated by the licensor forthwith by due written notice to licensee upon the failure of the licensee to pay any of the royalty payments provided for under and in accordance with paragraphs 2 and 3.

10. This agreement may be terminated by Licensor upon due written notice in the event of bankruptcy or insolvency of Licensee or in the event of licensee's making an assignment for creditors, in the event that an order for sequestration shall be issued against licensee's assets, or upon the merger or acquisition of the licensee's stock or assets with another.

11. This agreement and the relationship of the parties shall be determined in accordance with the laws of the State of _____ 14 _____ .

12. Any communication or notice provided for hereunder shall be effective if addressed as follows to the party to be notified:

                If to Licensor: _____ 15 _____

                          _____ 16 _____

                If to Licensee: _____ 17 _____

                          _____ 18 _____

IN WITNESS WHEREOF, the parties hereto have executed this agreement as of the day and year first written above.

        _____ 19 _____
        _____ 21 _____

        _____ 20 _____
        _____ 22 _____

altogether. (Author's Note: This clause has helped me remarket an invention several times.)

Always negotiate from a position of power! Remember that it is *your* invention. If a company wants the invention badly enough, it usually will negotiate in good faith and give you a better-than-average deal. Still, be sure to have your patent attorney help with the negotiations. Better minds than yours and mine have been hoodwinked by clever wordings in a contract.

Protecting Your Ideas and Products with Proper Documentation

Properly documenting a concept is a basic, yet vitally important part of the invention process. Without the creation of a proper "paper trail," it is often hard to prove ownership of an idea. You should work hard to document and keep track of your progress during the creation of an invention. One of the main elements of keeping good records is accurately recording important dates on the documentation.

Six Dates You Should Document

Keep track of six key dates as you document the growth of an idea into an invention, and finally into a product ready to market. These dates can have legal consequences for you in terms of your ability to claim proprietary rights—or lose those rights. The six dates are:

- The date of conception
- The date of reduction to practice
- The date of first public use
- The date of first publication
- The date of first offer to sell
- The date of sale of the invention to another party

These dates and their importance are defined and examined in the paragraphs that follow.

The Date of Conception

According to patent law, the date of conception is

> the date at which the idea is formed or complete enough to enable a person with ordinary skills in the pertinent art to proceed toward the completion of the invention without the exercise of inventive skills.

In other words, just getting a basic idea is not enough to satisfy the legal requirements of the date of conception. The idea must be complete enough on that date for others to act upon it and build the invention without further creativity on their part, if they have the basic skills to produce such a product.

The Date of Reduction to Practice

"Reduction to Practice" is defined by law as the actions involved in completing an invention after you have conceived it. Patent law describes two types of Reduction to Practice. They are: Constructive and Actual.

CONSTRUCTIVE REDUCTION TO PRACTICE   is demonstrating on paper that the idea works, through an explanation capable of being used to file a patent application.

ACTUAL REDUCTION TO PRACTICE   is building an actual working model of the invention that operates the way the invention is intended to operate.

Patent law allows you to use either date, constructive or actual, when establishing and documenting reduction to practice for an invention.

The Date of First Public Use

Patent law states that you lose the right to obtain a patent if you do not file for a patent within one year of the first date of public use. "Public Use" is defined as any commercial use or any public disclosure, or any private disclosure without a confidential relationship being established between the inventor and the person to whom the invention is shown.

The Date of First Publication

Patent law states that you lose the right to obtain a patent if your invention is "described in print anywhere in the world" before your date of Reduction to Practice. Additionally, patent law states that you lose the right to obtain a patent if you do not file for a patent within one year of the first date of publication of the information.

Date of the First Offer to Sell

Under patent law, you lose the right to obtain a patent if you do not file for a patent within one year of the first date of your attempt to sell the invention in the United States. The starting date for this year is often deemed to be the same as the date of your first public disclosure without protection by any sort of secrecy agreement.

Date of Sale of Invention to Another Party

This portion of the law states that you lose the right to obtain a patent if you do not file for a patent within one year of the first date of the sale of the invention in the U.S.

Creating a Paper Trail

Knowing how to create good documentation may be one of the most important skills you will need to master. Documentation enters into all phases of inventing. The initial concept must be documented and protected; the development of the concept must be documented for proof of "reduction to practice;" the business plan must be documented to raise capital; and the physical development of the product must be documented to provide data for production. Every phase in the life cycle of an invention requires the inventor to prepare some form of written information to build credible "paper trail" that will help move him or her to the next major step.

Specifically, here is how documentation is used in the invention process:

1. To establish a time frame for your invention's conception. This is to be used in case of a tight legal battle to establish who had the idea first.

2. To show evidence of "Reduction to Practice." This is a term used by the Patent Office to describe an inventor's efforts to develop the idea to a working product. This is also a way of determining who should have the final rights to the patent if it is in dispute.

3. To establish who the actual inventor was in the case of a partnership or a group of people who all claim the idea.

4. To show the inventor how on target his ideas are. In the event the inventor does not do anything with a particular idea, it is still gratifying to have a logbook of concepts to match against new products as they come out over the years.

5. To keep track of ideas that may not have formed fully into the final invention. Often, an inventor will get bits and pieces of an idea, but without the full picture, these bits and pieces are useless. Idea logs let you look back and say, "Now's the time to take *X* idea and team it with a newly developed material or technology to accomplish a goal that was thought to be out of reach beforehand."

Types of Invention Documentation

Some important forms of invention documentation are:

- Inventor's logbook
- Witness stamp
- Registered mail
- Notarization
- Disclosure Document Program
- Patent application

Inventor's Logbook

A hard-bound book is the best, but a spiral-bound notebook will work as long as the pages are numbered and kept intact. The inventor's logbook can cover many ideas as long as they are all witnessed. You should keep separate logbooks or project books on any major invention that will generate a large amount of data or drawings in the development of the idea.

Looseleaf notebooks sometimes do not work as well as hardbound books, because pages can be added and deleted at will. This could become a bone of contention with attorneys if your logbooks are ever required as evidence in a court of law. This is the reason for the development of the BIDS (Basic Idea Development Sheet) system of documentation discussed earlier in this book. The BIDS system allows the use of looseleaf sheets to successfully coordinate a project's development. These sheets are set up to be individually dated and witnessed. They can be arranged in a looseleaf notebook with other forms to form a comprehensive documentation package on an invention's development.

Witness Stamp

The witness stamp is useful for any idea document, and especially useful for loose sheets that contain the first recorded thoughts of an invention. Samples of inventor witness stamps can be found in Appendix III. Every inventor should have a basic witness stamp and someone to act as their regular witness.

Registered Mail

One old but still useful form of documentation is to send yourself a registered letter with the idea inside. By handling and dating the letter, the U.S. Postal Service will provide you with documented proof that the idea was yours by that date. Don't open the letter when you receive it. Keep it in a safe place, instead. This is a tried and true method, and it has stood up in many court cases involving invention documentation. Make sure the letter is in a good, solid, clean envelope. Do not cover the edges or seams of the envelope with any sort of tape. These areas must be clean and open to stamping by the Post Office in order to establish the registration process.

Notarization

Get all of your ideas notarized when possible by a local Notary Public. This method has its liability, since you have no real secrecy agreement with the Notary. The Notary only establishes that, on a particular date, you presented the material for notarization. Notarization does not ensure it will not be seen by others during the process, nor does it ensure the notary will not discuss the materials with friends and family.

Disclosure Document Program

You can send full disclosure information to the government for short-term (two-year) record keeping. See below for more information on the Disclosure Documentation Program and how to write a disclosure document.

How to Use the U.S. Government's Disclosure Document Program

One of the services provided for inventors by the U.S. Patent and Trademark Office is the acceptance and preservation (for a limited time) of "Disclosure Documents" as evidence of the date of conception of an invention.

What Is the Disclosure Document Program?

A paper disclosing an invention and signed by the inventor or inventors may be forwarded to the Patent and Trademark Office by the inventor or any one of the inventors when there are joint inventors, by the owner of the invention, or by the attorney or agent of the inventor(s) or owner. It will be retained for two years, then destroyed unless it is referred to in a separate letter in a separate letter in a related patent application filed within two years.

The Disclosure Document is not a patent application and the date of its receipt at the Patent and Trademark Office will not become the effective filing date of any patent application subsequently filed. However, like patent applications, these documents will be kept in confidence by the Patent and Trademark Office.

This program does not diminish the value of the conventional witness and notarized records as evidence of conception of an invention. But it should provide a more credible form of evidence than that provided by the popular practice of mailing a disclosure to oneself or another person by registered mail. The credibility of the program is in the fact it is registered with the Patent Office and not with oneself or an interested third party. Depending upon the use of the registration (i.e.: raising capital, sale of the concept, etc.) its value can vary. Most business people, once they learn of the program, respect it as valid and thus its value increases to the inventor who wishes to maximize his entrepreneurial abilities.

The Content of a Disclosure Document

Although there are no restrictions as to the content, and claims are not necessary, the benefits afforded by the Disclosure Document will depend directly upon the adequacy of the disclosure. Therefore, it is strongly urged that the document contain a clear and complete explanation of the matter and the process of making and using the invention in sufficient detail to enable a person having ordinary knowledge in the field of the invention to make and use the invention. When the nature of the invention permits, a drawing or sketch should be included. The use or the utility of the invention should be described, especially in chemical inventions. You can use the various forms in this book (IDF, BIDS) to describe, outline and draw your basic and advanced concepts for disclosure document preparation.

Preparation of a Disclosure Document

The Disclosure Document must be limited to written matter or drawings on paper or other thin, flexible material, such as linen or plastic drawing material, having dimensions not to exceed 8.5 inches by 13 inches. Photographs are also acceptable. Each page should be numbered. Text and drawings should be sufficiently dark to permit reproduction via commonly used office copying machines.

Other Enclosures

In addition to the fee described below, the Disclosure Document must be accompanied by a stamped, self-addressed envelope and a separate paper in duplicate signed by the inventor. The paper must state that he is the inventor of the concept and that he is requesting that the material be received for processing under the Disclosure Document Program. The papers will be stamped by the Patent and Trademark Office with an identifying number and date of receipt, and the duplicate request letter will be returned in the self addressed envelope together with a warning notice. The warning notice is to the inventor telling him that the Disclosure Document may be relied upon only as evidence of inclusion in this program and that a patent application should be diligently filed if patent protection is desired.

The inventor's request letter should take the following form:

The undersigned, being the inventor of the disclosed invention, requests that the enclosed papers be accepted under the Disclosure Document Program and that they be preserved for a period of two years.

The Fee

A fee of ten dollars ($10.00) is charged for this service. Payment must accompany the Disclosure Document when it is submitted to the Patent and Trademark Office. A check or money order must be made payable to "Commissioner of Patents and Trademarks, Disclosure Document Program, Washington, DC 20231."

Disposition

The Disclosure Document will be preserved in a secure location for a period of two years after its receipt and then will be destroyed unless referred to in a separate letter in a related patent application filed within the two year period. The letter filed in the related patent application must identify not only the patent application, but the Disclosure Document by its title, number and date of receipt. Acknowledgment of receipt of such letters will be made in the next official communication or in a separate letter from the Patent and Trademark Office.

A Warning to Inventors

The two year period should not be considered a grace period during which the inventor can wait to file his patent application without possible loss of benefits. It must be recognized that in establishing priority of invention, an affidavit or testimony referring to a Disclosure Document must usually also establish diligence in completing the invention or in filing the patent application after filing the Disclosure Document.

Inventors are also reminded that any public use or sale in the United States or publication of the invention anywhere in the world more than one year prior to the filing of the patent application on that invention will prohibit the granting of the patent on it.

TO: **Commissioner of Patents and Trademarks**
                 Disclosure Document Program
                 Washington, D.C.   20231

Date: _____

From: _____

                 _____

                 _____

                 _____

Ref: Submission of Invention Concept to the Disclosure Document Program

Concept Name: _____

To Whom It May Concern,

Enclosed please find:

[1] two sets of a _____ page disclosure document.

The disclosure includes_____ pages of text and _____ pages of drawings.

[2] a self addressed and stamped return envelope.

[3] a check / money order for ten dollars to cover the cost of the filing.

Please process this disclosure and return one set of my disclosure completed with PTO date stamp and Disclosure Document number.

INVENTORS DECLARATION:

The undersigned, being the inventor of the disclosed invention, requests that the enclosed papers be accepted under the Disclosure Document Program and that they be preserved in total confidentiality for a period of two years.

Signed: _____ Date: _____

If an inventor is not familiar with what is considered to be "diligence in completing the invention" or "reduction to practice" under the patent law, or if they have any other questions about patent matters, the Patent and Trademark Office advises them to consult a patent attorney or patent agent registered to practice before the Patent and Trademark Office. A publication "Attorneys and agents registered to practice before the U.S. Patent and Trademark Office" is available from the Superintendent of Documents, U.S. Government Printing Office, Washington, D.C. 20402. Patent attorney and agents may also be found in telephone directories of most major cities. Also, many large cities have associations of patent attorneys which may be consulted.

Patent Application

Filing a patent application is the most secure and lasting method of documentation. It also leads to a possible patent on the concept. During the application time, you may market and sell your product under the "Patent Pending" status. This is often used as a sort of protection, warning others of your application for exclusive rights to the idea. This may deter some people, but not others if your concept is easily pirated.

How to Write a Disclosure Document

Generally, *disclosure information* is the basic outline that a patent attorney uses in preparing a patent application. Carefully prepared disclosures are necessary for a well-prepared patent application and a good, solid patent. Following this discussion, you will find an Invention Disclosure Form that can help you assemble the information necessary to prepare a formal disclosure document.

To illustrate the information needed for the form, let's assume that you have invented a steerable parachute. The following basic details should be included in the disclosure:

OBJECTIVE OF THE INVENTION: What is it supposed to accomplish? For a steerable parachute, you might write: "To allow a person or object to float safely down from a great height to a specific landing site without damage; to allow a parachutist to direct his descent to a desired landing spot."

DEFINITION OF THE INVENTION: How would you describe its function? For the steerable parachute, you might write: "A parachute that has a continually adjustable venting system that is controlled by the user. This venting system allows the chute to spill air pressure in a desired pattern that affects the rate and direction of its descent."

FEATURES OF THE INVENTION: What makes it unique and patentable? Here you would describe how your steerable chute differs from a nonsteerable chute: how the venting system works and how the actual mechanics of the new system work.

COMPARISON WITH EXISTING TECHNOLOGY: What are the differences that are patentable? Your parachute is steerable; others are not.

USES OF THE INVENTION: How would it be used, and what are its markets? In the steerable parachute example, you might describe potential uses by the military and sport parachutists.

IMPORTANCE OF THE INVENTION: Why is it worth developing? In the case of the steerable parachute, you could point out that it could save lives in combat and enhance sport parachuting.

BACKGROUND OF THE INVENTION: What discoveries led to the invention; what prompted development of the idea; what was the need?

INVENTOR IDENTIFICATION: This should include all pertinent information, including your name and address.

You should make each section of the disclosure as detailed as possible. Disclosures typically require five to twenty typewritten pages. Give as detailed description as possible on what the invention does, how it operates, and how it is better than existing technology. Your patent attorney will use only the information you give him in preparing the patent search and application. The patent attorney will not add information to your disclosure, even if he or she thinks it is obvious, given the information you already have. If an attorney gave you information to add to your invention, then he or she technically would become a co-inventor on the patent application.

Another reason why you must give considerable thought to the disclosure information is that it will form the limits of the patent protection. Thus, you should always try to imagine the widest possible uses or applications for your concept. Also try to include every possible way the same goal might be accomplished, using different methods within the scope of your concept. This will save you from disappointment when another patent is issued that cleverly supersedes your patent by doing the same thing in a slightly more novel manner.

The same disclosure document that you prepare for your patent attorney can be submitted to the Disclosure Document program of the U.S. Patent Office. This is a good procedure to follow to ensure a dated, secure disclosure of a concept if your actual patent application is delayed because of financial setbacks.

When you fill out an Invention Disclosure Form, be sure to have a witness sign and date it before you submit it to any third party.

INVENTION DISCLOSURE FORM (IDF)

INVENTOR: _____ Date: _____
INVENTION: _____
PAGE 1 OF _____

A. OBJECTIVE: (CONTINUED ON PAGE _____ OF _____)
_____
_____
_____
_____

B. DEFINITION: (CONTINUED ON PAGE _____ OF _____)
_____
_____
_____
_____

C. FEATURES: (CONTINUED ON PAGE _____ OF _____)
_____
_____
_____
_____
_____

D. COMPARISON WITH EXISTING TECHNOLOGY:
(CONTINUED ON PAGE _____ OF _____)
_____
_____
_____
_____
_____

E. USES: (CONTINUED ON PAGE _____ OF _____)
_____
_____
_____
_____
_____
_____
_____
_____
_____
_____
_____
_____

Page 2 OF _____ Invention Disclosure Form
Inventor: _____ Date: _____
Invention: _____

F. IMPORTANCE: (CONTINUED ON PAGE _____ OF _____)

_____
_____
_____
_____
_____
_____
_____
_____
_____

G. BACKGROUND: (CONTINUED ON PAGE_____ OF _____)

_____
_____
_____
_____
_____
_____
_____
_____
_____
_____
_____

H. INVENTOR IDENTIFICATION INFORMATION:
(CONTINUED ON PAGE _____ OF _____)
NAME:_____
ADDRESS: _____
CITY: _____ STATE: _____ ZIP _____
HOME TELEPHONE:_____ - _____
WORK TELEPHONE:_____ - _____
SS#_____ - _____ - _____
DRIVERS LICENSE NO. _____ STATE: _____

MISC. INFO: (CONTINUED ON PAGE _____ OF _____)

_____
_____
_____
_____
_____
_____
_____
_____
_____
_____
_____
_____
_____

Page 3 OF _____ Invention Disclosure Form
Inventor: _____ Date: _____
Invention: _____

TYPE OF INFORMATION:
_____
_____
_____
_____
_____
_____
_____
_____
_____
_____
_____
_____
_____
_____
_____

IDEA GRAPHIC:

How and When to Use Secrecy Agreements and Meeting Forms

  To help protect your ideas, you should understand how and when to use two key documents: (1) the "Agreement to Review Confidential Material" (for brevity, it is referred to as "the secrecy agreement" in the remainder of this chapter); and (2) the "Product Meeting Disclosure Form" (referred to, also for brevity, as "the meeting form").

If you have these two documents and follow the simple procedures for their use, you can control the confidentiality of your ideas. The two forms, when used in the proper combination and circumstances, also can help you make money without developing a product past the documentation stage. I have done this on several occasions. I have made thousands of dollars using just this paperwork and common business sense.

The sample documents presented later in this chapter were drawn up by attorneys. However, keep in mind that the forms are not foolproof. You must take great care to always use them with the proper procedures or they can be valueless. Also, the forms will be most effective only if the people you deal with have some ethics—or have something to lose if they break the agreements. The agreements in the secrecy agreement and meeting form will stand up in a court of law in most states—but please ask your attorney to review them.

Before you can use these forms, however, you must register your product concept with the Disclosure Document Program at the U.S. Patent Office. Until an idea is registered, the usefulness of secrecy and meeting forms is limited. After the idea is registered, however, the registration and the two forms become powerful allies that can help you make money with a concept.

Basic Rules for Using the Forms

One of the basic rules for using these documents is that you should allow people to read the blank forms carefully before you ask them to sign. This is important for two reasons.

First, no one likes to be surprised with a contract to sign without first understanding what is in the contract. The secrecy agreement and the meeting forms are contracts which severely restrict the rights of the signers and how they can act in response to the information you are giving them. In a society where freedom of speech and free enterprise, are valued highly, these forms can be seen as both a godsend and a severe curtailment of rights—depending upon which side of the form you are on. For this reason, you should allow prospective signers to have an advanced viewing of the forms.

Second, letting the prospective signers review the forms in advance can save you time, effort, and money. If I am considering going to a company for hard core talks on selling a concept, I usually send the forms at least two to four weeks in advance, with a letter explaining the procedures for their use. This allows company executives time to review the forms and decline the offer for the visit, if they feel they cannot sign them. By declining in advance, they save the company time and effort, and you don't waste the time and expenses involved in making a trip to the company location.

Some companies will request that you sign their secrecy agreement, as well. Study their agreement carefully before you sign it. If it resembles the secrecy agreement I have designed, then the company's document may represent just a case of mutual precautions. If it resembles the "Company Confidentiality Agreement" example at this end of this chapter, then I urge you not to sign the document or even do business with the firm. Beware of any individual or company that wants you to sign such a form letter. It is designed to strip an inventor of his or her most basic rights. *Also, beware of any individual or company that will not sign your secrecy agreement for a basic review of your concept (even when money is not an issue).* The ulterior motives of such people have been, at least in my experience, not in the inventor's best interests. There is only one exception to this warning: It is okay to have your concept reviewed by an attorney with whom you are considering doing business. Attorneys are bound by their fiduciary responsibility *not* to disclose information about a client.

Secrecy Form and Meeting Form Examples

Before proceeding, carefully examine the secrecy agreement and the meeting form that I have used successfully. Pay particular attention to the ways that individuals and witnesses are identified and what they agree to when they sign the documents.

Using the Forms Separately or Together

The function of the forms is different when they are used separately or in combination.

USING THE SECRECY AGREEMENT BY ITSELF. Here is what to remember when using the secrecy agreement by itself:

- **The secrecy agreement should be used anytime you show anyone any of your ideas.** Make *no* exceptions to this rule, unless you feel so strongly about the person that you have unshakable faith they will keep your secrets. This usually means your parents, your wife or husband, or any other person who has an undeniable interest in seeing you succeed. Using the secrecy form will involve a personal decision on your part. I know of some inventors who use this form only when meeting with business people. I also know other inventors who make family members sign it before they will reveal their ideas.
- **The secrecy agreement should be used for only one idea or concept at a time.** The concept should be named on the blank lines in the center of the first page. A short description of the concept should be included after the idea name. *Never give a filled out secrecy agreement*

MUTUAL NON-DISCLOSURE AGREEMENT
Page 1 of 4

This AGREEMENT, effective during the DISCLOSURE PERIOD, defined below, is between

_____ , (hereinafter "Inventor"), having its

principal place of business and offices at _____

_____ and _____

(hereinafter "Company") having a principal place of business at _____

_____.

WHEREAS, INVENTOR and Company each have or may acquire certain "Confidential Information" (the "Concept" or "Invention") relating to the subject of :

_____

_____

_____

 related thereto which they desire to disclose to each other and each party is willing to confidentially accept the other's information during a DISCLOSURE PERIOD, defined as the period between the EFFECTIVE DATE and EXPIRATION DATE of this Agreement, and as limited herein. Either party may disclose information to the other party in confidence. Therefore, in this AGREEMENT, either party may be the disclosing party and either party may be the receiving party and all terms of this AGREEMENT shall apply to each.

NOW, THEREFORE, the parties agree as follows:

1.   **The EFFECTIVE DATE of this Agreement shall be the date of the last signature below. This Agreement shall expire 3 years after the EFFECTIVE DATE hereof unless extended in writing by the parties hereto. The EXPIRATION DATE shall be the date upon which this Agreement expires.** The obligations of the parties contained in paragraph 3 shall continue in effect notwithstanding the expiration of this Agreement.

2.   "Confidential Information" is defined as any device, graphics, written information or information in other tangible forms that is disclosed by <u>EITHER PARTY TO THE OTHER</u> during the DISCLOSURE PERIOD, that is marked at the time of disclosure as being "Confidential" or "Proprietary". Information disclosed orally or visually and identified at the time as Confidential shall also be considered as "Confidential Information" if such orally or visually disclosed information is reduced to a tangible form, appropriately marked or identified as being confidential by the disclosing party and delivered to the receiving party *within thirty calendar days* of its oral or visual disclosure to the receiving party.

Page 2 of 4
Mutual Non-Disclosure Agreement
Date: _____

3.   Unless otherwise expressly authorized by the disclosing party, the receiving party agrees to retain the "Confidential Information" in confidence for the DISCLOSURE PERIOD and **THREE YEARS** from the EXPIRATION DATE of this Agreement, during which period the receiving party shall not disclose the "Confidential Information" to any third party and shall not use or reproduce the "Confidential Information" for any purpose. These obligations with respect to the "Confidential Information" shall survive the termination of this Agreement but shall not apply to any information that is or becomes disqualified as "Confidential Information" pursuant to paragraph 5.

4.   Each party shall use its best efforts to limit dissemination of the other's "Confidential Information" to such of its employees, agents and associates who have a need to know for the aforesaid purposes.

5.   Notwithstanding any other provision of this Agreement, each party acknowledges that "Confidential Information" shall not include any information that:

> (a) is or becomes published through no wrongful act on the receiving party's part;

> (b) is, at the time of disclosure under this Agreement, already known to the receiving party without restriction on disclosure; except that the receiving party will notify the disclosing party in writing and at the time of disclosure, that it has already or knows of the disclosed technology (per the Meeting Disclosure Form): Failure of the receiving party to notify the disclosing party is proof that the receiving party has no prior knowledge of the technology;

> (c) is, or subsequently becomes, rightfully and without breach of this Agreement in the receiving party's possession without any obligation restricting disclosure;

> (d) is independently developed by the receiving party without breach of this Agreement: The receiving party will so notify in writing, the disclosing party for the duration of this Agreement;

> (e) is explicitly approved for release by written authorization of the disclosing party.

6.   Each party agrees to return to the disclosing party, upon written request, the devices, graphics, writings and information in other tangible forms containing any of the "Confidential Information" referred to in paragraph 1, and any copies of "Confidential Information."

7.   No license, express or implied, in the "Confidential Information," is granted to either party other than to use the information in the manner and to the extent authorized by this Agreement. No indemnification for damages of any kind, sustained by either party, by reason of the disclosure or use of the Confidential Information is granted or implied. No warranty or representation of any kind is granted or implied to either party.

Page 3 of 4
Mutual Non-Disclosure Agreement
Date: _____

8.   The receiving party acknInventoredges that:

(a) the Confidential Information is the exclusive property of Disclosing Party, and that Disclosing Party will provide the Confidential Information to Receiving Party only if the parties enter into this Agreement, and that this Agreement does not create or transfer any right of ownership in the Confidential Information in or to Receiving Party;

(b) the provisions of this Agreement are reasonably necessary to protect the confidential nature of the Confidential Information, and that a breach of this Agreement by Receiving Party would cause Disclosing Party irreparable harm for which it has no adequate remedy at law; and

(c) Receiving Party agrees to the issuance of an injunction in a court of competent jurisdiction to enforce the terms of this Agreement should Receiving Party breach or indicate that it ntends to breach its obligation of confidentiality under this Agreement.

9.   The parties acknowledge that they are not prohibited by the Office of Export Administration for the U.S. Department of Commerce from receiving technical information, know-how, data or other information and they represent and warrant that no technical data furnished to them by the disclosing party shall be exported from the United States without first complying with the International Traffic in Arms Regulations and Export Administration Act.

10.   In no event will the disclosing party be liable to a receiving party in any way related to a disclosure hereunder, for any actual damages, lost profits, lost savings or other consequential damages, even if the disclosing party has been advised of the possibility of such damages.

11.   This Agreement shall be governed and interpreted in accordance with the laws of the State of _____. Any action arising under or involving this Agreement shall be brought in a court of competent jurisdiction in _____ County, in the State of _____.

12.   This Agreement shall in no way require either party to disclose or receive Confidential Information. Notice hereunder must be in writing and shall be effective when delivered to the parties at their addresses set forth above by certified mail, return receipt requested.

13.   This Agreement constitutes the complete understanding between the parties of each party's obligations to the other party relating to said Confidential Information delivered during the Disclosure Period.

Page 4 of 4
Mutual Non-Disclosure Agreement
Date: _____

IN WITNESS WHEREOF, the Parties understand this Agreement and have caused this Agreement to be executed by their duly authorized representatives.

INVENTOR
By _____
Name (Print) _____
Company _____
Date _____
Drivers License Number or S.S. #: _____ State _____

By _____
Name (Print) _____
Company _____
Title _____
Date _____
Drivers License Number or S.S. #: _____ State _____

By _____
Name (Print) _____
Company _____
Title _____
Date _____
Drivers License Number or S.S. #: _____ State _____

By _____
Name (Print) _____
Company _____
Title _____
Date _____
Drivers License Number or S.S. #: _____ State _____

By _____
Name (Print) _____
Company _____
Title _____
Date _____
Drivers License Number or S.S. #: _____ State _____

to someone when first approaching them about signing the agreement. The reason for this is that they will be able to read your idea synopsis on the page prior to signing, and then they may not sign. Always ask a person to read a blank copy of the agreement first, so they will understand what you are asking them to sign.

- **Give those who agree to sign the agreement the filled-in agreement with several yellow Post-It Notes covering the actual idea information on the middle of the page.** *After* they sign the agreement, then peel off the Post-It notes to reveal the concept. This ensures secrecy until the moment of signing. Also remember to insert the state and county names in the blanks in the agreement. This should be the state in which you do business, not necessarily the state in which you are signing the secrecy agreement. This will allow you to start legal proceedings against the signer in your home state, if they violate the agreement.

- **Always get the full information on the bottom of the page from the signer.** His or her driver's license number or Social Security number is very important for confirming the identity of the signer and validating the signature. Don't be shy about asking to see the confirming document to make sure the number and signature are real. Remember, this is not a joke or an inconsequential action you are undertaking. You are revealing an idea from which you hope to make money. Take the use of the secrecy agreement seriously, and the signers will take your idea seriously.

- **Have the signers initial each page of the idea material shown to them.** This validates that the information was the actual information acknowledged in the secrecy agreement. Keep this original information with the signed secrecy agreement. Any major artwork presented during the course of a concept disclosure should be duplicated in miniature in the material covered under the secrecy agreement.

- **Always keep the original copy of the secrecy agreement in your possession.** If the signer(s) want a copy, then give them a blank. If they insist on a copy of the original, then admonish them that showing the copy of the idea information on it is an act of revealing the idea and thus is a violation of the secrecy agreement. When you return to your office, place the original secrecy agreement in a safe or a locked file for protection. The agreement is good for three years, with the option of more time if both parties agree to the decision to extend the time frame. Keep the agreement in a secure location until you feel it is no longer needed for your concept's protection.

You should use the secrecy agreement by itself only when you are *not* seeking to either raise capital, license or sell the concept. The secrecy agreement usually is used by itself when:

a. Showing drawings to potential manufacturers for pricing information;

b. Showing drawings to potential sources of prototypes or materials;

c. Showing drawings to potential end users for feedback and evaluation.

USING THE SECRECY AGREEMENT AND MEETING FORM TOGETHER.
The times to use the secrecy agreement and meeting form together are when you are seeking capital investment or seeking to sell or license your concept. You should use the two forms together because the secrecy agreement only requires that the individual or company keep the information confidential and not try to do anything with the concept. This works well with individuals who either have no real ability to take your concept and run with it, or whose best interests will be served by doing business with you and not trying to steal your concept. Unfortunately, many of the companies to which you will want to disclose your ideas may have a great interest in ripping you off, if you don't know how to protect yourself. These companies are not necessarily bad, just opportunistic. If they see the chance to take your idea without compensating you, they will. They will rationalize it as "free enterprise" or some other nonsense.

It was for this reason that I developed the Product Meeting Disclosure Form. The meeting form is like a steel box in which you trap the company into admitting that you're the inventor of the product concept and that they have no rights to do anything with it without you being compensated. The meeting form is also the fairest document possible for both sides, because, if the company proves to the inventor that they already have the concept in house, in any stage of development, then they are free of constraints of both the secrecy agreement and the meeting form. Most companies see and agree with the fairness and logic of the system after they review the form. See Appendix III for a sample Product Meeting Disclosure Form.

Here is how to use the meeting form in combination with the secrecy agreement:

1. At the time the initial secrecy agreement is signed, the top section of the meeting form is also filled in. Every person who signs the secrecy agreement must also sign on one of the top lines in the meeting form. This is to acknowledge that they were present at the meeting. The top third of the page (down to the insertion point of the inventor's name) should be filled out prior to turning over the idea information for review.

2. All people present at the meeting should be told that no one is allowed to leave the room (with one exception to be discussed shortly) until after the material is reviewed and the meeting form is completed. This is done because the meeting form requires proof from the company that the idea is already under development for the inventor to release the company from its obligations of secrecy and compensation. Any person leaving the room for any amount of time after the concept is revealed might be capable of fabricating a document as evidence of the company's prior development of the concept. If, after the idea is revealed, the company president or other highest-ranking member states that they have no such idea or concept under development, the meeting form should be fully completed with the signatures of those present on the appropriate lines at the center of the document. You can then allow people to leave the room and the discussions can continue for any length of time—with you in the driver's seat.

3. If, after the concept has been revealed, the president or any other member of the company states that this is an idea already under development, then you must request to see the evidence of this fact. They must know about this possible request ahead of time and agree that the evidence will be presented immediately upon your request. If it is in another part of the building or any location where it is said to take a while to bring to the office, then you should request to be able to go to that location and see it there. It is for this reason that all concept disclosures must be made at the company's location and especially where they do their research and development. If an inventor tries to do this at a hotel location or at any other location where the company has the chance to delay the viewing of the corroborating information, the company can fabricate enough details based upon the disclosure to them to get out of the agreement and steal your ideas.

4. If the concept is proven to be already under development, then you are obligated to sign the bottom portion of the agreement and give up any rights you have to the product that may come from that company. This does *not* mean that you cannot try to sell your concept to another company. As long as you do not disclose the proprietary information learned from the first company, and as long as no other agreement constrains your actions, you are still free to try to market the concept. You also still have the option to try to produce and sell the concept on your own, in competition with any and all firms.

Proper use of the secrecy agreement in conjunction with the meeting form can get you a contract with a company for the sale of the concept, even without further development or patents. Having proof of registration with the Patent Disclosure Document program *prior* to the meeting is the best way to totally lock up the concept when using these forms. One firm that was not presently capable of buying a concept outright at the time of the initial discussions put me on retainer to hold the idea while they evaluated the concept's practicality in their product line. This was to keep me from marketing the idea to their competitors. After more than a year of payments for "holding onto the idea," the company was unable to purchase it because of other business problems that took their cash flow. I still retained the product rights, however, and later sold the concept to one of their competitors. This demonstrates the ability of the secrecy agreement and meeting form to generate income in various ways while protecting your ideas from being easily ripped off.

Why You Should Avoid Company-Issued Confidentiality Agreements

Beware of "Confidentiality Agreements" offered by companies when you want to reveal ideas to them. Many of these agreements actually can help a company steal your idea.

Before you sign any agreement, it is always wise to show it to your attorney. Some company-issued confidentiality agreements are meant to be fair. The majority of them are along the lines of the sample "Company-Generated Confidentiality Agreement" that follows. This agreement is an actual form letter sent out by a company in the electronics business. I have deleted the company's identity and the inventor's name and address, but have not otherwise altered the content of the agreement.

The following items in the company-generated "Confidentiality Agreement" that follows on page 92 should be of great interest to an entrepreneurial inventor.

Item #1 urges you to protect yourself! Do so, by not signing any agreement that even remotely looks like this agreement.

Item #2 asks you to reveal the current status of patent applications. With this information, you reveal (a) if you have applied and (b) if not, that the invention is not covered by any formal protection. *Always* have your application for inclusion in the "Disclosure Document Program" on file prior to even making the initial call or sending the first letter to the company (the dates "A" and "B" referred to in the first paragraph of the agreement). Item #2 also asks you to send them copies of your drawings and specifications only, if you have filed for a patent. Patents are based upon claims, but, by revealing all of your technical specifications under this agreement, you will virtually give them the entire idea. It is then an easy matter for them to make their own claims based upon your information and to try and "One Better" your claims. It only takes one claim to get a patent. They may apply and get rejected on all of the claims that they can ascertain from your drawings and specifications, but get an improvement patent on an idea of their own that they have added to your idea.

Item #3 asks that if you have NOT applied for a patent, send them EVERYTHING on the idea. They are basically asking you to let them steal the idea, because they are asking you to sign and date the information. With that information, they can predate your documents with any data they want.

Item #4 is common sense, of course. You wouldn't send them the originals and forget to keep a copy for yourself. This clause in the agreement is on your side, yet smacks of "Don't keep anything back from us, only keep in your records exactly what you send us." In other words, send us EVERYTHING!

Item #5 takes away your right to discuss the fact that you are marketing the idea. This restricts (a) your ability to raise capital with that information and (b) your ability to use that information as leverage with other companies (such as parts manufacturers or another interested purchaser). They don't say how long their evaluation will take or if they will send you a letter telling you that the evaluation period is over. This basically ties your hands forever!

Item #6 says nothing about them applying for their own patent and fighting you in court to override your patent. Patents get overridden by other patents all the time. Since they know everything there is to know about your patent application or original idea, it may then be a simple matter to beat your patent.

COMPANY GENERATED CONFIDENTIALITY AGREEMENT

(Sample Agreement: Taken from Actual Contract Used Today in Industry)

NOTE: *Never sign any agreement that sounds like this agreement. It is designed to strip an inventor of all his rights and protections. All* <u>*underlined*</u> *items have been deleted and generic equivalents have been substituted.*

Dear Mr. <u>INVENTOR'S NAME</u>

Thank you for your letter received <u>DATE "A"</u> following your conversation with our offices on <u>DATE "B"</u>. <u>WIDGETS, INC.</u> has the following standard agreement we sign with inventors. We request you review and sign our agreement before we proceed any further.

CONFIDENTIALITY AGREEMENT WITH INVENTOR
To <u>The Inventor</u>:

1. WIDGET, INC. urges you to take all steps necessary to protect your idea and to safeguard your interests. You should consult an attorney and file an application for a patent.

2. If you have filed for a patent, please send us a copy of just the drawings and specifications portion of the patent application, keeping the claims to yourself.

3. If you have not filed for a patent, please send us a complete written description of your idea. Please include any sketches, drawings, or photographs which would help us to understand and evaluate your idea. All your materials should be signed, dated and witnessed.

4. Please keep an identical copy of the material which you sent to us, so that both of us will know exactly what is involved.

5. During our evaluation of your idea, you agree not to disclose our potential interest or otherwise use our name without first getting written permission.

6. By evaluating your idea, we will not receive any rights to any patent you now have or may acquire.

7. We are not required to hold your idea in confidence, and no confidential relationship is being established between us.

8. By reviewing your idea, no agreement to compensate has been entered into by us, and you agree to rely solely upon your rights under the patent laws.

9. After reviewing your idea, we are not required to return it to you, since otherwise we would have no record of what was disclosed to us.

10. We are not required to tell you about our own developments, or of other ideas which have been submitted to us, or of ideas which are already in use by ourselves or our competitors.

11. If we are interested in your ideas and material, you will agree to negotiate with us for rights thereto.

12. All of these conditions apply as well to any other information which you may send to us about your disclosure.

Very Truly Yours,

<u>Mr. X.</u>
President, <u>WIDGET, INC.</u>

AGREED:

BY: _____   TITLE:_____

DATE: _____

Item #7 is structured so that, although you can't tell people that you are dealing with the company, the company has no responsibility to you to keep your information confidential. They might market your idea around to find out if there is any interest in it, thus possibly making the idea public-domain material. They might also sell the idea to someone else and then come back to you to buy it for a song. They may just sell the idea and not even come back to you and tell you anything about their actions.

Item #8 again reaffirms their right to do what they want with your idea without compensating you for it. Your rights under the patent laws are based solely on your ability to exclude others from making your item commercially. If your idea is being produced by a company prior to your patent being issued, your only choice is to wait and see if the patent gets issued and sue the company. If the company is making money on the product, be prepared for an expensive court fight.

Item #9 is a real con job! They could easily photocopy your material and send you back the originals, but that would involve some sort of documentation on their part that they sent it to you. Thus, they could be tied up in a legal battle if you decided they had ripped you off. By not sending you anything other than this Confidentiality Agreement, they have no paper trail that connects you to them.

In clause #10, they take away your right to know what they are doing or even to get information from them on their current products that are in the field of the invention. They are asking you to abandon your right to request material from them that is already public material, which they would send to anyone who asked about it. This clause also allows them to say that your invention was similar to a product concept already under development, and this was why they didn't respond any further to your business advances.

Item #11 is the real killer! They tie you up in an agreement that allows them the first access to the idea if they feel that they must buy it from you. By agreeing to negotiate with them for rights to the idea, you place a block in the path of opening negotiations with another company that may be interested in your idea. By agreeing to this, you may have to include this company in any deal you make with another company.

Finally, item #12 basically ties all the information you might send them into this one agreement.

Understanding the Major Points That Have Been Left Out

Pay careful attention to the major points that have been left out of this example agreement and learn how to spot their absence in future agreements you may encounter.

1. Nowhere does it say what the agreement is about. The idea name is nowhere to be seen. Thus, if you sign this form, you have given them a blanket agreement that they can say is related to anything you may invent, now or in the future.

2. Nowhere in this document is there any sort of time frame under which this agreement operates. They may have tied you up forever, if you sign this agreement. But this may work in your favor because any document without a time frame may be judged invalid in a court of law.

For your own protection, always be careful and wary of anything you sign. At the same time, be certain that your own forms ensure the protection you seek for your ideas. Also, review this chapter carefully and often. The information presented here can be the difference between benefiting to the fullest from your ideas and losing everything to a competitor.

Chapter 6

Starting the Design Process

All that is comes from the mind;
It is based on the mind,
It is fashioned by the mind.
The Pali Canon
250 BC

Designing a new product is one of the most enjoyable and most challenging parts of being an inventor. Not everyone is cut out to design a concept from scratch, however. That is why learning how to communicate effectively with draftsmen, design engineers, machinists and graphic designers is essential. But most of the time, you can develop a basic concept to the point where the majority of technical and nontechnical people can understand what the idea is and how it works.

This chapter shows you how to get started in the design phase of product development. Two key areas are covered: invention artwork and establishing the design parameters for a product.

Invention Artwork

The ability to design any product centers around your ability to imagine the product in its final form—as a three-dimensional (3-D) object. Good drawings are vital in the early stages of the design process, as well as in the patent-application, prototype, and manufacturing stages. If you are not a skilled graphic artist or draftsman, don't be afraid to hire professional help. But first, you should develop at least a basic understanding of the types of drawings that go into the process of developing an idea into a product.

95

The Three Categories of Invention Artwork

All inventions require some sort of artwork during the course of their development. The artwork essential to entrepreneurial inventing can be divided into three general categories. The categories are:

- Developmental artwork
- Patent artwork
- Promotional artwork

1. DEVELOPMENTAL ARTWORK.   These are any illustrations used in the first stages of an invention. This type of art is used to conceive and develop the concept. These include rough sketches, and original drawings by you, the inventor. They can also include technical drawings for machinists to produce parts, or for model makers to fashion a working model or prototype. Developmental artwork can also include line art, exploded views, cross sections and cut-away drawings.

2. PATENT ARTWORK.   This artwork is specifically drawn in patent style and format to support the patent application. This artwork is usually produced by a patent draftman. It must be done to the exacting specifications of the patent system or it risks rejection by the patent examiner.

3. PROMOTIONAL ARTWORK.   This is any professional artwork that is used to promote the invention at any stage. Promotional artwork includes color renderings, line art, exploded views, cross sections and cut-away drawings.
    The types of artwork used most by inventors are:

- **a.** *Color Renderings.* These are full-color drawings that show the product in a three-dimensional perspective that allows the viewer to get a real sense of the product as it will appear in its final form. Color renderings can show the product by itself or in a setting that gives an indication of its size and/or intended use. Color renderings are usually done life-size or larger (with the exception being extremely large products shown in a smaller scale). These drawings are often used in presentations to investors, and then later used in product brochures and media releases.
- **b.** *Line Art.* Line art is any artwork that consists of lines and possibly shades of gray. There is no color. This includes all artwork types described in "c, d, e, f and g" below. All color renderings usually start as line art. Line art includes both two- and three-dimensional works.
- **c.** *Exploded Views.* Exploded views are drawings that show the component parts of an invention in a disassembled state to illustrate how they fit together. This type of drawing is valuable in product development work and marketing of the product to investors and end users.
- **d.** *Cross Sections.* Cross sections are two-dimensional drawings of a product that show the interior of the product as if it were sliced in

half. This type of illustration often allows a viewer to more readily understand the function of a product by revealing its inner workings in the simplest format.

e. *Cut-Aways.* Cut-aways are three-dimensional drawings of a product that have part of the exterior cut away (hense the name) to reveal the inner workings of the device. The interior parts may or may not be cut away, thus revealing their exact structure and how they interlink with other components of the product. This type of drawing is extremely useful to illustrate high-tech systems inside a product where they would not normally be visible to the viewer. Cut-aways can be color renderings for dramatic effect in promotional materials.

f. *Diagrams and Schematics.* Diagrams and schematics are used to show the overview of an entire system or series of connecting components in the simplest possible way. Diagrams show realistic components in three dimensions. Schematics show dialog boxes or simplified part icons in a two-dimensional layout.

g. *Product Specification Sheets.* Product specification sheets usually consist of three basic orthographic views (top, side, and front) of a product along with a three-dimensional view or photo. Product spec sheets usually supply the very basic information about a product including its dimensions, materials, and unique features. See Appendix III for sample of typical Product Specification Sheets.

How to Get Help from Artists and Illustrators

You should find—and develop a good working relationship with—several artists and illustrators early in your career as an entrepreneurial inventor. One such artist is Gary Whitten of Whitten Illustration and Design of Phoenix, Arizona. The drawings on pages 98–102 are samples from his brochures. Whitten specializes in artwork for new product development and marketing. Not every artist can fulfill the requirements of every job, so you should find and cultivate a variety of good sources who understand the three categories of drawings discussed above. Normally, an advertisement placed in a large newspaper will get many responses from artists willing to do freelance artwork. Be specific about the types of illustrations you need. If necessary, use the samples of art work on the following pages to make sure the artist you hire knows exactly what you need for a particular project.

Many artists advertise in trade journals and statewide artist resource guides. Always examine samples of an artist's work and ask for a list of other clients to whom you can speak for references. A good working relationship with a versatile illustrator, one who understands your concepts as you see them, is crucial to getting artwork that represents your inventions in the proper light.

Fees for invention-related artwork vary and are totally subjective. How much you will have to pay can depend upon the complexity of the work, your relationship with the artist, and how badly he or she needs the job. Illustrators

Exploded View Technical Drawings

Exploded views are usually
used in assembly sheets and
parts catalogs but they are
also valuable in new product
development and marketing.

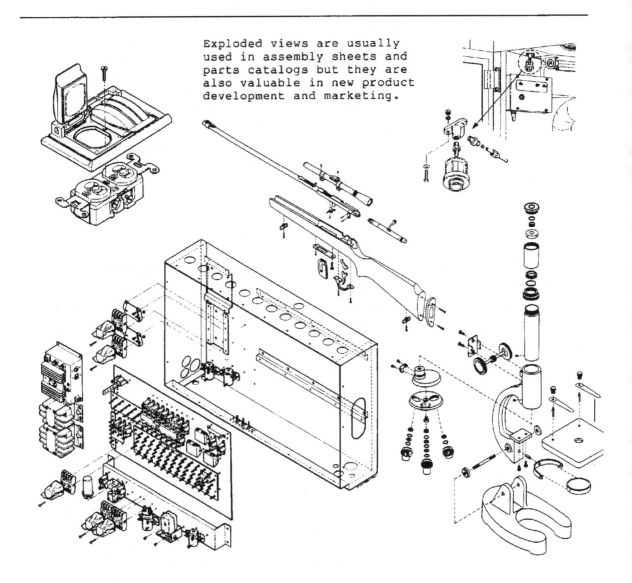

Illustrations Courtesy of Gary Whitten
Whitten Illustration & Design
Phoenix, Arizona (602) 491-6407

Cross Section & Cutaway Drawings

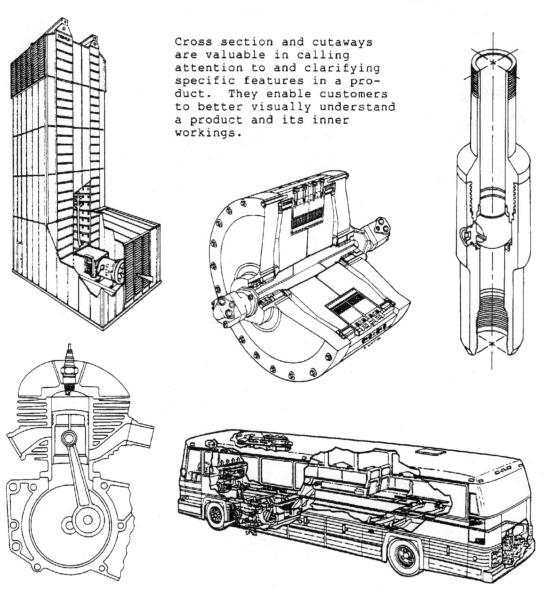

Cross section and cutaways are valuable in calling attention to and clarifying specific features in a product. They enable customers to better visually understand a product and its inner workings.

Illustrations Courtesy of Gary Whitten
Whitten Illustration & Design
Phoenix, Arizona (602) 491-6407

Diagrams & Schematics

Schematics & diagrams are used
to simplify and show an overview of the major components
in a system, such as an
electrical wiring harness...

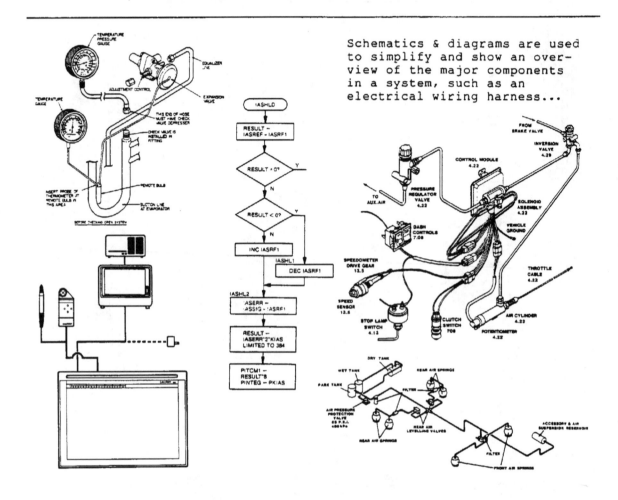

Illustrations Courtesy of Gary Whitten
Whitten Illustration & Design
Phoenix, Arizona (602) 491-6407

Product Specification Sheets

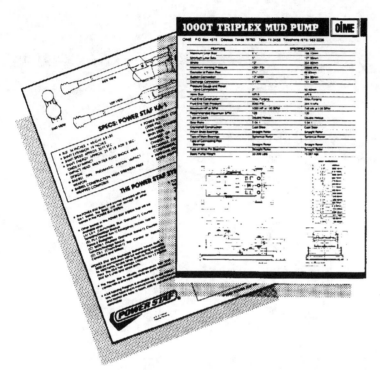

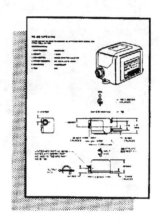

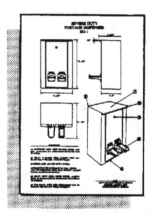

Product specification sheets supply the
basic information about a product and it's
specifications such as dimensions,materials,
unique features,etc. "Spec" sheets usually
include drawings of the three basic orthographic views (front, top, & side) as well
as an isometric or perspective drawing.

**(See Appendix III for actual sample of Power Staf® Product
Specifications Sheet.)**

**Illustrations Courtesy of Gary Whitten
Whitten Illustration & Design
Phoenix, Arizona (602) 491-6407**

Whitten Illustration & Design is a "high tech oriented" commercial art service with an extensive background in conceptual art for new product development and marketing. Realistic and technical illustrations rendered from blueprints, numerical specifications, prototypes or photos.

Some of our Services:
Airbrush Illustration
Architectural Renderings
Exhibit Design/Graphics
Logo & Package Development
Photo Retouching
Poster Design
Medical Illustration/Graphics
Technical Line Art

Airbrush
Illustrator

WHITTEN ILLUSTRATION & DESIGN

(602) 491-6407

Some of our Clients:
*(Direct or through affiliate agencies)
The Pointe
Calcomp (Digitizer Division)
Greyhound Corporation
Paddock Pools & Spas
Arizona Automotive Institute
Sperry Corporation
U.S. Homes
Valley National Bank

such as Whitten are in high demand, of course, because of their levels of expertise and client list.

As a general rule, however, don't offer the work to the first artist you interview. Try to check out a variety of artists in your area. You may find one, like Whitten, who has the proper balance of skill, personality and fee structure to accommodate your budget and requirements. Or, you may find several who have individual strengths that can help your project in different stages of its design and development.

Product Design and Ergonomics

The physical size and shape of most inventions relate directly to people in some way. There are exceptions, of course. People are much bigger than microprocessors and much smaller than giant well-drilling bits. But, for the most part, whether an invention is to be operated by a person or will act upon a person, it is designed with people in mind.

The basic design information that relates to people is called *ergonomics*. This is the science of how mechanical devices relate to the human body in reference to design characteristics. The term "ergonomics" today is often used to refer to the physical comfort of a product, as well as how easily it can be operated or used. The science of ergonomics is fairly new. It was started during World War II when the War Department needed fighter pilots to be able to operate their small but complicated planes during long and arduous missions. The planes were cramped, and it became obvious that the pilots could only operate at their maximum capabilities if their fighters were designed with the pilots' comfort and ease of flying in mind. This concept in design later was carried over into industry, where today it is well known that proper ergonomic design of the workplace, its tools and furnishings can lead to increased productivity and less absenteeism.

Designing Products Sized for People

The following series of human figures (page 104) give you important dimensions that can help you design products to work with people. The dimensions shown for each of the letters (next to a particular part of the figure) are average distances for the general population. The first number shown is for males, and the second figure (in parenthesis) is for females. Additional information on specific body-part dimensions can be obtained from design books found at your public library.

The Design Specifications Checklist

The Design Specifications Checklist is a tool that can help you evaluate the exact parameters for the final specifications of an invention. The use of the checklist is simple, yet the information you put into it will form a sophisti-

BASIC DESIGN DIMENSIONS

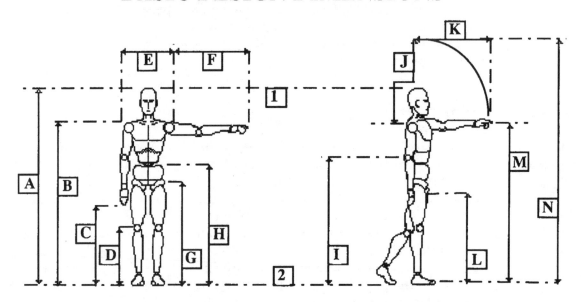

All dimensions are approximate for the average U.S. adult population and may vary from your own specifications, or the needs of a particular group for whom you are designing a product. All dimensions from the floor up to a particular body area are for the individual standing barefoot on a flat floor. [1] = Head Level   [2] = Floor Level.

Male	Female	Legend
A - 5' 10"	[5'4.5"]	Floor to Top of Head
B - 4' 10"	[4' 5"]	Floor to Shoulder Pivot Point
C - 2' 1"	[1' 10.5"]	Floor to Finger Tips
D - 1' 8"	[1' 6"]	Floor to Knee Joint (center)
E - 1' 8"	[n/a]	Shoulder Width to Outside of Arms (with arms folded)
F - 2' 4"	[2' 3"]	Arm Reach to Side of Body
G - 3' 1"	[2' 11"]	Floor to Hip
H - 3' 6"	[3' 2"]	Floor to Waist
I - 3' 8"	[3' 4"]	Floor to Elbow
J - 2' 7.5"	[2' 3.5"]	Arm Reach Above Shoulder Level
K - 3' 2"	[2' 10.5"]	Arm Reach in Front of Body
L - 2' 9"	[2' 7"]	Floor to Groin
M - 4' 8"	[4' 3"]	Comfortable Arm Reach Level (front of Body)
N - 7' 5.5"	[6' 8.5"]	Total Upward Reach

cated set of criteria that can help you determine all aspects of the product you are trying to create. The "envelope" created by this checklist is the form the invention must take to perform successfully.

To use the checklist, pose each question as a separate important factor in the product's development. Ask each question as an adjunct of all other criteria. Determine what elements of the design interlink to form a criteria that must satisfy them both.

The successful use of this checklist, by itself, can give you important design and prototyping information. When this checklist is used in conjunction with the Idea Development Checklist discussed in Chapter 3, the two checklists form a powerful evaluation technique for developing the final product parameters.

The questions below are the ones used in the Design Specifications Checklist (pp. 115–119). The blank form itself follows the questions' explanations. The blank checklist should be copied and used for all invention projects.

☑ A. SIZE

1. Who must use the product?

If designing the product in one size makes it unrealistic for all possible end users to wear, handle or control the product, then it must be designed in several sizes. Otherwise, a large part of the market may be lost.

2. By whom, and where, must the product be maneuvered?

The ability to use the product in the environment where it is regularly going to be used is crucial to its marketability. If the end user has problems taking the product where it must go because of its designed size, then the product does not serve the end function of the purchaser. An example of this is a product designed to be carried by a passenger aboard an aircraft. It must be stored beneath the seat or in the overhead bin. If it does not fit this size characteristic, it will not be a marketable product.

3. Where must it be stored?

As pointed out above, storage is an important aspect of a product's design. If a product needs special storage facilities or a special environment that is in conflict with the size of the product, then the product design will not be functional.

4. How does its size affect its end use?

Size is often an important factor in the end use of a product. If the product is unnecessarily large or small, it may be awkward to use. The interrelationships of the type of user, the environment it will be used in and the product's end use are linked together to form a direct design criteria for almost every product.

5. *How does size affect its salability?*

This is an important criteria because a product that won't sell is a product that was a waste to develop in the first place. Size and salability are also linked by concerns regarding shipping and packaging costs. Many products have a low density but are extremely bulky, thus increasing their shipping costs. The higher costs, in turn, are reflected in the overall sales price to the end purchaser. Another factor of size and salability is the perception of the end user and the function for which he wants the product. If the end user wants, or needs, to have a compact device, then a large product, regardless of its functionality, will not be suitable.

6. *Is size linked to its safe use?*

Does the size of the device cause it to have any detrimental side effects or possible hazards in use or storage? Would an increase or decrease in size improve safety without devaluing the product in some other respect?

☑ B. WEIGHT

1. *Who must use the product?*

Will the weight of the product hamper its use by the intended end user? Is it necessary for the device to have different weights for different end users, categorizing them by age, market group, or other factors?

2. *Who must maneuver the product?*

Will the end user be capable of handling the expected weight of the product in the intended environment of use? Would a higher or lower total weight make any difference?

3. *Where must it be stored?*

Weight is a special concern when storage is a factor. Make sure the typical storage location is suitable to handle the weight of the product. Many products must be stored in high cabinets or other areas. This can make it difficult or unsafe to lift them, depending on the weight of the product. Keep in mind that most bowling balls are not stored on upper shelves for this reason. If the product is intended to be stored in an awkward location, it is important to minimize its weight for best handling.

4. *How does its weight affect its end use?*

If a product is too heavy to carry around, it better be intended for stationary use, or at least have wheels to facilitate moving it! A lightweight sledge hammer may be great for carrying to the job site, but may not really do its job because its effectiveness is based upon a factor of its mass. Your product should have the proper weight to fulfill its purpose, but usually no more than is needed.

5. How does weight affect its salability?

This is sometimes a direct contradiction of the statement above. Many products are often weighted to give them a solid feel. Sometimes a lightweight product has a lower perceived value than a comparable, heavier product. In some cases, just the opposite is true. For example, a light running shoe is regarded as more desirable and thus perceived to be worth more to the purchaser than a heavier running shoe. The military often judges a product by its weight, as well as by many other factors. For example, some items must be transported by foot soldiers into the field. A lighter-weight product is perceived as a greater value because it is less fatiguing to the soldier who is carrying it.

6. Is weight linked to its safe use?

This is often the case when a product's overall design is taken into account. Many products are inherently safe or dangerous because of their weight distribution. A ladder or a car are perfect examples of what motion, gravity, and inertia can do to a safe-looking product that has a bad weight distribution. Many products that have excellent designs are still hard, and possibly unsafe, to use because of poorly designed weight distribution. Improper weight distribution simultaneously fatigues the user and causes balance and control difficulties.

☑ C. COLOR

1. Does color affect its use?

The ability to see a product against any number of backgrounds is always a factor when designing a device. This is the reason that almost all safety-related devices are colored bright yellow or orange. Those colors stand out against almost any background.

2. Does color affect its salability?

Many products will not sell in their intended markets if they are not the proper color. Weapons painted bright pink would not be purchased by the military, nor would black wall paper sell extremely well (although there may be a small market for both). Keep this in mind: *People are swayed by color more than any single factor in the selection of many products.* Advertising companies and even the military know that certain colors affect people in very specific ways. Selecting just a single color for a product may decrease its sales. Providing a selection of colors may increase sales. For that reason, even weaponry comes in an assortment of grey, blue, black and stainless steel finishes for every possible market and taste.

☑ D. POWER SOURCE

1. Does it need one? Can it do its job without one?

Not all products need a power source. Artistic, display and personal items of non-electronic nature do not, for the most part, have any need for power to fulfill their operational goals. Many products that, in the past, have used a power source can now, through modern technology, create the same effect without power. An example of this is the reflective and phosphorescent surfaces on clothes or products. These surfaces produce their visible glow from reflection or absorbed light radiation.

2. Who must charge or power up the product?

Creating an access for power is also a concern for the design in relationship to its end user. There is a major difference between plugging a product into a wall outlet and changing batteries in a device. Many parents do not want their children playing with anything that requires them to plug or unplug a product at a wall outlet, but they have no concerns over the same child changing batteries in a device.

3. Where must it be stored? Used?

Devices requiring any type of electrical power have different storage concerns from mechanically powered, fuel powered or fluid-powered types. Every type of powered product also has safety requirements regarding its proper use, handling and storage. Designing the use of a power source requires that you look into the safety aspects of the device in relation not just to use, but non-use and storage, as well.

4. How does its power source affect its end use?

The difference in power sources is a great variable in the end use of many products. Products constrained by electric power cords have a limited distance that they can be used from conventional outlets. Otherwise, they will need portable generating equipment to operate. Battery-powered devices are very portable but lack the capacity to do many jobs, at least for long, because of their power consumption curves. Solar-powered devices are at the mercy of the weather and have no access to power in darkness. Gasoline and compressed natural gas-powered devices can be easily refueled in the field, providing you have the fuel, but usually are noisy products only useful for certain tasks. They do, however, have great power-to-weight ratios in relation to the work they are capable of doing for the fuel expended. Compressed air and other gas-powered devices have their own special limitations that make them effective in only a limited number of situations. Always take the power questions into account when designing a product. If you can use low power or no power, you are probably way ahead of the competition.

5. How does its power source affect its salability?

The price of power is always increasing and that has a direct relationship to the cost of operating any device, regardless of its power source. If a product has a high operating cost, either in batteries, gas or electric charges, then it is less likely to be sold competitively.

6. Is its power source linked to its safe use?

If you design your product to work off nuclear waste, you may have problems clearing it for use in homes around the nation. But seriously, the power source should be considered in light of its possible dangers to the end user and the environment. Rechargeable, reusable or renewable energy sources are the best bet for the inventor of the Nineties and beyond.

7. Availability of power source?

Make sure that the power source you design into your product will be available when and where it is needed by the end user. There are no power outlets in the outback, and there are very few specialty battery stores in Smalltown, USA.

8. Types of power sources:

Several different types of power sources are available. Each should be considered for its merits and drawbacks in respect to the invention on the drawing board. Here are the key issues:

a. *Disposable:*
Usually batteries. These present a serious environmental threat. If batteries must be used, please try to make them long-life and low current drain. This will lower the number of times they need to be replaced. Batteries of all types are excellent for portable applications.

b. *Rechargeable:*
This can mean batteries as well. The nickel-cadmium variety is the most popular of the rechargeable types and can often last for years with regular recharging. This can be done with a removable battery or by using a power cord to the wall outlet to directly recharge the internal battery in a device. Other rechargeable power sources include compressed air, gasoline, and natural gas.

c. *Semipermanent*
This means some sort of connection to a stationary power outlet. This includes wall plugs for all appliances that can be moved from one location to another.

d. *Permanent*
This means a hard-wired power connection that is neither moveable nor rechargeable. This usually entails being hooked directly into a power grid of a building or vehicle.

e. *Renewable*
This means any power source that is naturally renewable, such as solar, wind, wave, or geothermal power. These are the wave of the

future and should be considered in the basic design elements of your product ideas. If you can use a naturally occurring power source that is free and unlimited, doesn't it make sense to do so? Additionally, most processes for tapping into these sources do not create any environmental hazards or pollution.

☑ E. MATERIALS

1. Who must use the product?

The selection for the types of materials to be used in a product is directly related to the end user. This is due to price, weight, durability, appearance and a host of other factors that will make the purchaser actually purchase it.

2. Where must it be stored?

Products are stored under various temperature, light and atmospheric conditions. These conditions can adversely effect the product, depending upon the materials from which it is constructed. When designing a new product, you must have the foresight to design it for worst-case scenarios or it may fail the end user at the most unexpected of times. Products with component parts made from most plastics must be kept away from extreme heat and cold; products with ultraviolet-sensitive materials must be kept out of direct sunlight, and so forth.

3. How does the material it is built from effect its end use?

The material you choose can have a direct bearing on a product's ability to fulfill its role. A foam-rubber crutch or knife is funny, but not extremely useful. A steel mattress is not going to provide a comfortable sleeping environment for the majority of people. Selecting the proper material is critical to making the product operate correctly.

4. How do the materials effect its salability?

Selecting the proper materials is also crucial to pricing the product so that it will sell in the marketplace. Although many products can use higher-quality components, many manufacturers opt for the cheapest possible material that will safely do the job. The reason is strictly bottom line. If some products are priced too high, they will not sell! On the other end of that spectrum is the top-dollar product that uses only the finest-quality materials. These products sell very well to the people who can afford them. In this case, the perceived value of the product is not the fact that it is expensive, but what makes it so.

5. Are materials linked to its safe use?

The proper design and materials to fulfill that design will usually result in a safe product. But this is not always the case. Take materials such as asbestos, for example. Once considered a wonder material for fireproofing almost anything, it has since proved to be a health hazard. As an entrepreneurial inventor, you cannot predict the future. But you can at least stay informed about the current safety aspects of the materials you select for use in your products. If the product is to be used in an environment that is likely to place it in contact with various solvents, acids or other chemicals, you must carefully research the effects of these chemicals on the materials in the product. The same reasoning goes for environmental conditions such as sudden temperature changes or rainfall. See the section on "Destructive Testing" in the next chapter for a testing plan that can help you do this type of product research.

6. Types of material properties.

The following are some considerations you should always remember when selecting materials for a product:

a. *Fireproof*
Fire-resistant and fireproof materials can often mean the difference between a saleable product or one rejected by mass merchandisers. Government specifications outline the products that must be made fireproof before they can be sold in the USA.

b. *Nontoxic*
You will almost certainly want to use nontoxic chemicals and materials in most products that come into contact with people. Many products cannot be produced without the use of some very toxic processes that transform the material into another state. You should review the processes needed to manufacture your concepts during the initial design stage to limit these processes later during the manufacturing stage.

c. *Flexibility/Rigidity*
The actual physical rigidity or flexibility of a material can greatly enhance or detract from a product's perceived value. You should consider different physical values of a specific material before deciding upon it as a component of your product.

d. *Magnetic/Nonmagnetic*
The use and combination of magnetic and nonmagnetic materials can create some very interesting product applications. Many products such as audio and video tape are strongly and adversely affected by magnetic materials. You should be careful to limit magnetic materials in your products to the absolute minimum, unless needed as part of the operational design of the device.

e. *Transparency/Opacity*
The ability of a component to allow light to pass through or to block light is integral to the operation of many devices. Many new materials have been invented in recent years that have unusual optical properties in relationship to electrical current (i.e. LCD) and light itself. You should look into these new materials for ideas in creating new products.

f. *Organic/Inorganic*

The use of organic or inorganic materials can play an important part in the ability of a disposable product to be biodegradable. You should be concerned about the future of our planet and look into the long-term disposition of any product that you design.

7. Availability of materials.

Are you designing a product from a material that is hard or impossible to get in any manufacturing quantity? If so, you may be designing yourself into a corner. Always make sure that several companies can supply your materials at a reasonable price and on a schedule you can live with.

☑ F. ERGONOMICS

1. What is its intended use and who are the end users?

Every product must be specifically designed for either a function or an end user—usually for both. Is your product designed to be used comfortably in its specific purpose by the intended end user?

2. How will it be handled?

Is the design specific to the needs and handling characteristics of the end user? Is it built to be carried by hand, on your back, over a shoulder, or at all? If it is portable, can it be accessed in a way that is easy and fits with the clothing or accouterment of the end users.

3. Will one size fit all?

Do you need several designs for different size people? Will one design work if it is made in several sizes?

4. Will custom sizes be manufactured?

Is there enough of a market to warrant the manufacture of more than one size, if one size will not fit all?

☑ G. COSMETICS

1. Will the look of the product offend any section of the public?

Have you researched the like and dislikes of the typical end user? Is the product offensive in any way (sexist, religious, racist, etc.)?

2. Does the look of the product convey its purpose?

Can you tell what the product is from its appearance? If not, is that good or bad? A toy doesn't need to look childish, but it should not be mistaken for a weapon. Just the opposite also is true. A device that is intentionally built to convey a serious, powerful image should do just that.

3. Does the look of the product convey any special meaning?

Some products need to have an exterior design that conveys a sleek, fast feeling. Others should appeal to a more conservative, slow-paced lifestyle. Your design criteria in this area is again dictated by your end user. If you build a sports car that looks like a slow, middle-of-the-road car, most sports car enthusiasts will not buy it. But you may create a whole new market of more conservative car buyers who have always longed for more power and zip in the style of vehicle they prefer.

☑ H. CONSTRUCTION

1. Will it be built of stock parts or custom parts?

Always try to build all your products with as many stock parts as possible. This will dramatically reduce your research and development time, as well as costs. It will also put you in a position to get free sample parts for most prototypes you build. Only create custom parts when it is absolutely necessary for a competitive edge or secrecy of construction. Many state-of-the-art products are a combination of tried-and-true components mixed with custom parts that help create the next step in that particular technology.

2. Will parts be interchangeable with other vendors' parts?

Having interchangeable parts is always a good idea. Even if you are in direct competition, the use of the same part means two things: (a) a good supply for manufacturing; and (b) a good supply for customer-replacement parts.

3. Is the product designed for assembly (DFA)?

DFA is the latest concept in design technology and manufacturing thought. It means that the product was designed with the express idea that the assembly will be as simple as possible when the device actually gets to the production room floor. DFA also makes a product easier to repair, by service technicians and by the end user. DFA usually entails more thought in the design process, but it is worth it at the bottom line.

4. Are parts available in general commerce?

Always use parts that are readily accessible to YOU! This may not mean in general commerce, and such, may give you the competitive edge over other products. But make sure the parts supply is strong and infinite. If you start to build a product with a part from a supplier that is known only to you and it gives you a competitive edge, great...until that supplier can't supply you any longer. Then you may be forced to raise prices unexpectedly or even stop manufacturing if you can't get equal parts for your production line.

5. Are any special molds needed for production?

If yes, make sure you own the mold and have the option to change your molder at any time. Otherwise, you may be over a barrel if the molder raises prices, makes parts for someone else or does any number of other typical business tricks that many businesses try when they have an upper hand with a small inventor and his company.

6. Are there any special production requirements?

If you need zero noise during manufacturing, or you must have one hundred people on hand for twenty minutes a day, but at no other time to make your product, you may want to rethink the process or the product. No product will come to fruition if the complications of its production outweigh its profit potential or your patience.

DESIGN SPECIFICATIONS CHECKLIST

Inventor's Name _____   Signed: _____
Project Name: _____   Product Field: _____
Invention Name: _____
Date of Invention: _____   Date of this Checklist: _____
Page 1 of 5

DESIGN SPECIFICATIONS CHECKLIST

(A) Size:

1. How does size effect who must use the product?
_____
_____
_____

2. How does size effect who must maneuver the product?
_____
_____
_____

3. How does size effect where it must be stored?
_____
_____
_____

4. How does its size effect its end use?
_____
_____
_____

5. How does size effect salability?
_____
_____
_____

6. Is size linked to its safe use?
_____
_____
_____

(B) Weight:

1. How does its weight effect who must use the product?
_____
_____
_____

2. How does its weight effect who must maneuver the product?
_____
_____
_____

Design Specification Checklist   Invention: _____
Page 2 of 5   Inventor: _____

3. How does its weight effect where must it be stored?

_____

_____

_____

4. How does its weight effect its end use?

_____

_____

_____

5. How does weight effect its salability?

_____

_____

_____

6. Is weight linked to its safe use?

_____

_____

_____

(C) Color:

1. Does color effect its use?

_____

_____

_____

2. Does color effect its salability?

_____

_____

_____

3. Is color linked to its safe use?

_____

_____

_____

(D) Power Source:

1. Does the power source effect who must use the product?

_____

_____

_____

2. Does the power source effect who must charge or power up the product?

_____

_____

_____

3. Does its power source effect where must it be stored; Used?

_____

_____

_____

Design Specification Checklist   Invention: _____
Page 3 of 5   Inventor: _____

4. How does its power source effect its end use?
_____
_____
_____

5. How does its power source effect its salability?
_____
_____
_____

6. Is power source linked to its safe use?
_____
_____
_____

7. Price & availability of power source?
_____
_____
_____

8. Types of power sources: (Check appropriate boxes)
□ Disposable □ Rechargeable □ Semi-permanent (Cord-wall)
□ Permanent (Hard wired) □ Pneumo □ Hydro □ Solar □ Other □ _____
Notes: _____

(E) Materials:

1. Who must use the product? How will the materials selection effect the user?
_____
_____
_____

2. Who must handle the product? How will materials selection effect its handling?
_____
_____
_____

3. Where must it be stored? How will materials selection effect its storage?
_____
_____
_____
_____

4. How does the material it's built from effect its end use?
_____
_____
_____

5. How do the materials effect its salability?
_____
_____
_____
_____

Design Specification Checklist   Invention: _____
Page 4 of 5   Inventor: _____

6. Are its materials linked to its safe use?

_____
_____
_____

7. Types of material properties: (some considerations, check appropriate boxes)
☐ Fireproof ☐ Flammable ☐ Non-Toxic ☐ Flexibility ☐ Rigidity
☐ Magnetic ☐ Non-magnetic ☐ Transparency ☐ Opacity ☐ Organic
☐ Ingoranic ☐ Other: _____

(F) Ergonomics:

1. How will its shape effect its intended use and end users?

_____
_____
_____

2. How will its shape effect how it be handled?

_____
_____
_____

3. Will one size fit all? Are special sizes needed?

_____
_____
_____

4. Will custom units be manufactured for special people or groups (ie: Handicapped)?

_____
_____
_____

(G) Cosmetics:

1. Will look of product offend any section of the public?

_____
_____
_____
_____

2. Does look of product convey its purpose?

_____
_____
_____
_____

3. Does look of product convey any special meaning?

_____
_____
_____
_____

Design Specification Checklist   Invention: _____
Page 5 of 5   Inventor: _____

(H) Construction:

1. Will it be built of stock parts or custom parts?

_____
_____
_____

2. Will parts be interchangeable with other vendors' parts?

_____
_____
_____

3. Is product designed for assembly (DFA)?

_____
_____
_____

4. Are parts available in general commerce?

_____
_____
_____

5. Are special molds needed for production?

_____
_____
_____

6. Are their any special production requirements?

_____
_____
_____

NOTES ON DESIGN AND DEVELOPMENT OF THIS PRODUCT/PROJECT:

_____
_____
_____
_____
_____
_____
_____
_____
_____
_____
_____
_____
_____
_____
_____
_____
_____

Chapter 7

Building and Testing Your Ideas

Genius is the ability to reduce the complicated to the simple.

C. W. Ceran

 Once you have completed the design phase, it is time to start creating the *prototype*. This is a working model or sample device that you can use to perfect your design, set up the manufacturing process, and show to potential backers, buyers, or customers. This chapter shows you how to create prototypes and how to test them for durability and safety. It includes information about setting up a home workshop capable of producing simple but sophisticated prototypes. This chapter also shows you how to get parts, usually for free, that can help you assemble a high-quality prototype.

Prototype Construction

 A prototype is the first physical evidence of a new product concept's ability to leave the drawing board and become reality. A prototype is also a valuable tool for acquiring data in an invention project. Every prototype will teach you a new lesson in building techniques, data acquisition and, most of all, patience. Building prototypes can be a fulfilling, if somewhat tortuous, process that is never the same from invention to invention. You should always keep your prototypes in a safe place, because they are a valuable asset and a source of pride and accomplishment. Prototypes also are dots on a time line of progress that will show you if you are learning the tools of the trade.

120

Types of Prototypes

Many types of fabrications fall under the heading of "Prototypes." Although you may build each of these fabrications for the same product, each type is different in construction and use. These types include: the **mock-up;** the **working model;** the **scale model;** the **first prototype;** and the **preproduction prototype.**

THE MOCK-UP.   There are two types of mock-ups:

a. The design mock-up looks like what the final version of the product is expected to look like. It is used for engineering and design purposes. It creates the envelope in which all final components must reside. The design mock-up is a very realistic model that is the final evolution of engineering and research work.

b. The presentation mock-up can be a design mock-up, but more often, it is a pre-engineering and research "wish" of what the creation team wants the final product to look like. It is a model that is used for publicity and promotion purposes such as raising capital and attracting media attention.

THE WORKING MODEL.   The working model is a functional invention that does exactly what the final product is expected to do, without any cosmetic concerns. The working model can look nothing like the final product as long as it is completely operational. The purpose of the working model is to demonstrate the product's usefulness and practicality. Many working models often demonstrate new and effective design parameters that are then incorporated into the final cosmetic design.

THE SCALE MODEL.   The scale model can either be working or nonfunctional, depending upon its intended use. The scale model is always exactly what it says, a smaller or larger scale than the projected final product. Most scale models are smaller than the product they are portraying. They are used in trade show exhibits or to raise capital. They are usually built to be easily transported and displayed. Scale models of very small and complicated products are made larger so the technology can be displayed and discussed.

THE FIRST PROTOTYPE.   Often called the "Proof of Concept," the first prototype is any device built around the idea for a product. It may be close in design and function to the final product or it may be a working model with partial cosmetic appeal. First prototypes are starting points for inventors to build on. You should never despair if your first prototype is awkward and slightly dysfunctional. Its main purpose is to fortify your belief that a product can evolve out of it and to give you a starting point for future development.

THE PREPRODUCTION PROTOTYPE.   The preproduction prototype is a last chance to make functional and design changes before going into production. Ideally, the preproduction prototype looks and functions just like the final production model. Preproduction prototypes are often used to market products before final production is even underway, thus creating a demand for the product's first production run. The preproduction model is also used for final destructive testing (see page 135) so that any final modifications based upon the testing can be incorporated in the production model.

Trends in Prototyping

The future of prototyping is fantastic! In the last several years, two important new processes for making prototypes have become available. Within the next decade or so, according to industry speculation, every inventor may have access to desktop prototyping, the same way printers and marketing people now have access to desktop publishing. The two advances that will make this a reality are:

1. CAD-CAM: The use of computer-aided design hooked directly to a CNC (Computer Numerical Controlled) type milling/lathe machine. You will only have to design the part on the computer and it will be fabricated by the CNC machine out of steel or plastic. This technology is available to a limited extent in some machine shops. The basic technology has been available for almost a decade, but it must be refined further for desktop applications.

2. Sterolithography: This technology was invented earlier in the 1990s, and it is as close to science fiction as modern science had come, thus far. Parts are fabricated by the solidification of a liquid chemical via application of laser light to that chemical. A computer analyzes the part design, then tells the machine where to apply the laser to solidify the compound to create the part. As this technology becomes more refined, it may replace certain types of manufacturing for custom parts. It will definitely become a source of quick prototyped parts for designers in the future. Its usefulness to you is limited only by its refinement and your imagination.

Most prototyping work still is based, however, on what you can fabricate using your own resources and your own finances. This does not have to limit you to crude prototypes. Many impressive prototypes are manufactured every year by entrepreneurial inventors using their own imaginations to adapt common materials to create new products.

Once the first prototype has been built, additional capital can be sought so the project can advance to the next phase of development, which usually will include professionally fabricated mock-ups and working models.

How to Find and Use Prototype Parts

Prototypes can be made from almost anything. A large part of the prototype process is determined by the type of invention you are attempting to prototype, your operations budget and the level of the prototype (mock-up, working model, scale model, etc.). Most inventors cannot afford to make complex and costly prototypes to exacting specification. But you can try to: (1) make an initial working model to prove a theory; or (2) make a mock-up to show how something will look in its projected final configuration. Both of these proto-types usually can be fabricated out of parts that are readily available to be modified to your needs. There are several ways to get proto parts. They include finds; hobby and model shops; machine shops; manufacturers; and model makers.

Finds

Finds are a prototype resource that many people overlook. Finds are items that you can find around the house (and/or business) or within the group of products you may normally purchase. What many would call rubbish, you may recognize as a find.

Here are some examples of finds:

1. Cardboard of all types (boxes, tubes, sheets, etc.)
2. Plastic containers of all types (soda bottles, cosmetics enclosures, packaging, etc.;
3. Rubber bands, plastic bags; and
4. Molded parts of any kind, such as those found on used toys, games, cosmetics, or any other product with prefabricated structures.

Additional parts can be found in the waste from manufacturing plants. Contact local plastic and metal shops to see if you can get parts from them before they are thrown out. Many places will be glad to supply you with large quantities of scrap that they would normally discard. When you come across a source of supply that has a steady output of a specific piece of scrap material, think about what you could do with that part. Use your inventive talents to see if that part can be made into an actual product. It may turn out that in your search for a prototype resource, you find a free product source.

Hobby and Model Shops

Hobby and model shops carry a wide selection of plastic, wood, paper, and metal parts that can be used to create mock-ups, display models, and working models. Hobby and model shops are some of the best sources of small hand tools for crafting mock-ups and scale models. Hobby shop owners and workers are usually a great source of knowledge about the production of scale models and the use of miniature power sources. Another resource found in hobby shops are the small gas and electric motors plus gearing and control systems to work them. These can be crucial to fabricating working models of many inventions, without the need to build special power sources. If you are designing a large structure or device, you can use many of the miniature parts available (trees, people, vehicles) to show scale. Hobby shops are a major resource that you should get to know.

Machine Shops

Machine shops are capable of producing parts for almost any project that requires cut lathed or milled metal parts. Machine shops are an expensive option ($25–$75 per hour plus materials is an average cost) and require detailed drawings to assure getting back a correctly sized and fabricated part. A good relationship with a local machine shop is an advantage for any inventor. Contact your local machinist trade union for information on local machine shops. Look in the yellow pages under "Prototypes" to locate shops that specialize in helping create new products. Ads in the classified section of the newspaper can also lead to good freelance machinists, many of whom have shops set up in their garages.

Local Manufacturers

Local manufacturers will often give you small samples of their parts that you may be able to use in your prototype. A face-to-face approach is often the best. But you also can write them a letter. See the discussion on sample request letters later in this chapter, page 125.

Model Makers

Model makers are people who make mock-ups, scale models, and sometimes working models for companies and independent inventors. Model makers are talented individuals who may be the answer for you if you can't master the various skills needed for a particular phase of prototyping. Model makers are only as good as the input they are given. Most model makers are fairly expensive. They usually base their prices on either a flat fee for a project, or an hourly rate for ongoing consultation services.

Not every invention needs a prototype, but I've yet to see a project that wasn't enhanced by having a nice working model to play with or model to view. Some inventions are so simple that the first mock-up can be the final preproduction prototype, but this is rare. More often the prototype process will use various materials to get the point across. Several of the most common proto parts are:

1. Foam Core: A lightweight sheet that comes in various sizes. It is a stiff foam with a paper backing on both sides. It can be used to create three-dimensional objects through layering or hollow box construction techniques. It is available at most hobby stores.
2. Balsa Wood: a lightweight wood that is easily cut and shaped. It can be painted, sanded, etc. It is available at most hobby stores.
3. Plastic Sheets and Struts: most hobby shops also carry these items for the scale manufacture of towns and railroads. These include "I" beam and rail-shaped plastic strips that are ideal for construction of various types of prototypes.
4. Spray Paint: all types of model, finishing and house paints can be used to create various effects. These are available at a variety of stores.

5. Bondo and Spackle: are two common prototyping compounds that have the ability to be shaped by hand while wet and soft. When dry, they are hard and stiff, ideal for sanding, painting, drilling or otherwise modifying into a final form. Bondo is a brand name for an auto body filler compound that uses a two-part epoxy type compound. Spackle is a premixed wall joint compound. Both are relatively inexpensive and easy to find in automotive and hardware stores.

6. Chicken wire: all types of wire and open-air type structures that can be used as the base for application of bondo, spackle or other hardening compound. Use the wire to create a framework to give the prototype a basic body shape.

7. Clay: can be used to make molds that plastics and foams can be poured over or into to create 3D structures of complex shapes and sizes. Clay can also be used as a body element in prototype construction.

8. Polyurethane foam: is available in a two-part mix or in an aerosol spray can that premixes it. This foam comes out like shave cream but hardens to a dense Styrofoam type texture within minutes. It can be used to give structural strength to almost any prototype. It can be used to fill interior spaces, to protect components from movement or damage. It can be used to create molds around clay structures (which are later removed). Plyurethane foam is one of the most versatile prototype tools.

Almost anything you can find or buy can be used in a prototype. Roam through good hardware stores and art supply stores and look at the multitude of items on display. Imagine how you can use them as something else to fabricate your new piece of technology. The idea is to make it look, feel or work like the final product. Try and have fun while you're building the prototype. This will keep your energy high for the project. One thing to remember is that it doesn't have to be perfect, so don't be disappointed with initial attempts. The only rule you have to remember is that there are no rules when it comes to individual prototypes. Good luck!

How to Get Prototype Parts and Information from Companies

 One of the best ways to get prototype parts and information from companies is to write them some letters. Here are some useful sample letters. Tailor them to your own needs.

 ### *Information and Parts Request Letter*

The letter that follows is a generic format that you can modify and use to request information and/or parts from manufactures. I have found that it will bring you a fast response and follow up by the manufacturer. Here are some tips on writing and sending the letter.

1. *Call the company first.* Get the name of the customer service person who will fill your request. Try to develop a rapport with that person, without giving away too much about your project concept. This may help you get more information and free samples. If you feel that you may be forced to give out too many sensitive details about your idea to the vendor, don't talk with the actual person, but instead just get his or her name for your letter.

2. If this company doesn't make parts exactly like those you need: (a) Ask who does! Don't be shy about asking for information on their competitors; (b) Ask if they make custom products and discuss what you need with the vendor. Be sure to get a sample of their parts for your parts collection. Even if it's not exactly what you need, it may spark ideas!

3. Don't appear to be the single small inventor just starting to develop an idea, even if you are. Most companies will not want to waste time with you. Use your company image and letterhead and phrase your letter so that you present a professional image.

4. In information gathering and prototype part requests, offer the impression that their company may profit from their association with you and your product. In reality, this may or may not come to pass, but the possibility exists that your idea may result in major purchases of their products. This will allow you to pick their brains for ideas about the adaptability of their products to your concept.

5. A good technique to use for getting information without giving it out is to act as a middleman consultant for a customer who remains anonymous. Because you could be representing a very large client, most companies will be happy to provide you with any samples and general information you request. Don't lie about who you're working for; just don't give out information. Referring to your client as "the client" usually works well.

Example of an Information/Parts Request Letter

```
Widget Manufacturing Corp.
1234 Anytown Road
Anytown, Your State 12345

ATTENTION: Customer Service Rep. I.M. Helpful
Ref: Plastic Widget Spring

Dear Ms. Helpful:

It was a real pleasure talking with you on the phone today.
Per our discussion, we are currently working on the development
```

of a new product that could use your plastic widget spring. I am in need of all current specifications on the service life of the spring, and its fabrication and failure rate in sustained use. It would also be helpful if you could supply as much information regarding its current and future availability, price, and specification variables (colors, additional sizes, etc.)

Also per our discussion, please supply me with several samples of your widget spring No. a12SP5 and b12SP6. If you feel any other springs that you produce have similar qualities, please send samples of these parts. I will contact you with feedback on our decisions regarding the final use of the springs as soon as they are rendered.

Presently, our development program forecasts between 120,000 and 300,000 parts per year for domestic applications. Our projected foreign market is currently in review. I would appreciate your response as quickly as possible, and I look forward to doing business with you in the future.

Sincerely,

I.M. Inventor
Director of Research
IMI/mac

Request for Quotation Letter

Quotations are the written prices that a company will charge to sell or produce given items. You should use this information when you are establishing wholesale and retail prices on a given invention. The information will allow you to make ballpark estimates and projections of production costs, as well as prototype costs for short runs.

The following is a sample "Request for Quotation" letter to send to any company. The number of units needed per item is up to you. The letter can be short or extensive, depending upon the level of information needed to attain your goals. Requests for quotations, by their very nature, must reveal a lot about the specific part you are seeking, but do not necessarily reveal the nature or working parameters of the final invention. Be careful not to give away more information than is absolutely necessary when talking with companies. Your great idea may be saleable to them if you protect it. On the other hand, your opportunity may be lost for no compensation if you carelessly disclose information over the telephone or in a letter.

Sample Request for Quotation Letter

This letter is written to request parts that a company already has in stock. It may be changed to reflect specifications for a custom part by substituting (for the italicized second line in the top paragraph) the phrase "Please quote on the parts described in the attached quotation sheet."

```
Any Company, Inc.
Mr. Parts Manager
AnyTown, USA

Dear Sir:

We are in the process of pricing parts for an upcoming
production run. Currently, we are using your parts listed
below. Can you please send a firm price quotation on these
parts in the quantities specified. Also, please include
information on delivery time, terms and shipping.

Part       Part       1000       Per        50,000     Per
Number     Name       units      10,000     units      100,000

_____   _____   $_____   _____   _____   _____
_____   _____   $_____   _____   _____   _____
_____   _____   $_____   _____   _____   _____
_____   _____   $_____   _____   _____   _____

Thank you for your time and consideration in this matter.
Please send all information as soon as possible to the address
shown on this sheet.

Thanks,


I.M. Inventor,
Production Dept.
```

Prototype Tool List

Once you have your design and the necessary materials and parts, you are ready to begin constructing your prototype. To do this, of course, you will need the right tools. Some inventions may require specialized devices. But every entrepreneurial inventor should have a basic set of tools. The amount and diversity of tools you can gather will enhance your ability to tinker with prototype devices. Tools are important for a variety of reasons, including:

1. Disassembly of existing products to examine construction and operation.
2. Disassembly of existing products to scavenge parts for a prototype.
3. Building and fine-tuning prototypes.
4. Data acquisition and design.

Tools fall into five categories: (1) display and model-making tools; (2) fabrication equipment; (3) adjustment and calibration tools; (4) chemical compounds; and (5) electronic equipment.

A Basic Tool Kit

A basic entrepreneurial inventor's tool kit should include as many as possible of the following tools in each category.

1. *Display and model-making tools*

a. Exacto knives: Very sharp, very precise cutting knives; they come individually and in sets. Handles accept replaceable knife heads.

b. Scissors: Have two types of scissors, one for paper and one for all other materials (i.e.: plastics, cardboards, etc.).

c. Marker sets: Two sets, one of various shades of black and gray, one set of various colors (watercolor and indelible types of both).

d. Putty knives: Various sizes, metal and plastic.

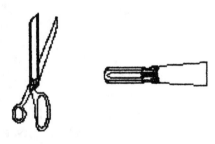

e. Vise grips (various sizes): Adjustable, locking pliers; have several types that range from miniature needle nose to large, broad, flat-mouth type.

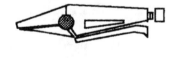

f. Velcro (various pre-cut configurations): Interlocking hook and fiber material; have various types (i.e.: adhesive-backed, wide band, etc.) available for use with parts that need to be attached and disassembled multiple times. Long pieces of Velcro can also be used as clamps for irregularly shaped parts that need to be held together during gluing or construction.

g. Various types of tape: clear, double-sided, electrical, strapping, and reinforced.

h. Paint brushes: different types and sizes. Foam,

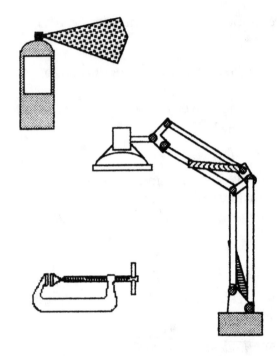

bristol and other types of brushes give different textures.

i. Paints: sprays and cans in basic colors and primer gray.

j. Sandpaper: various types give different surface textures and different levels of finish to a prototype.

k. Glues: various types; Elmer's white (for wood and porous surfaces), two-part epoxies (for filling and bonding dissimilar surfaces), Super Glue type (for bonding glass or other smooth surfaces).

l. Good light source: combination regular and florescent, plus a good, powerful, but small flashlight.

m. Small hand clamps and vises: various sizes and configurations for clamping irregular-shaped objects.

n. Calculator: handheld type; best if it has a paper tape to keep track of multiple calculations or a number of surfaces.

2. *Fabrication Equipment*

a. Dremel™ motor tool: handheld, motorized drilling and shaping tool capable of working various types of materials including wood, metal and plastic. The tool has interchangeable heads that allow very exact manipulation (cutting, buffing, sanding, drilling) of all materials.

b. Glue gun: with glue sticks of various types of adhesives. Glue guns are useful as filling tools; the quick drying glues are useful for setting parts in place, especially plastics.

c. Pop Rivet gun: (with steel and aluminum rivets). Pop Rivets are small connectors that can be placed in a hole drilled in two surfaces. When the pop rivet gun is used, it crimps one end of the rivet, thus attaching the two surfaces together. Joint of a pop rivet can also act as a swivel.

d. Plastic/rubber hammer: useful in hammering surfaces without damage that can be caused by a metal hammer. Good for adjustments without marring surfaces.

e. Set of screwdrivers: Phillips (x) and flathead (-)

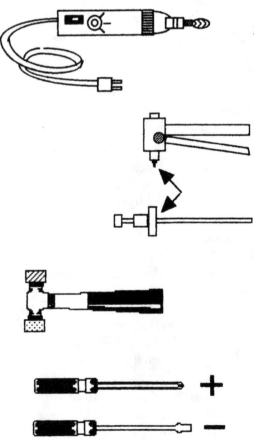

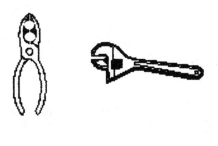

(slot) types. Get a range of different handle lengths. There are other specialized sets of screwdrivers, and every entrepreneurial inventor should try to collect as many types as can be obtained. Various types of screws allow for different types of screw connections (i.e., metal to metal, metal to wood, or nonremovable).

f. Pliers: various types, such as needlenose (for small spaces), slip-joint pliers (for normal and wide jaw use), lineman pliers (for cutting heavy wire), snippers, and others.

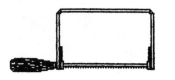

g. Wrenches: Adjustable type, also called a monkey wrench, can be used on many sizes of nuts and bolts. Combination open end and box wrench set for all types of nuts and bolts. A nut driver is a type of wrench that looks like a screwdriver, except it has a space that fits a nut in the end.

h. Dust brush: (Various sizes) for cleaning works in process and for removing the debris from the work area.

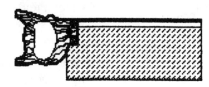

i. Hand saws: at least three types; hacksaw for metals; coping saw for cutting small-diameter curves in wood and plastic; and a backsaw with its reinforced edge for quick powerful cutting.

3. *Adjustment and Calibration Tools*

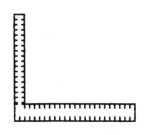

a. Jeweler's screwdriver set: set of ultra small screwdrivers for fine work (usually comes in flat/slot style).

b. Good rulers: length optional; steel type with fine graduations and a tape measure.

c. Level, bubble type: to indicate if work and workspace are level via moving bubble. Sometimes very important to know if a device works in various states of off-level condition.

4. *Chemical Compounds*

a. Cleaners and thinners (for paints and glues): used for cleaning up after use of various paints and chemicals.

b. Bondo (fiberglass auto-repair compound): used for creating solid models or surfaces for prototypes. This is a mixable putty-type compound that dries into a hard, sandable, cutable, drillable surface.

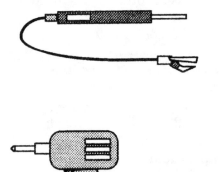

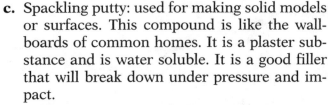

c. Spackling putty: used for making solid models or surfaces. This compound is like the wallboards of common homes. It is a plaster substance and is water soluble. It is a good filler that will break down under pressure and impact.

d. Modeling clay: used in preliminary structures for molds and to hold other parts during the prototype construction process. Various types of clay have different properties. Several types of clay can be baked to a very rigid, yet workable composition.

5. *Electronic Equipment*

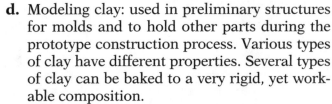

a. Simple circuit tester: used to test for open and closed circuits and for the presence of electrical power in a system. This is important if any part of a prototype is made with electrical components.

b. Soldering gun (with various types of solder): used for connecting or disconnecting electrical circuits, plus simple soldering of components.

An Advanced Basic Toolkit

An "advanced basic" prototype tool kit builds on the basic list and is composed of the following additional equipment in each category.

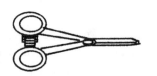

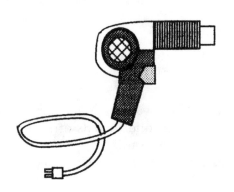

1. *Display and Model Making Tools*

a. Benchtop WorkMate™ multi-vise: The Benchtop WorkMate is a combination adjustable vise and stable working platform for all manner of prototyping. It has a vise mouth that is sixteen inches long and can be configured to hold any shape material. The vise can hold materials inside its grip or via a series of moveable pegs that are placed in holes on top of the face of the Workmate. The entire platform is also capable of being tilted up by an adjustable hinge to give access to the work from any angle.

b. Hemostats (various configurations): a type of locking, surgical clamp that is very useful in detailed protowork. A hemostat can be used to pick up, manipulate, or clamp small parts.

c. Heat gun (blower type): can be used to shrink wrap parts with shrink wrap tubing or sheets.

Heat guns can also soften plastics for configuring or to soften paint for removal from surfaces.

2. *Fabrication Equipment*

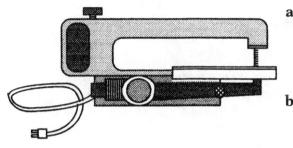

a. Electric scroll saw: is a type of jigsaw that operates via reciprocating high-speed blade held in place on a platform. It is used to make detailed cuts and shapes in wood, plastic and some metals.

b. Electric screwdriver: is a time- and effort-saving device when building a prototype that involves a number of screws or bolts. Most can be adapted to handle all different types of screw heads as well as various bolts with English and metric sizes.

c. Hand-held vacuum: is an important tool for keeping the work area free of litter and dust made by various other tools. It can also be used to keep prototypes free of particles that may foul their internal operations.

d. Standard hand drill (with a set of drill bits): will provide the capability of creating holes for screws and bolts in most materials. The drill, which should be variable speed and reversible, will allow you to polish, sand, and cut various size holes in many materials with the addition of selected attachments and accessories.

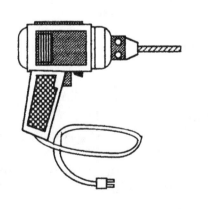

e. Welding torch: is a unit that consists of two high-pressure tanks containing acetylene and oxygen, which are combined in a hand unit to produce a flow that is ignited. The acetylene burns, and the oxygen enhances the flame heat to produce a pin-point torch capable of cutting through metals of all kinds. With proper training, you can use the torch to cut, braze, and weld metals into all types of prototype configurations.

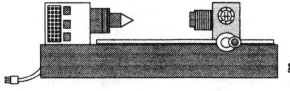

f. Miniature lathe: Similar to a full-size lathe, the miniature lathe can turn metal, plastics, and wood at high speed. This turning action, combined with proper cutting tools, allows the shaping of custom parts.

g. Miniature mill: Similar to a full-size mill. The miniature mill can cut plastics and metals in precise patterns. The mill is a powerful motor,

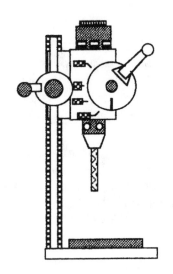

like a drill that is fixed above a moveable table. The table (called a bed or a platform) is moved by hand-turned precision crank wheels that allow the material to be worked upon and moved in any direction left to right and front to back. The actual moving bit of the mill can be lowered and raised with great precision. This allows the material to be cut in all three directions.

h. Drill press: is a powerful drill that is fixed in a stand to allow for precision drilling of wood, plastic and metal. It is best used for repeated operations where accuracy is extremely important.

i. Tap & Die Set: is a set of precision cutting tools that can make and repair all manner of screw threads. One set (taps) create threading within holes in materials (metal usually—wood sometimes). The other set (dies) create threads on bar stock or exterior of tubes. This tool allows you to create attachment points for most prototype applications.

3. *Adjustment and Calibration Tools*

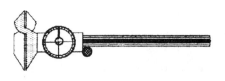

a. Precision vernier calipers: a hand-held measurement tool that allows for ultra-precise measurements of distances up to eight inches (in most cases). The exterior and interior dimensions of parts can easily be taken with this tool, as can the depth of a hole. The calipers can be used to measure square, round, and cylindrical surfaces to within 100,000th of an inch. This tool is important when dealing with machine shops or designers who need precise measurements to complete their tasks.

b. Digital scale: for measuring the weight of parts. Commonly used for postal weights, a digital scale is a handy device for prototyping.

4. *Chemical Compounds*

a. Urethane foam (two part mix): this is a liquid that is mixed of two parts which turn into a Styrofoam type substance. It is ideal for creating simple molds, support structures or basic parts. Urethane foam also comes in cans that automatically mix the two parts as they are dispensed. It is used for insulation and building purposes, but inventors will find many applications for its unique properties.

b. Molding plastics: come in several types and consistencies. Their final properties can be clear or opaque, hard or flexible, depending upon the compound chosen. Most have a cure time from several hours to several days. They can be used for molds or the fabrication of sturdy and intricate parts when poured into a clay mold.

5. *Electronic Equipment*

a. A computer capable of creating reports and graphics. I recommend a Macintosh system but there is software written for IBM compatible systems with comparable graphic and word processing functions. I constantly generate disclosure documents, parts drawings, reports, articles, proposals, business plans, and product specification drawings with the word processing and graphics capabilities of my Macintosh system. This is an invaluable aid to any entrepreneurial inventor. It gives a professional, polished image to your work while providing the convenience of data storage for your files and projects. In today's competitive, high-tech era, people won't really take you seriously without a proper presentation. Be sure you have an adequate computer, so you can put your best foot forward in the business and technical world.

Destructive Testing

Once you have a prototype, you should put it to the test. *Destructive testing* is a research testing system that determines the limits of operation of a product. Every product should have destructive testing procedures performed so that the operational envelope of the product can be documented. This allows you and the manufacturer to know if the product will stand up to the rigors of the market for which it is planned. For example, a product that is expected to function in military service under extreme climatic and operational conditions will usually exceed the specifications for a similar product intended for civilian use. Destructive testing often determines many of the variables on the Design Criteria Checklist. The following generic destructive testing checklist can help you set up your own tests. A generic destructive testing worksheet is included after the checklist.

Checklist for Destructive Testing

☑ 1. Water Resistance Test*

Test object is exposed to constant or simulated rainfall for 24 hours.

☑ 2. Salt Corrosion Test*

Test object is exposed to constant saltwater spray for 24 hours.

☑ 3. Heat Test**

Test object is exposed to various heat settings in a controlled test oven for 24 hours.

☑ 4. Compression Test

Test object is placed in a compression vise that is gauged to place an exact and symmetrical pressure on the object for a specified length of time.

☑ 5. Sand Test

Test object is buried in sand for 24 hours. Sand is agitated hourly to ensure that any possible interaction with, or penetration of, the test object by the sand will happen.

☑ 6. Drop Test

Test object is suspended above a steel deck or concrete surface from various heights and then dropped. The object is oriented in the drop to impact upon the most sensitive areas of the product, as well as upon flat surfaces.

☑ 7. Acid Test***

Test object is subjected to an acid spray (various acid content) for 24 hours.

TEST NOTES

*Water and saltwater corrosion tests involve a spray of water. This test is done on all products that must face marine or outdoor use. This test should not be done on electrical items that use wall plugs, except where they are expected to function in an exterior capacity without damage.

**The Heat test is gauged to the type of materials that the test object is made from and expected to withstand. For example, automotive products expected to be in a car trunk in Arizona during the summer must be able to withstand temperatures in excess of 250 degrees.

***These sprays do not need to be constant, but instead must keep the test object wet with the compounds.

☑ 8. Solvent Test***

Test object is subjected to a solvent spray (various solvent content) for 24 hours.

☑ 9. Base Test***

Test object is subjected to a base spray (various base content) for 24 hours.

☑ 10. Sunlight Test

Test object is subjected to direct sunlight for periods of time from one hour to several months, depending upon its intended end use.

☑ 11. Freezer Test

Test object is placed in a freezer for 24 hours, then used or operated.

☑ 12. Notch Test

Test object is notched with a razor or knife and then subjected to various impacts on or around the notched section.

Consult the various industries and others who will use your invention on a regular basis. This will supply critical information on the specifications of each test level and duration of the test. Many government agencies have specific testing criteria that you may want to test your products against before submitting them for possible evaluation or purchase.

The best way to use these destructive tests is to conduct them in-house to determine what your product's survivability range is in each category. The range will allow you to determine if you need to redesign the product in a somewhat tougher configuration. Then you should allow an independent, outside laboratory to do the same tests as a backup to your results.

Keep track of your destructive testing data on copies of the generic worksheet provided on the next page. This test information will provide valuable insights into the durability of your designs, as well as provide additional evidence of "Reduction to Practice" via a well documented invention "paper trail."

DESTRUCTIVE TESTING WORKSHEET

TEST NAME: _____

WATER [ ]   SALT CORROSION [ ]   HEAT [ ]   COMPRESSION [ ]   SAND [ ]
DROP [ ]   ACID [ ]   SOLVENT [ ]   BASE [ ]   SUNLIGHT [ ]   FREZZER [ ]   NOTCH [ ]

Date:_____   Project Code:_____

Product Name:_____

Page _____ of _____   Researcher/Inventor: _____

Test No. _____   Part No. _____   Generation No._____

D/O List™: Page No. _____   Line Number _____   Code: _____

TEST NOTE: _____

Test Needed?   _____ Yes   _____ No   _____ Unknown

Test Performed?   _____ Yes   _____ No   Date _____   Length:_____

Test Parameters: Application of:_____

                        Application Rate: _____

Misc. Test Parameter Data:_____
_____
_____
_____
_____
_____

Results of Test: _____
_____
_____
_____
_____

Notes on Test: _____
_____
_____
_____
_____
_____
_____
_____
_____
_____
_____
_____
_____
_____
_____
_____

Chapter 8

The Delicate Art of Raising Funds

**Money is the seed of money,
and the first guinea (dollar)
is sometimes more difficult to acquire
than the second millions.**

Jean Jacques Rousseau

 The goals of this chapter are straightforward: (1) to give you factual information about the entrepreneurial inventor's side of the fence in the delicate process of raising capital; (2) to describe the necessary presentation documentation; (3) to discuss how you can protect your ideas during the capital-raising process; and (4) to highlight the importance of a presentation method known as the dog-and-pony show, which can help you capture the attention and money of investors.

This chapter does not show you how to write a business plan, nor does it list possible venture capital sources and other money resources. These things are detailed in countless other books and sources found in libraries and bookstores across the country.

The entrepreneurial inventor has many different capital resources and various types of finances available, including friends and family, local investor groups, Small Business Administration (SBA) loans, venture capital firms, and some exotic deals formulated by inventors and interested parties. Capital sources are available, but they are individual and unique to every deal. To try and cover every possible case would be impossible and unproductive. Instead, I describe the most important tools for maneuvering within the superstructure of the world of money, secrecy, and documentation.

Raising Capital

  The process of raising capital is very important to the invention process. Most inventors are not independently wealthy, nor do they have the financial resources needed to pay for basic invention stepping-stones, such as prototypes, patent applications, and presentation artwork. To further your inventions and your career as an entrepreneurial inventor, you must learn the skills of raising capital.

Raising capital for an invention can change the entire way an invention is created, developed, marketed, and sold. These outcomes can depend upon who the capital comes from and under what circumstances. If you can make your invention and get it on the market without using other people's money (OPM), then I strongly suggest that you take that course of action. Once you've accepted outside capital, it often changes the way you interact with all phases of the development process. Sometimes this change is for the better, and sometimes it is for the worse. Here is a general rule of thumb about raising capital: *Raise as much as needed to do the job right without giving up control of the project.*

Techniques for finding people with money include talking to friends and family, networking, and placing advertisements.

Friends and family are the basic resource, because they already know and trust you. They know what your background is and what your basic motives are in taking on this project. You can be totally yourself with your family. Of course, depending upon how you get along with your family, this may work against you. Some family members may not want to help you, because you pose a threat to the status quo or because of jealousy. If this is the case, keep looking among immediate and extended family members and friends for the seed capital you need.

It is within this circle of family and friends, however, that most inventors find their initial capital or seed monies. The main reasons for getting your primary seed capital from either your own pocket or a source close to you is:

- You need a certain professional image to attract substantial investor support. Creating that image must be done prior to approaching outside investors.

- Your family and friends don't care about image, they know you already and will invest or loan you the money based upon a deeper trust and commitment.

- The last thing you want to do is approach an investor outside of your close inner circle for capital to create your image. You should already have this *before* you approach investors.

Networking is a term used for a person's ability to make contacts and progress through the establishment of relationships with other people and businesses. To raise outside capital, you must use every contact you can imagine. Leave no stone unturned in getting the word out that you have an investment opportunity in a new and special invention project. Talk to friends, relatives and co-workers. Never pass up an opportunity to talk up your project. This will bring you in contact with many different people who, in turn, may know other people who may want to invest in the project. Networking can bring you in touch with a large number of possible investors in a short time if you approach it actively. NOTE: Chapter 10 focuses specifically on the art of networking and how to build up and benefit from your contacts.

Be careful not to give out details of the invention to everyone, unless it already has been granted a patent. If the product is unpatentable or a patent is pending, only reveal the field of the invention and talk about how great it is for what it does. Don't give away the exact concept. The only person who should get full details is an investor candidate who signs a secrecy agreement at a presentation you give.

Advertisements for investors for an invention usually get good response. The catch is that the people who reply usually are not the people with whom you really want to talk. Many so-called "investors" that respond to ads are merely con men looking to swindle fledgling inventors. They may want to get your idea or con you into paying them for investment services.

Others who respond to your ad may profess an honest desire to invest, but what they really want is to be entertained! Some people with money have too much time on their hands and like to involve themselves with active, creative people, like you. Basically, you will entertain them with the ins and outs of your project development. It is rare that these people actually invest in a project, but, of course, it is not entirely out of the question.

Unfortunately, every inventor must make a number of presentations, or "Dog and Pony" (D & P) shows, to possible investors without anything ever coming out of it. This is the price that has to be paid for getting exposure to possible investment capital.

Answering ads that offer investment capital is also fruitless. The same scenarios exist. Most of the time, there will be ads placed by an "Invention Marketing" company claiming to be able to place an inventor with a capital source. Once you've contacted the company, they will want money for their services. Beware of "Invention Marketing" firms. Most (about 95 percent) are outright frauds. Ask for lists of other inventions they have successfully gotten capital for or have marketed to a successful conclusion. Ask for name and telephone numbers of satisfied customer. Any real company that does this full-time should have dozens, if not hundreds, of happy clients for you to talk with. Also check with the state's Better Business Bureau and the attorney general's office about invention marking companies before seeking any sort of capital help. These contacts can often provide a list of potential rip-off companies before you find them the hard way. More warnings about invention marketing companies are presented later in this book.

The bottom line on ads is this: *Ads will bring good and bad contacts.* Be cautious of everyone and check out all investors before disclosing information to them. Remember, your time is as valuable as theirs. Don't waste your time on dead ends and companies that are looking to rip you off.

When to Use Your Money and When to Use Other People's Money

  Your Money

Your money includes your own personal money and seed capital from family members and friends. This money should be used to create a stable base for presenting yourself as a professional inventor. This needs to be done regardless of whether you intend to pursue entrepreneurial inventing on a part-time or full-time basis. The following six basic items should be included in your spending of the initial seed money:

1. TO BUILD AN INITIAL IMAGE: When approaching friends and family, a professional image is not necessary, because they know you and your history. They can see past any shortcomings and look at the project, because they already have confidence in you as a person. However, potential investors will most probably be total strangers. At best, you may have an introduction through a networked contact. You need to present yourself to the potential investor in the most professional light available to you. This means having the right personal appearance. The proper grooming (haircut, clean appearance) and the proper attire (a high-quality suit, proper shoes, tie, and so forth) will speak for themselves when you meet people. The first impression you make as a person will go a long way toward convincing the potential investor that you are someone with whom he or she can do business. The wrong personal appearance will put people off, even if you have a great product. Spend a little money on yourself, because investors really invest in people, not products. Your appearance will convey a feeling of your capability in managing the investor's money. This will create a "comfort level" that will instill confidence in the entire operation. If the investor feels ill at ease with you personally, he or she will be less likely to trust you with money.

2. PRESENTATION ARTWORK: The way that a concept is presented to an investor is almost as important as the concept itself. Naturally, the concept comes first. But you will need to rely on some sort of presentation artwork, unless, in the lucky instance, you have a prototype device that looks and operates the same way as the final production device.

The presentation artwork may be one of several types, including a cut-away style drawing, showing the internal layout and components as if the product had an invisible skin, or a color rendering style that shows the product in full color in three dimensions. (See the examples and discussions of these types of drawings in Chapter 6.)

No matter which style of drawing or rendering you choose to display, the main concern is that the artwork looks professional and realistic. This will help convince the investor that you have done your research into how you will build the product. It will also show him that you have invested some time and money in the project prior to approaching him. No one likes to be approached with an idea drawn on the back of a napkin. It shows no forethought and will probably evoke a "Come back to see me when you have this project organized" type of response. Investors want their capital placed in projects that have a chance of succeeding, based upon what they see at the time of investment. Proper artwork can help convince an investor that the project is a solid concept.

The artists who helped you create artwork during the design phase may also be able to help you prepare the presentation artwork. If not, you can locate good artwork sources by placing an ad in a major newspaper. The ad should read: "Artist/Designer with rendering and cut-away drawing skills needed to work with new product development company. Send samples of work, résumé, and information to... ." This type of ad will get you numerous responses from which to choose. Compare rates, time frames for work completion, and personalities of the people who respond to find the best artist for whom to work for you. Remember, always have each artist sign a secrecy agreement prior to revealing any idea to him or her. Always review their style and do a personal interview to determine their working compatibility with you before exposing your concept to the artist. Only the artists who actually will do the work need to know what the project is about. An artist who is also a designer or design engineer is the best possible source of technical illustration.

Another source for finding a good artist may be a local arts council that publishes an artist directory. Look for artists who specialize in new product development drawings. You will need this type of artwork for the best possible presentation. For an example of this type of artist, see the illustrations by Gary Whitten of Whitten Illustration and Design in Chapter 6.

3. ESTABLISHING A COMPANY IDENTITY: Every entrepreneurial inventor needs a personal image and a company image. The personal image is how you are perceived by people when they meet you. The company image is everything else, including the presentation artwork. The company image includes the product name, the company name under which you are working, the logo for the company, the promotional materials about you and your product, as well as simple things such as your business cards, company stationery, and business address (a post office box will do).

You must create an image for yourself and your product. This is one area where the seed capital is incredibly important. This bears repeating: You cannot go to an outside investor and ask him for money to make you look the way you should have looked when you met him. This is why seed capital must come from your own pocket or people close to you.

4. PATENT SEARCH: The patent search is a very important tool to have in your bag of tricks when approaching an investor. It is evidence that you have researched the concept. It is also proof that you stand a good chance in getting a patent on the product. If the product is not patentable and is something that may just require a fast jump into the marketplace, then you may skip the search and patent application. If, however, the product is patentable and you decide that patent protection is wise for the long-term sales and viability of the product, then a patent search is a very important first step. Most investors

will not want to put capital into a project without some proof that it can be a secure investment. Additionally, you will want to use seed capital to conduct the patent search, so you can avoid the prying eyes of investors. If a search comes back and proves the concept is too close to an existing patent, the investor may pull out of the deal. But by doing the search first, you can modify your product to take the other patents into account. This way you can still progress with your project and successfully raise capital. An average patent search will cost between $500 and $1,000.

5. PATENT APPLICATION: If the patent search comes back in favor of going ahead with the project, then the next logical and powerful step is to proceed with a patent application. Use your seed money for this, since the patent application is the second most important tool in your inventor's bag of tricks. If you already have a patent application in which the investment capital is sought, it puts you in a more powerful position. In this way, the investor can't demand to have his name put on the patent application as a form of security for his investment capital.

Technically, only the true inventors of a product can have their name on a patent, but I have seen several cases where inventors were bullied, by investors, into adding the investors name to the patent.—Beware of ever doing this! The reasons is the investor now has all the rights the inventor has in the invention—ie. to sell and license the invention without compensating the inventor.

A patent can be assigned to an investor so that the investor's name appears on the patent as the assignee. I hesitate to do this unless the inventor's deal is very lucrative and binding on the investor. The reason is the same as before—the investor gets too much control.

You are in the driver's seat, because the patent is now pending, and you can use it as if it is already issued in terms of contracts and negotiations. You are the sole owner and creator. It is your "Intellectual Property" and, as the center of the project, you have a stronger negotiating position. An average patent application will cost you $2,000 to $3,500. The final patent may run anywhere from $2,500 to $7,500 (or higher, depending on the individual concept and patent attorney) before it is actually issued.

6. EXPENSES RELATED TO RAISING CAPITAL: Use the seed capital for all other expenses related to raising capital. You can't ask an investor for money to pay your car fare to meet him, nor can you get a lot of pre-meeting details cleared up without using the seed money. If you want to make a major presentation to a group of investors from various sources, it may be less expensive to rent a room at a hotel and give a major demonstration, rather than to make many separate trips to various locations over a period of time. All expenses like this must be paid for with seed capital.

Other People's Money

Use this money for EVERYTHING ELSE! Once investment is made in the project, stop using the seed capital (if you have any left). Keep it in reserve for important items that concern you, as the inventor, but for which the investors may not want to pay. Never let the investors know exactly how much seed capital you have raised already or how much you have left. Use approximate figures to show that you have already gotten some investment in the project.

All projects started with seed capital should now become supported by the investment capital. This includes the patent application.

How to Negotiate Capital

  Negotiating capital is a very individual process. It is intertwined with all phases of the inventing process, because everything takes money. You must establish a personal rapport with your investment sources. The only time this is not entirely necessary is when capital is raised through a middleman.

Middlemen are money brokers and people with connections who arrange deals for a percentage of the capital raised. They can often make the deal by acting as the in-between agent who negotiates for both sides. This does not happen very often. The more frequent scenario is that the middleman will introduce you and the investor for a percentage and then step out of the picture.

Negotiating capital can be a very frustrating and time-consuming process. It involves many egos all trying to get what they want for their secret agenda. Always keep in mind that the entire project and reason for the negotiations is your invention. Never let investors browbeat you into taking a deal in which you feel uncomfortable. You can always find other investors, but more likely than not, they can't find another invention like yours. Always make sure that you have signed secrecy agreements and meeting agreements with all investors and their associates who see your information.

Although inventors have been stereotyped as poor businessmen, you, as an entrepreneurial inventor, must learn to negotiate from a position of power. Remember your position in this deal, and keep it in mind: *It's your creation, your idea and your business!* You are in the driver's seat!

Contracts and Deals

 "It's a done deal!" Until you have the money in the bank, *never* believe this line. Contracts don't mean much if they aren't fulfilled. Many people will ask you to do things based upon agreements, pending money coming in. Beware of people who continually have excuses for capital delays. Your idea isn't going anywhere until the contract is completed by a capital transfer.

Any deal that requires you to put up personal guarantees of cash, properties or future earnings is not a deal for which you want any part. You are contributing the concept, complete with patents pending and all the effort it took to get the investor to want to invest in the first place. You already have seed capital at risk. You shouldn't accept any deal that delegates you to a position of payback or puts your personal finances in jeopardy if the deal falls through.

Always shop for the best deal using multiple avenues simultaneously. Don't limit your capital-seeking potential to one source at a time. You can end up wasting valuable time with an investment group that doesn't pan out. Additionally, if you have multiple sources and multiple offers, you can pick the best one and sometimes play one off against the other to get the best possible deal for your situation.

Basic Investor Rules

Pay attention to the following rules before becoming involved in deals with investors:

1. Do a background check on your investors, and ask for references. This will make you look more professional, and also prevent you from getting involved with con men. Reputable business persons will have no problem giving you verifiable references.

2. Don't give out proprietary information on your concept without getting secrecy agreements signed and, better yet, money in the bank. Keep important information secret that will protect your interests until you are secure in the fact that you have a firm deal.

3. Don't believe that money is on the way without proof. Structure the deal so it can be negated if money fails to materialize, or if the investors or middlemen go back on any part of their agreement with you. This will keep someone from marketing or brokering your deal as a secondary middleman.

4. Middlemen (money brokers) are okay as long as they represent themselves to be just that. Get a contract from them outlining their position in the deal and what their responsibilities are to you. Make sure the contract or terms of agreement show that the middleman only get paid if he is directly responsible for arranging the cash or line of credit.

Making Estimates and Projections

Raising money means you must be able to project where and why the funds will be spent. This is a key element in establishing credibility with any investor or investment group. There are many good books available on making business plans and doing estimates and projection for business purposes. It is wise to get one of these books and learn the terms and applications of the various types of spreadsheets and projection systems prior to talking to investment people. You also should locate an accountant and attorney who can help you plan estimates and projections for an invention-related business.

Estimates and projections should not be taken lightly. They will be the cornerstone of how much, if any, capital you will get and how you will be able to use the money. Investors will take your projections of expenses and sales very seriously. Always project the "Worst Case Scenario" for all expenses and sales. This means to show the most amount of money that you think it can take to make the project work (and then add 20 percent to give a margin of safety). On the sales side, show the best and worst cases you foresee in sales revenues. This will give the investors some "pie in the sky" to shoot for in the best numbers, and some low-ball figures to expect if all the worst things happen and sales are extremely low.

How Estimates and Projections Are Used

Estimates and projections are used to generate the following figures:

(a) *Money you need for each phase of development of the invention.* Try and take everything into account. If you don't, you may have the project fail because of lack of funds. This is the number-one cause of failure in invention-related businesses.

(b) *Money your invention will earn via sales over time for repayment of investment, as well as profit revenues.* This figure is very near and dear to the investor's heart. Your numbers should indicate that the invention will make enough money over a reasonable amount of time to pay back the investors and then give them a substantial profit.

(c) *Time line projection of what you expect to do, in what amount of time.* Always give yourself extra time in a time line projection. Things always go wrong (Murphy's Law). If you make your time frame too conservative for completion of a project, it will make you look bad when you are late. On the other hand, if you give yourself extra time and you come in early and under budget, the investors will have increased confidence in you and your abilities. It can help you in other areas of your dealings with the investors, as well.

(d) *Estimates of market share and projections of market penetration.* These can usually be obtained from current industry literature and associations. Contact the appropriate industry associations for details.

 NOTE: Raising capital is a hard and often infuriating process that takes a lot of personal energy. It will tax your abilities to the maximum. Remain calm and cool, and remember you want to get this done, because the invention is the important thing. Ask for help from professionals such as bankers, accountants, lawyers, and others who go through the process on a regular basis. They may be able to help locate and negotiate capital for you. Always remember that people do not often do things for nothing. Be prepared to get various people involved for either a percentage of the deal, or a percentage of capital raised in return for their help. I prefer to pay out a percentage of raised capital as opposed to giving away a percentage of the company. Remember to choose initial stockholders and partners as carefully as they choose you. You will have to live with them inside your company once they own any part of it. Also always remember to retain at least 51 percent of the deal, or you will find you have lost control and may even be ejected from your own company as a commanding force in the enterprise. Best of luck!

The Art of the Dog-and-Pony Show

 A *Dog-and-Pony Show* (D&P) is the term used to describe the physical presentation of a product concept or business idea to an interested party or group. It is a term usually used in conjunction with presentations involving the raising of capital, but it can also be any time you, the inventor, goes before any group of people to promote your invention.

When Do You Need to Do a Dog-and-Pony Show?

You need to demonstrate your concept in various fashions on a regular basis. These include:

1. Initial and sustained capital-raising efforts;
2. Demonstrations to manufacturers for various types of support;
3. Presentations to the media for publicity and promotional purposes;
4. Explanatory discussions with prototype builders and/or engineers.

Types of Dog-and-Pony Shows

There are two types of dog-and-pony shows: the mini D&P and the maxi D&P.

The *mini D&P* is great for limited time frames. It can be packed with information, or it can be a mere introduction of things to come. In either case, it must be concise and straightforward, leaving no doubt in the minds of the viewers of the points you are stressing. It is essential that the mini D&P have a powerful theme and good *leave-behind* literature. Literature that you leave includes brochures and other descriptive materials, which the attendees at the D&P show get during the demonstration or talk. The mini D&P is often used before a busy group of potential investors or the media. It can range from fifteen minutes for investors to three minutes for news media. The mini D&P may also be the first demo you do before a group. It is enough to start an interest in your invention and give the group enough information to discuss the project among themselves. In this way, you can present your concept to a busy group, but leave enough to come back for a full presentation. The hope is to generate enough interest with the mini D&P that your audience will want to know more.

For the media, the information should be hard-hitting and concise, so it won't lose appeal during the editing process. Most news stories, especially video, are very short and must pack a lot of information into a small space or small amount of time. The mini D&P works well for this format.

The *maxi D&P* is a full-blown presentation that explores all aspects of the project, depending on the audience. The maxi D&P should use any and all presentation media you have at your disposal, including charts, video-tapes and handout material.

The Maxi D&P should have:

- An introduction to the concept (with the background of the invention's development;
- Full marketing information, your niche in the market and how you expect to grab the maximum share;
- Investor and company profitability information;*
- A live presentation of the invention (if applicable);
- A question-and-answer period to tie up loose ends.

The Criteria for a Good Dog-and-Pony Show

The following four items are important both as a group and separately for a good D&P show:

 1. *People with money; people in a position to do you some good.* Don't waste your time doing a presentation for every person who wants hear about your idea. Many people will want to see a presentation just for the amusement value or possibly to steal the idea. Be selective; screen your potential investors. Ask for references when the concept is in the early stages of disclosure, especially if you're looking for capital investment. Make sure the people are who they say they are prior to committing to a D&P. Remember, your time is valuable, and you're not a traveling carnival doing demos for other's pleasure.

 2. *People with interests that coincide with your invention.* Doing D&Ps for groups who have a vested interest in your product can lead to valuable contacts. If your product is the "Pet Care" line, you might want to show it to a group of pet shop owners or veterinarians. The exposure can generate letters of reference about your product and leads to capital sources, manufacturers or sales outlets. Most importantly, the feedback may point out shortcomings in the product that can be corrected before the invention project progresses any further.

 3. *Have a functional invention or interesting presentation to show the audience.* Make sure that what you have to show is worth watching. A boring presentation can kill even a great product. A good D&P is a sort of controlled craziness, a mini circus with you as the ringmaster and your invention as the lion act. A good presentation will leave the crowd with a sense that their time was well-spent. It will also leave them talking and thinking about your product. A functional invention or prototype is the best possible thing to have at a D&P. People like to play with a new product and, if possible, try it out for themselves.

*When the Maxi D&P is used for any media attention, it should not have any mention of investment or profits.

Even a mock-up (nonfunctional model) can evoke greater interest than mere words or drawings.

4. *Hand out information and visual materials that grab the attention of your audience.* Make sure the leave-behind materials and visual aids look professional. In this age of desktop computers and laser graphics, investors and the media expect professional-looking presentation materials. If your materials look like they were done on a cheap typewriter and your visual aids are of high school show-and-tell quality, your credibility as a potential moneymaker will plummet even before they get a real grasp of your invention's potential.

Market is everything for an invention. Your presentation material must reflect the invention's market potential. Poor-quality materials will indicate (whether true or not) that there is limited potential in the product. Poor-quality materials will also hurt you in other ways. First, they will not hold the attention of the viewers during the presentation. This will distract from the important features of the product. Secondly, the leave-behinds will present a poor picture of the product after you are no longer there to defend its credibility. On the other hand, first-rate literature will always project a good image, even if the actual presentation did not go as well as expected. Good literature will also open doors with people who have yet to meet you in person, or see the product. Don't skimp on quality presentation materials!

Key Elements of the Dog-and-Pony Show

There are four distinct elements to every D&P show. They are: the **artwork,** the **written presentation,** the **oral presentation** and the **audio-visual aids.**

The artwork includes line art, renderings, cut-away art, and other presentation artwork that enables you to get your point across with maximum visual impact. Poorly executed art can put even a great product concept in a poor light in the eyes of investors and the media.

The written presentation includes all handout information. It must be of the best quality that you can generate. Computer-generated and laser-printed documents have proven the most effective and the least expensive. Your handouts are what must represent you when you are not present to explain your invention. Be concise and accurate. Don't make written claims you can't live up to later!

Your *oral presentation* should be well-rehearsed and specific. Make points that are cogent to the concerns of your audience (i.e., the media should get one type of talk while possible investors will require another). You should be prepared to answer questions without hesitation. Know your topic! If you don't have complete information on your invention, who will? Your answers to questions and the gist of your prepared speech will reflect the level of development of the invention.

Any *audio-visual (AV) aids* usually will enhance your presentation. They include slides, video tapes, overhead projections, audio tapes, and other methods. When used correctly, AV aids can create a dramatic presentation even for mundane inventions.

Every entrepreneurial inventor eventually must go through his or her own Dog and Pony "trial by fire." According to several studies, getting up and speaking in front of a group of people is the number one fear of most Americans. Getting over your fear and learning to give concise, informative presentations is an important ability you must have if you expect to ever raise capital or promote your product. Once you overcome this fear, public speaking can help you in many other areas of personal and business life.

If your invention has merit, and you have the nerve, doing dog-and-pony shows can become an exciting experience that opens investor checkbooks and the doors of opportunity.

A Dog-and-Pony-Show Checklist

The following checklist can help you plan, organize and keep track of successful D&P presentations.

DOG AND PONY SHOW CHECKLIST   Date: _____

PRODUCT NAME: _____

INVENTOR'S NAME: _____

SPONSOR / D&P DONE FOR:_____

LOCATION: _____

ADDRESS: _____

NUMBER OF PEOPLE EXPECTED:_____ MAXIMUM: _____

DATE: _____ DAY: _____ START TIME: _____ AM / PM

TRAVEL TIME TO PRESENTATION _____ Hr. _____ Min. SET UP TIME _____ Min.

LENGTH OF PRESENTATION: _____ Hr. _____ Min. Q&A TIME: _____ Min.

TELEPHONE AT LOCATION:_____

FAX AT LOCATION: _____

MAIN PRESENTER: _____

BACK-UP PERSONNEL: _____ Job: _____

EQUIPMENT NEEDED FOR D&P: Slide Projector [ ]   VCR [ ]   TV / Monitor [ ]
Overhead Projector [ ]   Movie Projector [ ]   8mm [ ]   16mm [ ]   Projection Screen [ ]
Blackboard [ ]   Loud Speaker System [ ]   Flip Chart [ ]   Other: _____

PRESENTER PREP:

[ ]**Artwork:** _____

[ ] **Written Presentation:** # of Handouts _____ Number: _____ Printed _____ Collated _____

[ ] **Oral Presentation:** Written [ ]   Ad-Lib [ ]   Rehearsed [ ]   Sync to A/V Show [ ]

[ ] **Audio/Visual:** Slides [ ]   Transparencies [ ]   Video Tapes [ ]   Audio Tapes [ ]

Charts [ ] Props: _____

COSTS INVOLVED IN D&P:

Presentation Materials and Handouts: $ _____ Items: _____

Audio Visual Materials (Event Specific) $ _____ Items: _____

Rental of any Equipment (Event Specific) $ _____ Items: _____

Transportation Costs (Event Specific) $ _____ Items: _____

Personnel Expenses & Salaries: $ _____ Items: _____

Postage and Mailings (Event Specific) $ _____ Items: _____

Misc Expenses: $ _____ Items: _____

TOTAL FOR D&P SHOW: $ _____

NOTES ON THIS PRESENTATION:_____

_____
_____
_____
_____

POST D&P FEEDBACK ON THE PRESENTATION:

Presentation went: Poorly [ ]   OK [ ]   Normal [ ]   Well [ ]   Very Good [ ]   Excellent [ ]

Response was: Poor [ ]   Conservative [ ]   Good [ ]   Very Good [ ]   Excellent [ ]

Business Prospects from D&P: Poor [ ]   Conservative [ ]   Good [ ]   Very Good [ ]

FOLLOW UP NOTES: _____

_____
_____
_____
_____
_____

Chapter 9

Getting Help When You Need It: Key Sources of Information and Support

**A single idea, if it is right,
saves us the labor
of an infinity of experiences.
Jacques Maritain**

 Inventors tend to be generalists, with a particular affinity for certain areas of expertise. For example, my own great technical loves are pneumatics and magnetics, but I don't know enough about either specialty to work on a complicated project without expert help. So, rather than trying to clutter my brain with formulas and equations, I turn to outside sources when I need help. This lets me spend my time working on the overall project and gives me more creative freedom and a wider range of options. More often than not, I also get inspiration from an outside source, which might not have happened if I had pursued the idea without relying on external help.

The entrepreneurial inventor can draw upon many sources of information and assistance. I call these sources "tools of the trade."

Three Tools of the Inventor's Trade

 As an entrepreneurial inventor, you must use every tool at your disposal to create a new technology. The information tools available to you cover a wide range of resources, but they fit into three basic categories:

1. Data acquisition
2. Consultants
3. Field Work

Each of these categories is examined in this chapter. I also examine one type of "help" you definitely do not need and should avoid: invention marketing scams.

Data Acquisition

To me, *data acquisition* is the most basic and important of these tools. This is collecting and cataloging important information related to your invention from various fields. The data then can be used for brainstorming and reference.

There are at least three ways that you can collect and catalog useful information: (1) a personal library system of catalogs and brochures; (2) a computer log or handwritten log of important information; and (3) a collection of articles taken from magazines and other sources. I use all three of these techniques in combination. I keep the gathered information in looseleaf notebooks and clear folders. Reading through these notebooks and folders has proven to be a great way to start a brainstorming session and to jog my subconscious into high gear. The result has been many serendipitous interactions of technology that were not even remotely connected. This system works for articles, photos, brochures, and other materials—virtually anything that you take from another source and wish to save for future reference. You can edit the information at any time, adding to or deleting from as you wish.

To set up a system similar to mine, you need several looseleaf notebooks and a box of clear vinyl plastic sleeves that have been punched for use in looseleaf notebooks. I place copies of all of my miscellaneous ideas in one notebook, magazine articles about new technologies in another, newspaper articles in another, catalogs in another, and so forth. This creates a fast-growing but very organized system of data that you can access at any time.

Using Public and Private Libraries

Much of the data I accumulate comes from public and private libraries. Libraries are invaluable assets for entrepreneurial inventors, because you must know as much as possible about the field in which you are inventing. There are two reasons why this is so. First, *you don't want to reinvent the wheel.* If you don't know the ins and outs of a particular field, you may be inventing something that has been a tried and accepted (or abandoned) concept for a long time. Researching and knowing your subject will let you start your developmental efforts from currents events in the field. Second, *your credibility is at stake.* If you don't understand your invention, its historical significance and position in the marketplace, you can easily lose your investors, vendors, and market.

Key Resources at the Public Library

Public libraries are storehouses for a vast amount of published materials, including newspapers, magazines, and books. These can be used to get important contact information, including people and companies that already have done groundwork in your invention field. Articles from publications can be used to bolster your case for why an invention is needed. The basic way to search for these articles is through the computer database available in most public libraries. You could spend the rest of your life researching a single concept if you attempted to physically go through all possible magazines and newspapers on file. The computer database search will pull out any references to your field of inventing or to a particular individual or event. Frequently, an article that is found in a database search will contain a reference to another source of information that can help you complete various parts of a project.

NOTE: Not all inventions need extensive research. These include "fad" inventions and "problem-solving novelty" inventions that have made many of their creators a bundle of quick cash. Even with these types of inventions, however, you still must use many of tools of the inventor's trade to get from the idea stage to the finished product.

Many books at the public library also can give you invaluable information on construction, marketing, and sales of almost any product. In addition, several books are particularly valuable resources for entrepreneurial inventors. These include *The Thomas Register,* the *Encyclopedia of Associations,* and the general encyclopedias and specialized atlases.

THE THOMAS REGISTER.   This is a set of approximately 23 books listing almost every type of industrial good or service available in the United States today. Over the years the set has grown from just a few volumes to its current size. I have found it to be a very important entrepreneurial inventing tool. The books are broken down into three sections: the main "Thomas Register," the "TOMCAT Guide," and the "Company Profiles."

The main *Thomas Register* is composed of fourteen large books that contain the actual listings. Some listings contain just a name, a location, the size of the company, and the heading under which the company appears. Other listings are full-page advertisements that show products, describe services, and give telephone numbers. Sometimes, these advertisements also present enough information on their product line that you can decide whether to contact them for help or parts. The Thomas Register is published by the Thomas Publishing Co., One Penn Plaza, New York, NY 10001.

The TOMCAT Guide consists of seven books that contain catalogs from selected companies listed in the register. Many companies place their catalogs here for 2 reasons: (1) to save customers the time and trouble of having to call or write for information; (2) to save the company the expense of mailing out brochures to all inquiries. The TOMCAT Guide gives inventors a convenient place to see what products and samples are available to them for their prototypes.

The Thomas Register's "Company Profiles" consist of two books that list all companies in the register by their actual name, rather than by the type of products they manufacture. This listing is helpful for looking up companies that you have heard about, but have no information on what they produce.

THE ENCYCLOPEDIA OF ASSOCIATIONS.   This multivolume set lists associations and organizations in the United States. Every association and organization holds a wealth of information on all aspects of their particular field. Most have newsletters, meetings, and other services that are listed. Contacting an association or organization can put you in contact with numerous experts in a particular field. *The Encyclopedia of Associations* is also an important networking resource. It is published by Gale Research Co., Book Tower, Detroit, MI 48226.

GENERAL ENCYCLOPEDIAS.   These are a basic resource for finding generic information about a field. Consult these first when you have a question. For tough problems, general encyclopedias often can give you several related options to explore to get to your next angle of attack.

SPECIALIZED ATLASES.   Many public libraries have a large selection of specialized atlases. These contain different information related to population distribution, marketing and other matters. The atlases can help you determine certain aspects of a market plan or product sales test area, for example.

Private Libraries: Building Your Own

You may also have access to the private libraries of various experts or other inventors. And the books you already have accumulated, as well as others you will come across, can form the nucleus of your own entrepreneurial inventor's library. I recommend having the following books on your shelves:

1. *The Way Things Work*, an illustrated encyclopedia of technology published by Paramount Publishing, New York, NY. This book and several like it are compendiums of knowledge about the technology that makes the world function. *The Way Things Work* explains more than 275 processes and machines that make up the backbone of most major technological systems. It also explores the dynamics of complicated machines and manmade systems. You may find this book extremely helpful for understanding certain technologies that you want to incorporate into a larger invention.

2. *The How and Why of Mechanical Movement* by Harry Walton, published by Popular Science Publishing Co., New York, NY. This is a basic book for inventors and everyone else who has wondered how and why things work. The book progresses from basic information on what work and power mean to the lever, simplest of all machines, and then through the wheel, pulley, screw, inclined plane, gears, and motors. This is the type of book that you may refer to thousands of times in the course of your career. It has insights that will trigger ideas and solve problems, and it was written and illustrated to be understood by everyone, not just the mechanically inclined.

3. *Up Your Own Organization* by Donald M. Dible, published by the Entrepreneur Press, Santa Clara, Calif. This is an excellent handbook on how to start and finance a new business. As an inventor, you need this entrepreneurial bible to help guide you through the winding paths of businesses plans, raising capital, and good management. Dible's work touches on many subjects discussed in this book, including idea developing, networking, and how to project a good image.

4. *Handbook of Business Finance and Capital Resources* by Dileep Rao, Ph.D., published by Interfinance Corp., Minneapolis, MN. This book is a major source of financial contact information, including venture capital firms and all types of lending institutions. It gives information about the sources that can be vital to how your business plan is structured and how you approach the financial institutions. This book also contains a comprehensive section on the fundamentals of business finance. Unfortunately, this book is rather expensive. Try first to find it at a library.

5. *Government Giveaways for Entrepreneurs* by Matthew Lesko, published by Information USA, Kensington, MD. This book is an excellent compilation of information about every section of the United States government and private resources that have money and materials available for free, cheap, by grant, or otherwise at a discount for entrepreneurs. It offers information that up until its publication was not available anywhere else in one source. The book has telephone numbers and addresses for many agencies and other sources. It has information on programs run by the government that have capital to give away for any reason. This includes hundreds of invention-related programs and all sorts of funding for new business and technology.

6. *The Writers Market: Where and How to Sell What You Write* published by F & W Publications, Cincinnati, Ohio. Most inventors will have the opportunity to write about their inventions at one time or another. This is the source book for breaking into the writing field. It is the writer's bible for information about all of the publications in the country that buy freelance articles. It doesn't cover newsletters, an important resource for inventors. However, newsletters can be sought out through the various organizations that publish them for their members. These groups can be found in the Encyclopedia of Associations listings. The *Writers Market* covers thousands of publications that accept material. The book tells everything that a writer needs to know to approach the publications. It also can put an inventor in touch with the information network for an entire industry he wants to explore.

7. *COLE-PARMER Catalog*, published by Cole Parmer Instrument Company (1-800-323-4340) Chicago, IL and *THOMAS SCIENTIFIC: Scientific Apparatus and Reagents* published by Thomas Scientific, Swedesboro, NJ (Eastern region, 1-800-345-2103; Northeastern region, 1-800-345-2101; Southern Region, 1-800-345-2100; Far Western Region, 1-800-345-2102). These catalogs are very useful to inventors researching what instruments and equipment are available for scientific experiment, setting up a workshop and use in prototype devices. These catalogs can cost a small fee but it is refunded with an initial purchase. If you approach the companies from the angle that you are an inventor looking to equip your lab, they may supply the catalogs for free. These catalogs are impressive publications in full color and have as many as 1,000 to 2,000 pages. The catalogs give prices of the equipment, which can help an inventor with estimates and projections. Inventors will find equipment in these catalogs that will not only solve problems but inspire new ideas.

8. *Edmond Scientific Catalog*, NJ. This company, long a favorite of every tinkerer, magician, inventor and fun seeker, covers the "holes" in most prototype applications. Edmond Scientific has made a career of having the most unusual, most off-beat and useful parts, gadgets, tricks, materials and tools. It is a definite *must* for every entrepreneurial inventor's private resource library.

Using Industrial Statistics

Industrial statistics are compiled by a particular industry or by the government about a particular industry. They can be extremely helpful in pinpointing specific information which can be used to:

1. determine needs that can be filled by inventions;
2. show investors the size of a market; and
3. show the inventor a target market for a particular invention.

Many government agencies, universities, and business associations also can supply an inventor with other information related to their particular field. State, regional, and local government agencies may also prove helpful. The information from these sources often is free for the asking. Some sources of information from federal agencies and universities are described in Chapter 14.

Two examples of government statistical information sources are the Uniform Crime Report (issued yearly by the Justice Department) and the Statistical Abstract of the United States (issued yearly by the Department of Commerce). These two massive texts reveal every thing that their respective agencies have learned during the year under study. This information may seem obscure at first, but an inventor must learn to see past all the numbers to the patterns that indicate which information can be used to support the cause of an invention.

An example of how I used this type of information is the development of a product called "Power Staf," which I invented. You will see references to Power Staf in various parts of this book. I have used the Power Staf product as an example in this book because it was a learning experience that took me to the extremes of the light and dark sides of inventing. Statistics helped play a role in the creation of the Power Staf idea by presenting information about a need to be filled and the size of the market.

The Power Staf is a pneumatically (air pressure) powered piston device that is designed to deliver a substantial impact to an aggressor up to six feet away via a moving shaft that reciprocates from the device. The device was originally conceived of as a weapon to be housed in a cane that could be carried by an elderly person or anyone desiring a nonlethal device for fending off muggers. The concept, after some review of design criteria checklists indicated that its intended market (the elderly and general public) was not appropriate for the action and complexity of the device. I then looked for another market because I knew the device itself was viable, but I understood the most basic premise of good entrepreneurial inventing: Market is everything! By looking to the next obvious market, law enforcement, I found the larger and viable market I was looking for. This was proven by the statistics in the Uniform Crime Report that showed 95 percent of all law enforcement officers injured during assaults in the line of duty are hurt with hands, feet, sticks or knives at distances of less than six feet from the aggressor. With almost no modifications to my original design, the statistics provided a perfect match for my device. The statistics also showed that more than 500,000 police officers might use the device. This, coupled with prison guards, national guardsmen and private security forces, provided a substantial base market. Using these statistics, I was able to generate interest in the product, and eventually, I raised more than a million dollars to develop, patent, and market it.

Using statistics from industrial sources is important for any product that will be sold in the private sector. Many industrial statistics forecast the growth of an industry. You can use some of these statistics to give credence to investing capital in a new device aimed at a particular market.

Consultants

Consultants are independent business people who have a special knowledge in a particular field. And they usually have some specialized credentials to back up their expertise. Illustrators, patent attorneys, and machinists are examples of the consultants inventors hire to help them accomplish their goals. The main advantage of using consultants is that they are only called in when you need them.

Be careful when hiring a consultant to help you with an invention-related project. Many people advertise themselves as invention consultants—and aren't!

Consultants typically charge a per-hour fee or by the job. Do *not* offer a consultant any equity as a trade for services, unless that consultant's services will be used extensively throughout the entire development of the invention project. Most consultants are happy to talk about what they can do, without charging a fee, until you ask them to perform some sort of work. If you are skillful at conversation, you may be able to get useful information from some consultants without paying any money. But inventors typically hire consultants to give expert advice on a project's development or to add credibility to a piece of presentation material.

Through your work as an inventor, you will amass a great deal of information and experience. As a result, you may become a consultant, as well, and develop a lucrative business serving companies in your specialty field, and other would-be inventors.

Field Work

Field work is another type of data acquisition you can use to help the invention process move from one stage to the next. Here are three important approaches to field work:

1. Working in a specific field to accumulate firsthand knowledge of a subject.
2. Becoming an observer in a specific field to accumulate firsthand knowledge.
3. Placing a prototype invention into a field situation to evaluate its abilities.

These approaches can give you different types of feedback and advantages when trying to develop, market, and sell a product.

The first approach, actually working in a specific field, enables you to get firsthand feedback on a situation and how your invention must function to be of value in that situation. This approach also is useful for convincing investors to risk capital in your project. Your hands-on experience in the field will be much more valuable than any academic degree. This type of field work often can give you insights that cannot be gained from merely thinking through the project design on paper.

The second type of field work, becoming an observer to the conditions that create the need for your invention, is the next best thing to actually doing the job or being part of the situation. Many times, a job associated with your invention, may require years of training and experience. One example is a police officer's job. When developing the Power Staf, I couldn't actually be a police officer, but I was able to ride along with the street officers. By doing that, I got a firsthand sense of what was needed in the product. Becoming an observer also lets you interview the end users to get their thoughts on what should be included in the product. Their spontaneous feedback is a form of brainstorming that can be a powerful asset.

You can pursue the third type of field work, also known as a "Beta Site," when you feel that your prototype is ready for the rigors of a field test. By actually placing it in the field, you can see what needs to be changed or improved to make your product more viable. Beta Test Sites are a form of test marketing. If the product works well, you will get positive feedback and find out if the need for your invention is greater or less than you expected.

How to Avoid Invention Marketing Scams

You can get to the point in a project where you are willing to do anything to get access to someone who knows what they are doing and is willing to help you. It is at this point that inventors are most vulnerable to one of the most dastardly of evils that can befall them: the invention marketing company (IMC). IMCs can be found almost everywhere in our society. They are a plague upon inventors that account for almost a billion dollars in losses to creative individuals every year. The Justice Department has said that IMCs today are one of the fastest-growing white-collar crimes in the United States.

IMCs are thriving because most inventors have no "real" place to turn to for advice and guidance. Inventors in general are average people who tend to believe most of what they read, and they usually don't think the world is out to do them wrong. What inventors tend to fear most is having someone steal their ideas. An IMC usually will care very little about stealing your idea, but it *will* care about emptying your bank account.

HOW INVENTION MARKETING COMPANIES WORK.   The typical IMC runs advertisements in major magazines and national newspapers. Some even advertise on TV. Look in the back of almost any magazine under the classified section for headings such as "Inventions," or "Of Interest to Inventors" or "Ideas." There, you will find ads for IMCs. If you look at the ad rates for these magazines, you will quickly understand that the IMCs must be doing a brisk business if they can afford to have these solicitations in every issue of many magazines for years on end.

The ads promise help in getting your idea protected and marketed. If you answer these ads, the IMCs will send you slick brochures about their services and trade shows. They will persuade you that they are the best thing you can do for yourself, your family, and your invention. And, of course, this will all sound like what you've been looking for—someone to take the load off your shoulders and make you rich. But it is simply too good to be true. Once an IMC has your name and number, you will get incessant calls from its sales force, offering to get you started on the road to prosperity from your ideas.

Most IMCs operate with a tried-and-true strategy, one designed to create a comfort level that blinds you to the obvious questions you should be asking. An IMC will offer to prepare an initial report on your invention. The report will take several weeks to prepare, you will be told, and the price likely will be between $350 to $600. You will be told that you can use the initial report as a preliminary business plan to raise money for your invention—"in the unlikely event that you don't want to continue with our program." This helps make the investment seem like a small price to pay for large potential benefits. The IMC then will keep up the pressure until you decide "What can I lose?" and send off the check.

When the initial report arrives in about a month or so, it usually will look impressive and appear to contain a wealth of information about you and your invention. A closer look, however, will reveal the truth: The report is made up of what is commonly known as "boilerplate." Boilerplate is a reusable script with blanks in it. Those blanks are filled in with information personalized to the particular invention and inventor, plus some general database statistics already at the fingertips of the IMC staff. Most of the information about the invention and inventor will be the same wording you have supplied to the IMC! Remember, IMCs prepare thousands of these reports every month for people around the country. There is no way they could ever do a "custom" report for the relatively small amount of money and time they are requesting.

Once the initial report has been in your hands for a short time, the IMC will contact you about the process of helping you make money with your idea. Unfortunately, the statistics clearly show that only the IMC will profit from the association. The IMC will make great claims about what it can do for you, but they will never have any real success stories that you can verify. They will flood you with information on products they are marketing, yet they will have no references that you can follow up on, to see if their system of idea development and marketing really works.

The easiest way for you to get to the bottom line on an IMC is to ask for information on products that currently are selling in retail markets or actively being sold via any legitimate sales and marketing system. The excuses and rebuttals that you will hear from the IMC salesperson will have little to do with the question at hand.

One of the most revealing documents that an IMC can show an inventor is not even required in most states. Some states *do* require disclosure documents, however. Texas, for example, requires full disclosure from any company that acts in the IMC role within the state. Texas requires an IMC to reveal how many people have contracted with it during the past five years. The same disclosure sheet also must tell an inventor how many of these people made money back (via the IMC's efforts) in excess of the amount they paid the IMC. This is where the real con takes visible form! In Texas, the page with this information is formatted so that the number of clients the IMC has is handwritten or typed in. This is done because the information changes all the time and must be updated by law with each new person. However, the IMC usually buries the next bit of information in the fine print of the disclosure sheet text. Set in type, the text discloses that the number of people IMC has made money for in excess of the amount they have paid in is "0" or "zero." They hope that most people might read right over this with little comprehension. But by setting this statement in type, the IMC makes a de facto admission that they *never* make any money for their clients, and they don't plan to make any for them in the near future!

HOW TO AVOID THE IMC TRAP.   Many inventors will continue to be blinded by the glitz of IMCs and the hype of their salesmen. The IMC industry will continue to pull in millions of dollars a day from unsuspecting and ill-informed inventors. What, in the long run, do inventors get if they stick with an IMC's program? Besides a substantially smaller bank account, they often get a mediocre brochure, a list of companies to which it has been sent, and possibly some representation in the IMC's in-house magazine, which is then used to hook more inventors.

Instead of turning to an IMC, you should look inward to your own creativity. You can do all of the things an IMC claims to do for about a tenth of the money. And you will gain new skills, knowledge, and confidence in your abilities along the way.

Don't, however, let this information on IMCs dissuade you from using resources in the marketplace that are real and worthwhile. Numerous companies are available that can create brochures, produce prototypes, and write advertising copy. You may want to try to do these things yourself, to see if you have a flair for it and enjoy it. If you don't, then try these other services.

But be sure to ask for business references and check with other inventors for their recommendations.

Life isn't a spectator sport, especially if you are trying to succeed in entrepreneurial inventing. Don't hand your dreams over to someone else in hopes that they will make your life's goals come true. Learn how to help yourself and how to seek out the right kind of help when you need it.

Chapter 10

Building and Maintaining Your Network

One man may hit the mark,
Another may blunder;
But heed not these distinctions.
Only from the alliance of the one,
Working with and through the other,
Are great things born.

Saint Exupery

 To "network" is to have and rely upon a group of contacts and resources who can help you in the right situations. In fact, networking is practically a systematic friendship acquisition program. Your contact network as an entrepreneurial inventor consists of a collection of friends and acquaintances from your business, school, and social life. Your immediate family and extended relatives also are part of your network.

The basic purpose of networking is to gain access to information, resources, and opportunities through the people with whom you are acquainted or well known. The greater the number of individuals in your personal network, the greater your chances of success with any given project.

Do not be concerned if your present network seems small and unable to help you. You probably have a larger network than you realize, one that you can activate through simple techniques. Networks don't pop up and stay the same forever. Think of networks as dynamic organizations that constantly interconnect and link up in amazing ways. Your network will grow quickly and usefully as you learn to see it and use it for what it is. It is your second greatest asset after your own creativity!

Networking Basics

 Remember and pay attention to the following basics when you start working to build up your network.

1. Networking is something that must be worked at to work at all. It must become part of who you are and how you view the world. You may meet people almost anywhere on this planet who may become part of your network. Always be on the lookout for a good contact.

2. Networking involves a concept that most people shy away from: the idea of "using" someone else to help you accomplish something and "being used" by them when they need your help to accomplish something.

3. Networking must work both ways, or it won't work past the first time you "use" someone. When you cultivate a contact, you are initiating the understanding that you are open to doing favors on a variety of levels. You, in return and without saying as much, expect that person to be helpful to you in some way in the future.

4. When possible, be the first to do something for a new contact, especially if the favor is easy and without consequence to you. This puts you in the receiving position for a favor from the new contact. This is all unsaid, but keenly felt when you establish the right rapport with a new contact. The more unexpected and needed the favor is, the better.

5. Listening and understanding are important parts of the networking system. These can help you identify people who can be useful to your network. By listening and understanding, you can identify favors and activities that would be most appreciated by your new contacts. Also, you can tune into opportunities that your contacts may have for you. A simple conversation at a party with a contact may tell you how you can help him, in areas where he doesn't know you have resources. Conversely, your contact may tell you, without knowing it, that he has an answer to a major problem facing your inventive efforts, such as lack of money, resources, or contacts. Listening and understanding can bring you a clear picture of problems faced by your contacts—keeping in mind that every problem is an opportunity for an invention to solve that problem. Almost no problem is totally unique, so if you create a solution to a contact's problems, you may also open up a new market for sales and profits.

6. Networking can lead to social and business entertaining. Some of the best friends you may ever have may start as newly acquired contacts in your network. Social and business meetings can lead to other contacts who may inspire new ideas and lead to profitable business opportunities through consulting contracts, investments, or business services.

7. Keep track of all of your contacts. Collect their business cards and other important data on them. Keep notes on when and through whom you met, what topics the contact enjoys, and on what level you mutually get along.

Remembering someone's wife's name the next time you meet or remembering a new friend's birthday or child's graduation can go a long way toward cementing a relationship that can span the years and generate help, opportunities and business.

NOTE: Keep your networking sheets and data private and confidential! This is valuable information. Also, you may not want others to read what you have written about them or someone else. See Appendix III for a sample Networking Contact Sheet.

Types of Contact Networks

 It is often said that in a good network, you are only three phone calls away from anyone else in the country. This may be overstating the case a bit, but it illustrates the importance of networks. Networks are all around you, waiting to be joined and explored for new possibilities. The following are some basic types of contact networks. Others will come to mind from your private and business life.

FAMILY.   Your family is your number-one network. Most people really don't have a good idea of what type of business or personal contacts their parents, siblings, aunts, uncles, or cousins really have. Let them all know what you are attempting. They may have a valuable contact you can get to know. Unless your family feuds like the famous Hatfields and McCoys, even distant relatives may be glad to help you. After all, if you turn out to be the next Edison or Ford, they will want to say "I knew him when... ."

FRIENDS, ASSOCIATES AND NEIGHBORS.   These are all part of your current, active network. Consider anyone you have ever worked for, or with, as part of this network.

FRATERNAL ORGANIZATIONS AND RELIGIOUS GROUPS.   These can provide a strong network system. Don't be afraid to go to club or religious meetings and talk up your inventing endeavors. You may meet many people who are interested in knowing a "real, live inventor." Their interest and connections can help you widen your contact network.

ALUMNI ORGANIZATIONS.   Join any these for which you qualify. Read their publications and take note of who has been promoted to which position. Use this information to your advantage by sending them a letter of congratulations. This often will get you a warm reply and a warm welcome if you later call them. Also attend alumni functions and mingle with the others in attendance. The connections you can make often will be amazing.

SCHOOL.   Going back to school at least part-time is a good way to meet people with similar interests and ideas. Try to talk to each person in your classes, as well as the teachers, to find out who is worth adding to your network.

CIVIC GROUPS.   These usually are composed of local people who want to change or better their living environment. As an inventor, you likely will be welcomed with open arms as a new resource. Get to know your neighbors through the civic organization. This can lead to opportunities and more contacts throughout the city or area where you live.

PROFESSIONAL ORGANIZATIONS.   Whatever your regular profession (I am assuming you are not yet a full-time inventor), you can find professional organizations to join. (There also are professional organizations for inventors. See the listing in Appendix I.) These organizations are fountains of opportunities for making new contacts. Most professional organizations also have annual meetings, and these are worth attending to make contacts, as well.

MISCELLANEOUS ORGANIZATIONS AND FUNCTIONS.   Good contacts for your network can be made anywhere. You may even find them if you join a ski club or scuba club or attend various workshops in your area.

Maintaining Your Network

Anywhere you can meet people, you can establish new links in your network. You should follow up on these contacts and try to keep in touch with the ones that you feel have potential. There are several ways to practice network maintenance.

One way to keep up with the latest news is to invite a contact to have an informal lunch with you or to meet you for predinner drinks. People love to sit and talk after a hard day at work—and they enjoy getting away from the grind and having someone to talk to at lunch. Make yourself available to chat and develop the relationship. Occasionally pick up the check, as well, with a flair, of course! Talking to a banker over lunch about miscellaneous enjoyable topics will be remembered fondly when you ask him later to line you up with some investors for your next invention. Keep in mind that the way your contacts talk about you to others, when you are not there, is an important aspect of networking.

Another way to practice network maintenance is to do some unexpected favors for your contacts. One of the easiest ways to do a favor is to pass along some information. If you notice an article or news item that may be of interest to a contact, pass it on. Your phone call will not only be enjoyable, but possibly an important point in their day and will help keep the relationship active and positive. When you let people know that you're thinking of them, it can go a long way toward getting them to act on your behalf at other times.

If one of your contacts shows a real interest in your work and achievements, keep him or her informed with an occasional progress report on your life and times. They will appreciate the note, and it is a good way to introduce them to a new idea or plan you are developing, before you ask them for advice or help.

Another good way to keep your network alive is to entertain. Have a party at least a couple of times a year. Invite a lot of your contacts and people you would like to have as contacts. Introducing your contacts to one another can strengthen your network by making it interlinked. Have fun and advance your goals at the same time.

Networking Correspondence

The following examples show how to write effective networking letters and what should be included in each. The types of letters shown are:

1. Follow-up letter to a new contact
2. Congratulatory note to a contact
3. An update note to contacts
4. Letter to a contact met through an organization or association

Follow-up Letter to a New Contact

These are the essential elements for creating an effective follow-up letter:

- Send the follow-up letter within two to three days of meeting a new contact. People usually respond very well to immediate follow-up. Your letter will give your contact a good sense that your interest was genuine.
- Use an informal and friendly tone, but keep the tone of a peer. Use elements of your original meeting conversation to break the ice. This will help keep the relationship on the same footing on which it started.
- Let your new contact know that your meeting was a real pleasure (in the first paragraph), making sure to mention the place and circumstances. This will jog the contact's memories and reinforce the meeting in his or her mind.
- Mention (in the second paragraph) the ideas that arose during your meeting and that you are interesting in pursuing with the contact. This will show him or her that you are doing more than paying lip service with your letter. You will show the contact that you are continuing to think seriously about the ideas discussed. This is especially important if you are coming up with ideas to help the contact, via an invention or doing consulting work on a problem.
- Also in the second paragraph, indicate why you are interested in pursuing those ideas. Mention work you have done or are doing, which may have a bearing on the topic. Give a little background on your developments may entice the contact into deepening the relationship or possibly giving you information on how both of you can work together on a future project.
- In the third paragraph, suggest a possible follow-up meeting, letter

or phone call. If you propose a meeting, call within seven days to schedule it.

- Enclose materials for your contact to review, if the person was receptive to seeing your invention or business proposal. If they were stand-offish about business when you met them, they may be wanting to wait until they know you better. Don't send them a lot of heavy business proposals or invention paperwork until they are ready for it.

Sample New Contact Letter

Using the tips above, here is how to construct an effective new contact letter.

Dear_____ ,

    It was nice to meet you last night at Robert's cocktail party. I am so pleased that I had the opportunity to learn about your current research project. I knew, of course, about the fine reputation of your firm. Now I know why that reputation exists!

As I mentioned last night, I have been working with many design firms by assisting them in the area of new-product design. As you know, I have been in the new-product development field for quite some time.

Given what you said about your plans to expedite the design phase of the project, it might be advantageous for us to meet again and see if there is a chance we might work together. I am enclosing my personal history sheet and a recent article that the Austin *American-Statesman* did about my work with a client in your area.

I will call you next week to see about setting up a meeting. In the interim, please send me any other information on the idea that you feel will help me get a better idea of what you need. I would really enjoy having the opportunity to review it.

With thanks,

Sincerely,

_____

Note of Congratulations to a Contact

This type of networking correspondence is important for establishing and maintaining goodwill with a contact. The following are the essentials of writing a note of congratulations.

- Send this type of note to people you already know.
- Use a semiformal tone.
- If your handwriting is legible, the note should be handwritten. Otherwise, type it out, in a personal style.
- Compliment the recipient, naming his or her specific achievement. Be sure to let the contact know the source of your knowledge. If your source was the print media, enclose a copy of the article containing the announcement of the achievement. People always can use extra copies of such news or magazine clips. Be sure to keep a copy of the article for your files.
- If there are any business, personal or other connections between the contact's achievement and your efforts, or if you belong to the group or organization making the announcement or award, make sure to mention this in the note. This will reinforce your connection to the achievement and the contact.
- Indicate that you want to meet with the individual. You don't always have to have a meeting in mind; just let contacts know that you appreciate their efforts in a particular field. Leave the when and where of a meeting to the follow-up call to talk about the achievement.

Sample Note of Congratulations

Here is the format for an effective congratulatory note to a contact.

Dear_____

   Congratulations on your appointment as Chief Engineer at General Molders. I read about it in today's Austin *American-Statesman* and wanted to send my best wishes. What a splendid appointment for you, and what a boost to the company's ability to produce fine products.

I would very much enjoy seeing you again soon and hearing the inside story of your appointment. In the meantime, enjoy your new position.

With all good wishes,

Sincerely,

_____

Update Notes to Contacts

An update note is a good way to keep your contacts aware of, and interested in, your activities. You should send one to your contacts when you introduce any new service, publish an article of interest, or want to report something notable. Send out an update note if you are doing an informal seminar, raising capital for an idea, or just introducing a new concept (after secrecy no longer is an issue). Keep these basics in mind:

- Update notes should be typed. Better yet, laser print them as announcements. Use some eye-catching graphics and your logo.
- Use an informal and entertaining, yet professional, tone.
- Get to the point in the first paragraph. An update note is almost like a press release, written to people you already know.
- If you intend to follow up, indicate in the second paragraph how and when you will do so. Follow-ups are not always needed. You should, however, follow up with specific individuals with whom you want to do further business related to the update information.
- Conclude by expressing your hope that the recipient's business is going well. If the update note is to a friend, inquire about personal matters. Always end the note with an upbeat closing.
- Enclose all relevant materials with the update information.

SAMPLE UPDATE NOTE.   Using the tips described above, here is an example of how to structure an update.

Dear_____

You may remember our meeting at the last McMurphy pool party, during which we discussed your company's need for development assistance in the area of low-cost prototype manufacturing.

I want to inform you that my firm has a new associate, Joan Black, who is an expert in the field.

Black has expertise in assisting organizations to create effective prototype equipment while working within very small budgets. She has worked with such organizations as IBM, Ford and 3M.

I would like to have Joan call you next week to discuss your needs in detail.

By the way, I saw an article about stereolithography in The Austin *American-Statesman* last week. I was glad to see that one of the new prototype systems we discussed has now developed to such an extent.

With thanks,

Sincerely,

_____

Letter to a Contact Met Through an Organization or Association

When you meet a promising new contact through an organization, club, or professional association, you can cultivate the opportunity by sending him or her a letter. Pay attention to the following basics for this type of correspondence:

- Laser-print this letter on your stationery. The letter should look like professional business correspondence.
- Allow space to type an inside address and salutation.
- Use a professional, but friendly tone.
- Be sure to mention in the first paragraph your connection with the individual and the organization at which you met or both belong to. This will trigger the contact's memory of you.
- In the next paragraph, be sure to mention your invention, idea, service, or business reason for this letter. Be specific and refer to any previous conversation or correspondence that you both shared.
- In the last paragraph, indicate any intended follow-up on your part, or indicate if the contact needs to do anything specific to follow up on this letter.
- Enclose any pertinent materials, such as brochures, photos, or article clippings.

SAMPLE LETTER TO AN ORGANIZATION OR ASSOCIATION CONTACT.   Use the following example to structure your own letter to an organization or association contact.

```
Dear_____

   As you know, I recently have joined the Centex Diver Scuba
Club and am very glad I did so. Everyone has been most kind
and helpful. One thing that I have been asked about is my
business. I have decided to send the members some information
for their files.

I set up my research, design, and inventing business ten years
ago. My associates and I primarily offer technical assistance
to any business that needs new product concepts or help in
design, research or fabrication of new products. Our primary
activities include development of prototypes, brainstorming
alternative construction and manufacturing processes, design-
ing custom destructive-testing criteria, and certain aspects
of marketing new concepts.

The enclosed brochure provides greater detail about my work,
as does the enclosed article from the Austin American-States-
man.
```

```
If I can provide any further information, let me know. I look
forward to seeing you at our regular monthly meeting, and I
would be happy to drop by and discuss my work with you at your
convenience, if you ever need our services.

Sincerely,

_____
```

The proper use of networking correspondence can greatly improve your business efforts and your social life. It is sometimes a long and tedious process to keep track of the information, but it will really pay off in the long run. Good luck with your network and keep making friends and contacts on the road to your dreams, because you never know where one of those contacts will lead you!

Chapter 11

Establishing Your Credentials as an Entrepreneurial Inventor

Our deeds determine us,
As much as we determine our deeds.

 One of the most important things you can do to help yourself toward success in entrepreneurial inventing is to establish a set of credentials. Most people hear the word "credentials" and immediately think of college degrees or other semi-sophisticated awards that are difficult to attain. Yes, it would be nice to list the Nobel Prize on your résumé or personal history sheet, but that isn't possible for the majority of us. Although these items are part of some peoples' credentials package, you don't have to have them to succeed in entrepreneurial inventing.

Credentials are the everyday documentation of what you make of yourself through your efforts to attain a better life. What you do with your credentials once you have them is a matter of individual choice. Most people, as they assemble a set of personal credentials, see the value of the credentials as a spearhead to opportunity. Whether you are trying to raise capital, get in to see an important contact, or get a manufacturer to work with you as an equal, credentials can play a vital role. Credentials are part of your public inventor's image. They are the "envelope" in which the world sees you. The world at large tends to respect experience and prior accomplishment because it makes the individual with credentials a known quantity on whom people can rely or have respect.

Credentials are not something to be flaunted. They are the past that lays a groundwork for getting things done in the future. Credentials provide a "comfort level" for people working with an inventor. They represent a level of expertise, interest or accomplishment in some particular area. They are the reason many people and companies will invest time and money in an inventor's concept.

Ten Ways to Establish Your Credentials

There are ten basic ways to establish your credentials as an entrepreneurial inventor. They are: letters of reference; degrees and professional licenses; work history; personal accomplishments; news coverage; outside firms that establish credentials; certificates of accomplishment; membership in organizations; writing and teaching; and the creation of anything.

These ten categories will allow almost anyone to develop a set of usable credentials. Each category is completely different in the way the credentials are attained and type of credentials that are available. Many people, by the very nature of the tasks they undertake, will have credentials in all ten areas. Others may only attain a handful in one or two areas. Sometimes, it is not the quantity, but the quality of the credentials that counts. Other times it is how you, the entrepreneurial inventor, capitalize on a credential that really matters for any particular situation.

You should have some or all of your credentials available for review in one or more formats. The use of the credentials is totally discretionary to each individual. You should integrate your credentials into a personal history sheet, press release, résumé, or master accomplishment book. Individual circumstance will dictate the actual use or display of this information. Ideas on how to integrate this information into your personal history sheet or a press release can be found later in this chapter.

Although résumés are very individual, they are structured along a standard format. If you are unfamiliar with how to set up a résumé, check out the local library or bookstore for more material on how to best structure one.

Creating a Master Accomplishment Book

A master accomplishment book is simply a loose-leaf binder with plastic sheet protectors. The loose-leaf binder is used to hold copies or the originals of letters of recommendation, news articles, certificates of merit and any other printed materials that is part of your credential package. This book can be duplicated and spiral-bound for inclusion with business plans and other documents where it is important for an individual or group to get a major dose of who you are and what you are all about.

You should look for opportunities to develop credential in the following ten areas:

1. *Letters of Recommendation.* Most people will be interested in what someone in specific has to say about you and your invention, your accomplishments, abilities, and background. A letter of recommendation provides a specific, detailed mini-story that people enjoy reviewing. Many people will give more credence to a letter of recommendation depending upon who the writer is, and what the writer has in the way of his own credentials. For example, a letter from your city's mayor about your great public-minded business activities will carry more weight than the president of the local block watch association. But don't discount the potential of the block watch letter, if it's the only thing in your credentials portfolio. Everyone has to start somewhere and every letter will build a path to a bigger and better reference for you and your invention.

2. *Degrees and Professional Licenses.* You should have as much schooling as you can stand. Everyone has a different need and tolerance level for education, but degrees that come from higher education do look nice in a credentials package. Depending upon the area of expertise that you acquire in school, the degree may enhance your chances of finding funding, partners or other resources along the invention path. For example, an MBA (Masters in Business Administration) looks great on almost any list of credentials, especially when it comes to getting others to invest their hard-earned dollars in a venture that you are going to manage. An engineering degree goes great with high-tech ventures, a degree in fashion design dovetails with a clothing venture, and so forth. An important thing to remember is that having a degree is not key to making your venture a success. Many investors and businessmen who have been successful without their own degree (and in some cases, very little formal schooling) know this for a fact, so don't try to use a degree as an all-encompassing credential. It can make you look like you're all "book knowledge" without "real world" practical experience. And that can negate the positive effect of an important specialized degree.

Other types of degrees from trade schools and correspondence schools can be very useful credentials. If your invention is in a new device in the plumbing industry, a plumber's trade school degree and/or a professional plumber's license are proof that you know your stuff. These are "real world" credentials that hold weight when dealing with investors, industry, and the media.

Still another type of degree is the specialized certificate of learning. These are from highly specialized courses, seminars, and workshops. The information taught in these formats is esoteric and usually on the cutting edge of knowledge in that field. These courses typically impart a specific skill at a user- or instructor-experience level. These certificates are an excellent resource as credentials because they show you are continually educating yourself in areas pertinent to the ventures you are pursuing. For this reason, I give all the students who complete my University of Texas course an official "Practical Inventing Workshop" Course Completion Certificate. Sometimes, it is the first piece of their credentials package toward becoming an entrepreneurial inventor. Other times, it is just one of many degrees and licenses they already have to their name. (See sample, Appendix III.) Another great thing about this type of credential is that a large number of separate certificates can be attained over a relatively short number of months or years. This gives both a quality and a quantity look to your credential package.

3. *Work History.* The easiest part of the credentials package is your work history. The places you have worked make up a large part of who you are and what skills you have developed. Sometimes, these skills don't have any bearing on the invention at hand. When this is the case, the best thing to do is not to specifically use your work history as part of the credentials. This can be avoided and turned into a positive resource by stating that you "have a steady work history in an unrelated field, references available upon request." When your work history is related to your invention, play up the fact that this is connected. It shows that you have thought about your profession beyond the 9-to-5 mentality.

4. *Personal Accomplishments.* This says more about you personally than almost any other type of credential. These can include such things as athletic accomplishment, whether you were an Olympic medal winner or local high school track star; civic recognition for public service or heroism; business accomplishments such as being a "Million Dollar Salesperson of the Year" or "Employee of the Month;" being a competition winner or runner-up, such as being local homecoming queen or Mr. Universe. Whatever the accomplishment, it shows that you try to excel in your everyday life. It focuses attention on the fact that you are more than one of the crowd. It shows you are a competitor in the game of life. This type of information looks great in print when someone wants to do an article about you and your invention.

5. *News Coverage.* Press coverage of all types—newspapers, magazines, radio, and TV—is a very important part of establishing widespread recognition for yourself, your ideas and your products. More importantly, media attention is a credential that says to the world: "Look at me, I'm newsworthy." Being newsworthy is one of the most important goals in publicity and promotion. In establishing credentials, being newsworthy is much like having letters of recommendation, inasmuch as a specific source is making a specific statement about you and your ideas. Being able to quote a magazine or newspaper about yourself or your product is a powerful promotional tool and a great ego booster. People believe what they see and hear, even in this age of skepticism about the media. Sometimes, even negative or mediocre press can be good for you if it gets people to remember your product name. There are many ways to get press coverage, and these are discussed later in this book. Once you have received press recognition, it is yours to use forever. Selected quotes, photos, and entire articles are reusable in elements of your press kit. Always update your printed promotional media as more press coverage is received. Take all copies of any printed material and include it in your master accomplishment book. Use this material to show prospective investors, manufacturers, and other news media that you are a dynamic force unto yourself and that their investment, cooperation, and interest is warranted.

6. *Outside Firms that Establish Credentials.* Several types of commercial firms can actually establish certain forms of credentials for individuals. The best known are the *Who's Who* series of books published by Marquis Who's Who of Wilmette, Illinois (1-800-621-9669). The Who's Who books (*Who's Who in America, Who's Who of Emerging Leaders in America, Who's Who in Science, Who's Who in Commerce and Industry, Who's Who in the West,* and so forth) give a short biographical listing of a select number of Americans, who for one reason or another qualify for the honor. Most books list about six to ten persons per ten thousand of population. There is no charge to be included, and you must be invited to place your name in their book. The company makes its money from people and institutions purchasing the books yearly (at about $150+ per book). For information on the selection criteria for any particular book, contact the publisher. Many people consider being listed in *Who's Who* as a credential in itself. I have been listed as an inventor in four *Who's Who* books for several years and have found it does get people's attention when reading my résumé or my Personal History Sheet. That's all it has ever done for me, and if it never does anything else, I will still be happy to be listed. It is recognition that is unsolicited, unpaid, unbiased, and publicly distributed on a national and international level. Another type of commercially based recognition that you can generate for your product can come from publications such as the *Jane's* series of books. Jane's Publishing of London, U.K. produces a large number of massive books that list all sorts of equipment produced around the world. Most of this equipment relates to the world's military and law enforcement community (e.g., infantry weapons, ships, aircraft, and so forth), but other publications like the *Jane's* series exist in other fields. These directories of available goods are basically paid and unpaid advertising disguised as an encyclopedia of that particular industry. Inclusion in the main body of *Jane's* books is free on a space-available basis. The front of the books are devoted to paid advertising space. Like the *Who's Who* books, *Jane's* gets the bulk of its revenues from sales of the books to libraries and interested parties around the world. Most retail for $125+.

Another source of credentials on any individual or business is a current credit history and report. A good credit history can be invaluable, and a bad one can cause many serious problems. TRW Credit Data Reporting Service is among the largest credit bureaus in the country. TRW and companies like it can help or hinder an inventor (depending upon the report content) in many phases of his business life. Using your credit report as an asset and credential is a good idea as long as you know its contents and who is accessing it. TRW has set up a service it calls "Credentials" just for this purpose. Contact TRW at 1-800-262-7432 for more information about their "Credentials" program.

7. *Certificates of Accomplishment.* Recognition of personal, professional, and civic activities is a valuable credential to have for any professional business person, especially the entrepreneurial inventor. These are actual formal certificates of merit or recognition that public and private institutions give to show appreciation and recognition. These can be another valuable printed credential to place in your master accomplishment book. Sometimes these certificates will be issued because of some personal accomplishment, or they may be issued for things as mundane as being the best Scout leader in your area. One of my favorite certificates of accomplishment is one I received from the Lower Colorado River Authority citing me as a good citizen for participating in an underwater river clean-up with my scuba club. I love to dive and its nice to get recognition for public service when it coincides with a fun activity.

As an entrepreneurial inventor, you hope that at least sometimes the certificate may be issued to some activity relating to inventing, or best of all, to your invention itself. Of course, this can happen if your invention wins a design award or is recognized by an industry for one reason or another. If you work for a major company, such as IBM, your inventive capabilities may be rewarded with certificates reflecting your creativity and contributions to the company. All of these should be part of your printed credentials package, to be used as needed to accomplish your entrepreneurial goals.

8. *Membership in Organizations.* Some say it's not *who* you are, *but who you're seen with* that gives credence to your actions. This may be oversimplifying the issue, but it does have merit. Joining the right organizations in the industry you're inventing for, or just joining civic organizations will be a beneficial credential. It shows that you are interested enough to take an active role in something. Actual active participation in many civic, business and cultural organizations can enhance your perceived and actual standing in your community, local social structure, and the business world. These memberships may also introduce you to information and people which can benefit your entrepreneurial inventing efforts. This will generate many contacts that can be crucial to your networking efforts. One or more of these organizations in a résumé or Personal History Sheet helps to round out your overall image.

9. *Writing and Teaching.* Writing is a way of becoming an authority in a field. Authors are perceived as knowing their fields and thus having a position within the respective field of endeavor. This is an important way to gain credentials for yourself within any given field. The ability to write on many topics can help you in many ways. A list of articles written or a book published is a strong credential in a résumé or Personal History Sheet. You can turn the research on a new product idea into the opportunity to write about the subject for trade publications, newsletters and other sources that may readily accept your work. Some of these particular writing outlets pay for articles while others generally don't. Good writing is still essential (even without being paid for it), because no one wants to be bored with an article. But creative writing is fairly easy when your subject is thoroughly researched. A body of articles will soon become a powerful credential that may enable you to get paid for articles and even publish your own book on the topic.

Teaching is just a stepping-stone away from writing. Teaching requires getting up in front of people and talking, but you should become accustomed to doing some public speaking for your Dog & Pony shows and other presentations. This experience directly relates to teaching in your subject area. A teaching credential is a powerful tool that can be used to open many doors of opportunity. You can teach a topic related to your invention, or you can teach the skills a person needs to operate in the field of the invention. Teaching is a credential that shows you have mastered that particular topic and can now impart it to others.

10. *Creation of Anything.* As an entrepreneurial inventor, this will be your most basic and most asked-for credential: "What did you invent?" Your ideas are credentials, and they don't necessarily have to be revealed at the drop of a hat to everyone who asks. After you have one or more publicly revealed inventions, it is an easy credential to provide and an ego-satisfying procedure. The use of an invention in a credentials package is the centerpiece of your media kit, or resume, and may be a large part of your Personal History Sheet. If your invention is something that can be easily transported and shown to people, then use it at every opportunity where you can do so without a problem. A product specification sheet is a good credential and a great sales and marketing aid. You should have specification sheets available on your product as soon as it reaches the marketing stage. This is an effective credential to hand to people who ask, "What did you invent?" It establishes you as an inventor and promotes the invention to every person who comes in contact with the flyer.

Remember, credentials are only as good as what you make of them. Properly packaged and distributed, credentials can sway investor opinion, get media attention, help market a new concept and generally provide a good base for you to build your entrepreneurial inventing career.

How to Get Letters of Reference and Recommendation

  No entrepreneurial inventor is an island! To be successful, you need the backing of various people to give credence to your abilities, your product and your project. These people are usually potential end users of the product, experts in the product's area of use, and fellow professionals in the field. Without endorsements of various types, you will have a hard time convincing anyone that your product is worthwhile, especially in the initial stages of its development.

The best type of backing and endorsement is the "letter of reference" or the "letter of recommendation." These two terms are somewhat interchangeable, although an actual letter of recommendation is considered the stronger of the two. In a recommendation the person writing the letter gives his stamp of approval to your efforts, to your product's abilities, or to your project's success. The best letters of recommendation, of course, give all three.

A letter of reference, though not as strong as the letter of recommendation, can be equally important if worded right. A letter of reference may just be a "thank you" letter from an end user who enjoyed a Dog & Pony show that you did for his or her group. If the letter makes favorable mention of the product or you, then the letter can be useful to the continued success of the project.

During the course of your efforts, you will come in contact with people whose opinions could matter in relation to the project's success. You should make every effort to start and maintain a good working relationship with these people. When you show your product and get a positive response from people, you should immediately follow up the meeting with an in-person request (or a very quick letter) to the people (individually and as an organization, if appropriate) for a letter. This is not as bold as it sounds. You make a person feel important by asking for his or her written opinion of the product, implying the opinion is so important that you want to be able to show it to others. If approached correctly, this will establish a good rapport between you and the letter writer, which usually will result in a good letter.

Another time you have an opportunity to get a good letter about your product is when someone else gives a demo with the product. If that person receives a good response to their Dog & Pony show, then you should get a letter from him or her indicating who attended the demo and the good response the product or related-information received. This secondary type of reference letter is sometimes more convincing to some people than the actual demo.

It is important that you actually ask for the letter, because most people will not write one without some urging. They are usually very busy and even if they thoroughly enjoyed the presentation, it will slip into the past without your request. A very simple way to approach the letter is to say, "I'm glad you enjoyed the presentation. Would it be possible for you to send me a short letter on your letterhead, giving me your impressions of the product and its usefulness in your field?" This is direct, polite, and usually results in a nice, useable letter. Make sure to ask for the letter on the company, agency or other official letterhead. A great letter looks lousy on a sheet of blank white paper. Letterhead gives the letter punch, authority, and professionalism. When using the letters as part of your credentials, it is very impressive when someone leafs through a pile of important letterheads. That sometimes carries as much weight as what's in the letter's content.

Once you start to assemble a body of letters, take care to keep them well-preserved and safe. I strongly recommend a high-quality looseleaf note-book with flexible plastic sheet protector sleeves. Place each letter in its own sleeve on the right-hand side of the book. This way, each letter is highlighted by itself as a person flips through the looseleaf. Never leave this book with anyone! It cannot be replaced! If anyone, for business or personal reasons, wants to have the book to review, give them a set of photocopies of the letters in a professional looking booklet. This is easily done by making a Bristol board cover (a type of thin cardboard available at all quick printers) to go on the front and rear of copies. Have a laser-printed sheet made with the words "Letters of Recommendation" in the top middle section of the sheet, with your name, product name and your contact information (address and phone number) printed on the bottom of the page in smaller type. Have this copied onto the front Bristol cover. Place the same information on a regular sheet as the first page when the book of copies is opened. The next page should be a short and concise overview of the product, with a picture, if available. Then the letters should be placed in any order you feel is appropriate to best present the information. These booklets should be bound with the flexible plastic comb bindings available at all quick printers. These work best because more pages can be added to or re-arranged in the existing book at any time by the printer.

Several of these booklets should be made and kept on hand at all times. You should take several with you when you go to see someone who may influence your project. These booklets make great "leave behind" material for important contacts. Keep updating the booklets and your looseleaf as more letters arrive and when other written publicity occurs. Newspaper articles and press releases can be incorporated into the booklet by simply changing the front title cover to say "Letters of Recommendation and Public News Coverage of XYZ Widget."

On the following pages, you will see examples of various types of letters of reference and recommendations. Each letter is unique in its content, how it was obtained and what its usefulness has been. These letters are from my personal collection of credentials. They relate to a product called "POWER STAF," which I developed for law enforcement. These letters are the result of my personal relationships with the letter writers. I have included comments on each letter indicating the background of how I got the letter, why it is good, and ways to use that type of letter.

Personal Letters of Recommendation

These letters usually are received from people who have known you for a long time. These people often are friends, co-workers and business associates. When starting out, you are wise to try to get several of these letters about your character. Such letters are good to have on hand for initial meetings with investors and others whom you want to get on your bandwagon. These letters say nothing about your invention concept and thus can be used for any project from that point forward.

Letter 1: Whitten Illustration and Design. This is an example of a "Professional to Professional" letter of recommendation. I had worked successfully with Gary Whitten on many occasions, and I asked him if he would write a description of my capabilities in a letter that I could use to generate support for my invention projects and possibly use to get new consulting clients. This letter is the result of that request. It is specific about our business relationship and about the way he views my professional capabilities, ethics, and knowledge. This type of letter is very helpful to show to new business associates when first trying to establish a rapport with them. It is also valuable to use when raising capital for an invention. It lets people know you are capable, honest and dedicated to your work. This is both a character reference and a work reference.

Letter 2: Advent Technology, Inc. This letter is from the head of engineering for a company that I worked with on a particular project. At the completion of the project, I asked for his opinion of my interface with his department. The resulting type of letter can be used for both a character reference and a work reference. Like the Whitten letter, this type of letter can be used in a variety of ways to benefit you in any project.

Letter 3: Trade International, Inc. This letter makes a very personal and emotional statement about my character. It is written from the viewpoint of one professional evaluating the moral and ethical standards of another professional in the field. I had known Don Wynnyczok for several years and had been good friends with him for a while at the time this letter was written. This letter was written to support my personal efforts at a time in my life

WHITTEN ILLUSTRATION & DESIGN
Translating complex ideas into accurate and exciting images!

Reference: Letter of Recommendation

To Whom It May Concern,

    This is a letter in reference to a three year business relationship with Mr. Robert J. Gold; inventor, writer and consultant.

    I am presently the owner of Whitten Illustration & Design, an advertising art studio specializing in conceptual art for new product development.

    I have had the opportunity to work with Robert Gold on many projects over the past three years. I have found him to be honest in his business dealings and very easy to work with. His project management skills are very thorough and well organized.

    I have been very impressed with his keen understanding of all phases of new product development. From concept through completion; he has displayed a comprehensive knowledge of patents, prototypes and manufacturing processes as well as very creative and innovative approaches to marketing the final product.

    I have worked with many people in developing new products over the past eight years but I have found few who are as knowledgeable, enthusiastic, and dedicated as Mr. Gold is to the field of new product development. I can highly recommend him for any task in this field that requires a true professional.

Sincerely,

Gary L. Whitten

Gary L. Whitten
Whitten Illustration & Design

2701 E. CAMELBACK RD. SUITE 351
PHOENIX, ARIZONA 85016
(602)955-4118

TECHNOLOGY, INCORPORATED

METROPLEX   SECOND FLOOR   3404 WEST CHERYL DRIVE   PHOENIX, ARIZONA 85021   602-993-4184

January 13, 1987

Mr. Robert Gold
6869 W. Sierra St.
Peoria, AZ   85345

To Whom It May Concern:

During the past year I have worked with Mr. Rob Gold as a
designer and engineer and have found the work to be both
challenging and enjoyable. Rob has an eye for detail and a
well-rounded knowledge of the real mechanical world which have
made his projects easy to design and straight-forward in theme
function.

Rob Gold is very professional in all aspects of his day-to-day
work routine. Projects are well planned and well thought out
prior to commencement.

In summary, Rob Gold is well disciplined in design judgement, has
an excellent eye for detail, possesses solid day-to-day business
sense, and admirable project follow-through. I have found him to
be very honest and straight-forward.

Sincerely,

ADVENT TECHNOLOGY, INC.

Paul O'Grady
Director of Engineering

POG/se

TRADE INTERNATIONAL, INC.

403 SEWARD SQUARE, S.E. • WASHINGTON, DC 20003 • (202) 547-0777

February 18, 1988

TO WHOM IT MAY CONCERN:

This letter is in reference to my association, personal and professional, with Mr. Robert J. Gold.

I have known Mr. Gold for over four years and in that time have come to understand his character as one of honesty, compassion and law abiding integrity. His life's work in the development of less than lethal products and life saving equipment reflects the fact that his concern for the protection of law enforcement officers, and the community at large, is utmost in his mind. His writings in many national magazines reflect his concern for the preservation of human life and the well being of law enforcement personnel.

My business dealings with Mr. Gold have shown him to be a man of his word. I can say without hesitation that I feel that his word is his bond. I know numerous other law enforcement and business professionals who would say the same of Mr. Gold's character.

In addition to my international business background of nine years my experience in the human character also comes from my years as a commissioned Naval Officer with five years of combat duty in Viet Nam and as an Operations Officer with ten years of experience with the Central Intelligence Agency.

I beleive that my judgement of Mr. Gold's character is based on a background which gives me a keen insight into the human character and the forces that play upon it.

Please do not hesitate to contact me if you have any questions regarding Mr. Gold.

Sincerely,

Don B. Wynnyczok
Presidnet

TELEX 249810 TRADE UR   •   FAX (202) 861-0621

when I needed to make a personal, rather than a professional or business statement about myself. Mr. Wynnyczok's background as a CIA operations officer, naval officer, and businessman gave him solid credentials to make his observation. The letter is a strong statement that helps bolster all the other letters in my credentials package. This type of letter is extremely valuable because people invest in, and trust, a person rather than a product.

Letter 4: Law Enforcement Technology Magazine. I asked my editor to write a letter of recommendation about my work (after only one year of my three with the magazine). I had two reasons for doing this. First, because I was looking to do other articles for more prestigious "over the counter" magazines and the good recommendation of my editor could prove useful in the eyes of the editors to whom I was applying. Secondly, I knew my editor was moving on to another job in the very near future, and I wanted to get a good reference from the magazine before he left because I had already established a good rapport with him. Although the letter is short, it is to the point and gives all the information about my writing activities that a new publication might need to feel comfortable about hiring me.

Letter 5: The Arizona Bank. I asked my banker to write me a letter about my account, because I was in the process of applying for various credit privileges with other businesses. This short letter tells that I had my account with that bank for five years and didn't give them any grief. Additionally, I knew the Assistant Manager at the bank on a personal level, and she was more than willing to give me a good verbal reference if someone wanted to back up the letter with a call. This type of Letter of Reference is valuable to have in your credentials package. It shows you are a solid community person with a history of banking at an established institution. It can help you establish other lines of credit and shows you are known to the bank, which is typically a very conservative institution.

Product Letters of Reference and Recommendation. I have included more background and history on each of these letters because I want to clearly illustrate how this type of product letter can be obtained. A large part of the process is networking and being pushy in a nice sort of way. Remember, people will only toot their horn for you if one of two elements are present. Those elements are: (1) they are getting something out of the action (money, recognition, etc.), or (2) you ask them to do it at a time when it is appropriate for you to ask and for them to respond. That time is often right after you have impressed them with the product or project. Don't be shy, or the moment will pass. It is hard to go back later and ask for a letter, after the momentum of the demonstration is gone.

Letter 6: Col. Rex Applegate. As part of my research into "less-than-lethal" weaponry, I had read the book *Riot Control: Materials and Techniques* by Col. Rex Applegate, a retired U.S. Army officer. Colonel Applegate won recognition during World War II as the expert developer of the close-quarters combat techniques used by American soldiers. He is also a noted expert on riot control systems and devices. The Colonel had long since retired from active training, but kept his name alive with various business enterprises including appearances at conferences where he promoted his books and other products he

LAW ENFORCEMENT
TECHNOLOGY

Executive & Editorial Offices: 50 West 23rd Street, New York, NY 10010 (212) 645-1000

January 13, 1987

TO WHOM IT MAY CONCERN:

Beginning in January, 1986 Robert Gold has been a
contributing editor of Law Enforcement Technology.
In addition to offering counsel based upon his
knowledge of the law enforcement industry, he has
authored a regular column, "Less-than Lethal," and
written feature articles. His work has been accurate
and submitted on deadline. In addition, his enthusiasm
was often greatly appreciated.

Sincerely,

Reinhardt Krause
Editor

Western Office: 5455 Wilshire Blvd., Los Angeles, CA 90036 (213) 937-5311
Midwestern Office: 360 North Michigan Avenue, Chicago, IL 60601 (312) 332-5945

January 21, 1987

1910 W. Thunderbird Rd.
Phoenix, Az. 85023
602-863-8412

Re;   Robert Gold and Power Staf

To whom it may concern,

Mr. Robert Gold has had accounts with this office of
the Arizona Bank since 1982. Mr. Gold has always
handled his accounts in a satisfactory manner. If you
have questions regarding Mr. Gold or Power Staf, please
feel free to call me at 863-8412.

Thank you,

[signature]

Dee Dee Rotz
Assistant Manager

Col. Rex Applegate

May 24, 1983

Mr. Robert J. Gold
NEOTERIC, INC.
250 W. 57 Street
Suite 1502
New York,NY 10107

Dear Mr. Gold:

This is in reference to your letter of May 16, 1983 and the demonstration you gave me of the POWER STAF at the recent National Rifle Association convention in Phoenix earlier this month.

I was impressed with the POWER STAF and its potential as a tactical and psychological law enforcement weapon. It is a new, unique development in the field of non-lethal weaponry. I will be awaiting, with interest, news of its manufacture and availability to the military and law enforcement.

I have gone over the material which you gave me and find it sufficient for my needs for inclusion in the next edition of my book, "Riot Control- Materiel and Techniques"(Paladin Press, Boulder, CO.).

Please keep me informed of your progress. I wish you every success in the development of this weapon.

Sincerely,

Col. Rex Applegate

RA:cv

enc:

THE ARMY-NAVY CLUB
17TH AND I N.W.
WASHINGTON, D. C. 20006
(202) NATIONAL 8-8400

Box 366
YONCALLA, OREGON 97499
(503) 849-2187
(503) 587-3402

endorsed. I heard from a friend that Colonel Applegate was to be in Phoenix at the National Rifle Association Convention and thought that a man of his background might have an opinion about the POWER STAF, since the unit was intended for use in, among other things, riot situations. I located the hotel where Col. Applegate was staying and called him. He agreed to meet me at his room for a demonstration of the POWER STAF. I spent about an hour talking with the Colonel and he liked the product. I asked if he was ever going to come out with a new edition of his book. He told me he was considering an update in the very near future and that he would like to include my device. Before I left, I thanked the Colonel for his time and asked him for a letter about his thoughts on the POWER STAF. His reply was that I should write him and remind him of our meeting and request the letter in writing. I did this in a letter on May 16, 1983, and received his letter the next week. His letter is a prime example of how a simple reply letter can turn into a fantastic letter of recommendation for a product. In the first paragraph of his letter he referred to my demonstration at the NRA convention. Technically I never gave a demo at that NRA convention only in the hotel, but the letter gives the impression and it works well to make the following statements in his letter even more impressive. His second paragraph is pure promotional rhetoric of the finest type. I ended up using the bulk of the second paragraph as a quote in almost every press release and promotional piece of material. You seldom can get that sort of endorsement without paying for it. People who knew of the Colonel's reputation took the fact that he was impressed with the device as strong evidence of its viability. The last paragraph showed readers of the letter that the POWER STAF was destined to be included in a noted author's book on the topic for which it was designed. This gave credibility to the device and helped raise hundreds of thousands of dollars of investment capital to continue the project. This is one of the best types of letters of recommendation, because it is genuine, enthusiastic and based upon the word of a publicly known professional in the field.

Letter 7: Chief Richard R. Ryan, Borough of Watchung Police Department. This was one of the very first Letters of Recommendation that I received about the POWER STAF product. It was still in the very initial and crude first prototype stage at the time it was presented to Chief Ryan. At this stage, the product shouldn't have been shown to potential end users because it was, in my opinion, far too crude. I contacted all the people in my "network" to request help in locating a friendly law enforcement official who would give me a letter based upon an honest evaluation on what the product could be, as opposed to an evaluation of the product as it was at its current stage. One of my contacts introduced me to Chief Ryan. The chief was a true professional law officer with many years of street experience. He agreed that the product (at that time) was not ready to be used by street officers in its current condition. But he could see past the prototype (with the help of artist renderings and descriptive literature) to a fully developed product that could be of great use to law enforcement. Based upon his reaction to the demonstration, I asked him for a letter with his views on the product as he viewed it in its final stage. The result was this letter. Chief Ryan, at my request, made

BOROUGH OF WATCHUNG

POLICE DEPARTMENT
Richard R. Ryan, *Chief*

August 25, 1982

Mr. Robert Gold, President
Neoteric
250 W. 57th Street, Suite 1502
New York, New York 10107

Dear Bob:

Thank you for your invitation to preview the Power Staf. I thoroughly enjoyed the company and was very impressed with your invention. The law enforcement community is constantly seeking to upgrade and modernize the tools of the trade. We are particularly concerned with weaponry and the need to develop non-lethal devices which accomplish our objective without unnecessary bloodshed. I am delighted to endorse the use of the Power Staf for a number of reasons:

1. An excellent non-lethal weapon for individual officers as well as a riot control device.

2. The Power Staf has a "deterrent burst" capability which is an excellent means for preventing situations from developing that could prove to be injurious to both the police officer and the perpetrator. This could prove to save enormous sums of money in downtime, overtime for replacement officers and medical disability.

3. The design of the Power Staf appears to make it virtually maintainance free.

4. The unit is light weight and has a minimal recoil. Can be used easily by officers on regular patrols, walking or mobile; and when not used in its power mode, doubles as a standard baton.

5. In my opinion, because of its versatility and relative low cost, the Power Staf will become standard equipment for law enforcement agencies throughout the country.

6. The Power Staf is the perfect weapon to use in many circumstances in which the use of a firearm is excessive and a baton is inadequate.

Congratulations and good luck in your future endeavors. I certainly hope you will continue to focus your many talents in the field of law enforcement.

Sincerely yours,

Richard R. Ryan
Chief of Police

RRR/eb1

10 Mountain Boulevard • Watchung, New Jersey 07060 • (201) 756-3663

sure to word the letter in a way that could be used for promotional purposes and as quotations. This letter was the spearhead of the product credentials for almost a year until the Phoenix Police Department and Applegate letters gave real backbone to the product's image.

Letter 8: Assistant Chief Donald D. Lozier, City of Phoenix Police Department. I had moved the company to Phoenix, Arizona, from New York City in the time between the Chief Ryan letter and the next real law enforcement endorsement of the product. In the interim, capital had been raised to go into research and development to develop a true preproduction prototype of the product. I knew that another infusion of law enforcement comments was due, but this time it had to be really hardline feedback that had some authority behind it. I called the Phoenix Police Department and requested a meeting with the chief to demonstrate a new product for his comments. The chief was not available, but I did receive an invitation from the Assistant Chief. When I arrived to do what I thought was a one-on-one meeting (like I had with Chief Ryan), I was shocked to find myself in front of a room of twenty of the top brass of the Phoenix Police Department. I tried to give the best presentation of the **POWER STAF** that I had ever done. I brought up everything that I could think of in relation to its operation, durability, maintenance and safety. After thirty minutes, I let each of the officials, much to their delight, take a turn operating the unit. At the end of the demonstration, I caught the Assistant Chief by himself and asked if it would be possible to get a letter of his comments on the product. I was careful not to ask for a letter of recommendation. That could have been seen as pushing him to endorse the product. The letter I received was more than I could have hoped for in response to that request. The Phoenix Police Department letter opened doors to many other law enforcement demonstrations around the country, as well as being a featured item (along with several other letters) in the company's press kit.

Letter 9: Alfred J. Baker, City of New York Police Department. This "thank you" letter also encompasses an acceptance by the NYPD to test and evaluate the product. This letter, although peppered with disclaimers about purchasing and withholding judgments on the product's usefulness to their department, is a good letter of reference. This is because the NYPD has a reputation for being conservative, hard-nosed, and slow to accept any change unless it is overwhelmingly proven to be to their extreme benefit. By accepting our invitation to demonstrate the product and then writing a letter like this, the NYPD had provided **POWER STAF** with an excellent public relations and promotional tool. This letter was circulated to various large police departments to show them that NYPD was interested enough to test the product, and to ask if they would like more details on how they could get some to test, evaluate and purchase. This type of letter, although seemingly noncommittal, can be used to your benefit if it is always viewed from its best possible angle.

Letter 10: Lt. Robert Scanlon, County of Bergen, Office of the County Prosecutor. Robert Scanlon, besides being a prolific writer, expert weapons trainer and detective par excellence, also happens to be my friend. I try not to impose too much on my friends for business purposes, but after four years of his observing the **POWER STAF** in development, I was very curious about

**CITY
OF
PHOENIX**

OFFICE OF THE POLICE CHIEF

June 9, 1983

Mr. Robert Gold
Neoteric, Inc.
Post Office Box 39276
Phoenix, Arizona 85069

Dear Mr. Gold:

Thank you for the presentation and demonstration of the
Power Staf on June 7, 1983. Neoteric, Inc., obviously put
a great deal of research and thought into the development
of such a unique non-lethal device. I and other members
of our staff were impressed with the Power Staf.

Some of the features that I particularly noticed were that
the K/A-1 is lightweight and well balanced, it appears to
be very durable, and would not require maintenance or
lubrication. It appears to be a very reliable device that
has considerable law enforcement application.

I will contact you in the near future as you approach your
production date.

Sincerely,

RUBEN B. ORTEGA
Police Chief

DONALD D. LOZIER
Assistant Police Chief
Investigations Division

pam

620 WEST WASHINGTON   v   PHOENIX, ARIZONA 85003   •   TELEPHONE (602) 262-6747

POLICE DEPARTMENT

NEW YORK, N.Y. 10038

P.D. 156-151

September 18, 1984

Sergeant Alfred J. Baker
C/O Emergency Service Unit
World's Fair Press Building
Flushing Meadow Park
Corona, New York 11368

Mr. Robert Gold
Director of Research and Development
Neoteric, Inc.
6622 North 57th Drive
Glendale, Arizona 85301

Dear Mr. Gold,
    Thank you for your most interesting demonstration of "Power Staf"
KA-1 (Kinetic Armament One) which you presented for members of our Department at the Outdoor Range on Wednesday, September 12, 1984.
    As indicated in our subsequent discussions, further evaluation
of the "Power Staf" will be required before a judgment can be rendered
relative to the usefulness of this equipment within the New York City
Police Department setting.
    Your offer of issuing the "Power Staf" to our Department, on a
trial basis, for use under actual field circumstances, may provide the
needed experience with which to base a future purchase decision upon.
The New York City Police Department would, of course, make no purchase
guarantees at this time. Should you, however, decide to take advantage of this opportunity, I would suggest the following distribution
of "Power Staf" units:
    - Emergency Service Unit - 4 units (to be assigned throughout the
      City on patrol)
    - Police Academy Firearms and Tactics Unit - 1 unit (for evalua-
      tion by qualified New York City Police Department Range instructors)
    - Police Academy Physical School - 1 unit (for evaluation in conjunc-
      tion with physical training activities)
    I would further suggest that the time period for the field evalu-
ation be of sufficient duration so as to allow for a myriad of possible
settings in which to apply the "Power Staf".
    Pending your reply, and on behalf of my Department, I wish to
say "Thank You" to you and the other members of your Company for your
informative demonstration and cordiality.

                                        Sincerely,

                                        Alfred J. Baker
                                        Sergeant

Office of the County Prosecutor
County of Bergen
HACKENSACK, NEW JERSEY 07601

(201) 646-2300

LARRY J. McCLURE
COUNTY PROSECUTOR

DENNIS CALO
FIRST ASSISTANT PROSECUTOR

January 12, 1987

To Whom It May Concern:

In 1982 my second book, "Law Enforcement Bible II," was published and released. Due to this new publication I again started to represent my publisher at police related shows throughout the United States.

In the spring of 1983 I represented my publisher at a "Non-lethal Weapons Association" show which was held in Clearwater, Florida. At this show I first met Mr. Robert Gold and observed his state of the art "Power Staf" in action. I had previously seen photos of and read about "Power Staf" but seeing is believing. The first demonstration I witnessed amazed me and indeed made me a believer. The subjects that volunteered to be hit with the weapon were immediately knocked off their feet and left somewhat dazed by the concussion. The amazing part of the demonstration was that the weapon put the subject into a position where they could be controlled by the police, while leaving no long term effects or causing physical injury.

I was not the only person at the demonstration who was impressed. Representatives from foreign countries and our own prison systems, both State and Federal, soon surrounded Mr. Gold's booth looking for further information on the "Power Staf."

Since 1983 I have run into Mr. Gold and his "Power Staf" at several other police shows, the last one in 1986 at Picatinney Arsenal in Dover, New Jersey and by the Department of Defence Police. Not only were the police who attended impressed, but also the Provost Marshal and his staff. They openly discussed how handy the "Power Staf" would be during a demonstration or riot at the prison stockade.

At several of these shows I was lucky enough to sit down and speak with Mr. Gold. He explained to me theories behind the "Power Staf" and its accessories as well as several other police related inventions.

After hearing about the "Power Staf" and its accessories, which triples its effectiveness, and knowing how all the police agencies throughout the free world are concerned about the misuse of deadly force which could cost them millions of dollars in a law suit, I felt that the area for sales of an effective non-lethal weapon such as the "Power Staf" are almost limitless. Some of these sales areas are agencies that man the prisons (local, state, federal), private security, mental institutions personnel, Riot control police units throughout the free world, and with accessories S.W.A.T. units.

If I can be of any further assistance in this regard, please feel free to contact me.

Sincerely,

LT. ROBERT SCANLON
Weapons Training Officer

his appraisal of the device. I asked him for a letter about the POWER STAF, because he was one of the few people I knew in the law enforcement field who was more qualified than myself to write about nonlethal weaponry. This letter of recommendation is possibly the ultimate marketing and sales tool. It is written by a professional with well-known, expert credentials, years of hands-on experience, and connections within the field of the product. To say I was pleased with his letter would be a vast understatement. To add the final element of credibility, he referred to me as "Mr. Gold" throughout the letter. This made it appear less like the recommendation of a personal friend and more like an objective evaluation. Don't get the wrong impression; he wasn't trying to deceive anyone. His letter was true and reflected his opinions, but it left out the personal element which might have confused many people as to his objectivity. If any of your close contacts offer to write a letter of recommendation for you, please indicate that this format would be the most advantageous for the both of you.

Letter 11: Warden James O'Sullivan, North American Association of Wardens. This letter is not quite a full letter of reference, but it has important elements that are crucial to career advancement using "stepping-stone" techniques described later in this book. The basis of this letter was a presentation I had given to a special luncheon of the North American Association of Wardens. I was attending their convention as a regular exhibitor to demonstrate the POWER STAF. While visiting our company booth, Warden (and past president of the association) James O'Sullivan expressed his desire to see a more "hands-on" demo of the product's capabilities and he said if I could do a presentation then he could guarantee to have a group of other wardens present from his area of the country. He immediately told me that "A"-group of wardens from the U.S. and Canada were having a special luncheon that afternoon and that he would get us time for a presentation if we could do it then. I saw that this was a promotional opportunity that could not be passed up and immediately agreed. We did a live demo of the POWER STAF (on a volunteer who agreed to sign liability waivers) on stage in front of 100-plus wardens from across North America. The demonstration was a major success, and we received numerous requests for more information. After the luncheon, I asked Warden O'Sullivan for a letter about his reaction to the product demo. He was very busy and asked me to contact him with a letter outlining my request. His letter is the result. His letter, like the letter from Col. Applegate, makes the events that transpired seem much more grand than they were in actuality. Although I was a speaker at the convention, it was an impromptu affair. His letter gives the impression that I was the scheduled speaker at the luncheon. He clearly indicates his reaction of being impressed with the product, and his request for more detailed product information gives the impression of a definite desire to investigate the product for purchase. His spreading of the information to the other members of the association via their newsletter is also an obvious endorsement of the product. This letter opened many doors for presentations to correctional facilities across the country. I also used it as an indication (and rightfully so) to other organizations that I was an interesting speaker who might be booked

North American Association of Wardens & Superintendents

10 September 1984

Mr. J. O'Sullivan
Past President
North American Association of Wardens
Post Office Box 160
Prince Albert, Sask.
Canada, S6V 5R6

Mr. Robert Gold
President
Neoteric Inc.
6622 North 57th Drive
Glendale, Arizona 85301

Dear Mr. Gold:

Thank you for your letter dated 24 August 1984. I was particularly impressed with your presentation at the Wardens' luncheon in San Antonio. As a result, I would like to receive additional information concerning prices, availability, quantity discount, and any additional information you have on Power Staf.

Additionally, I intend to include a copy of your letter in the next issue of Grapevine which is the North American Association of Wardens and Superintendents' quarterly newsletter. This will ensure the membership will have access to your product if they so desire.

J. O'Sullivan

J.O'S/ar

cc: NAAWS Exec.

to talk at their next function. I used this to "step-stone" into more public speaking engagements.

Letter 12: Tom Ashmore, Tom Ashmore Enterprises, Inc. This letter is by a professional law enforcement trainer who had a **POWER STAF** unit for evaluation. Tom Ashmore teaches cops all over the country in everything from high-rise rescue to tactical assault. He is a Vietnam War hero and former cop who turned his talents to training. He also has a company that sells the equipment with which he trains. And because of this, he is very selective about which equipment he will represent. I was very pleased when he accepted a **POWER STAF** for evaluation and immediately started showing it around to various agencies for their feedback. At my request, he provided my company with several letters like this one over a period of time. This type of second-level reference letter is sometimes more convincing to some people than information regarding demos you or your parent company may give. This type of letter states who saw it, when, under what circumstances and what they thought of the product. This letter also stated that sales could have been made immediately at the site (the possible order stated in this one letter were in the area of $50,000). This is the type of letter that is ideal for raising capital, because the investors see where their investment will be coming back from. The only thing better than a letter like this is a purchase order for the product.

All of these letters are part of a total image that you should strive to generate. Even if a product fails in the long run, the credentials established will make it a hundred times easier to get started on the next project. This is because letters such as these are part of a track record, which you will always have available to call upon. Every project, whether it's a winning or losing proposition, will create credentials that can become a vital part of marketing the next concept to come off your drawing board.

Let the world know that your idea exists...then sell it to them!

TOM ASHMORE ENT., INC.

Tactical Rope Rescue
and
Assault Specialists
Training-Equipment-Sales

93 Sand Pit Road
Danbury, CT 06810
203/775-2374

August 5, 1986

Mr. Robert Gold
Power Staff, Inc.
21617 North 9th Avenue
Phoenix, Arizona 85027

Dear Mr. Gold:

I am very pleased to write this letter to praise you on the
"Power Staff" I have for evaluation. On July 31st, I held a training
session for the prison authority at Somers Correctional Facility
in Connecticut. Present were representatives from Springfield Correctional
Facility, Springfield, Mass., Woodbourne Correctional Facility for
the State of New York, along with a scattering of representatives
of both local and state police.

I had an overwhelming response to the "Power Staff". Without
exaggeration, we could have taken orders for 75 to 100 units, with
the most asked question, "when can we expect delivery"?

You have a wonderful product there and I would suggest that
you start production soon.

Sincerely,

Tom Ashmore

TA/lr

Encl. 1

Chapter 12

Creating and Building Your Image

Nothing great was ever achieved without enthusiasm.

—Emerson

 As an entrepreneurial inventor you must project three images to the public. You must have a company image, an inventor's image and a product image. These three images can be very different, and they must accomplish a variety of goals.

The *company image* is how you want your company to be perceived by the world at large. Your company may have a high-tech image or a down-to-earth image, but that image will represent the company in every instance where it will have a public "face." The logo, business cards and stationery of your company will reflect the type of image that you want to project for the company as a whole. Part of the company image is the company name. A company name that is specific to a single invention may limit you when it comes to future products, unless they are related to the initial invention. A more generic company name is best if you wish to branch out at a later time.

The *inventor image* can be completely different, but it doesn't necessarily have to be different. Your inventor image is how you want the world to perceive you as an individual. This can be as a serious individual or as a crazy inventor. Your inventor image can sometimes affect the company image, so you must be careful to separate the two if they are not compatible. You may have a lovable, free-wheeling image, while your company may have a stern, high-tech image. This may not be a problem if the two images can be played off against each other in a way that is beneficial to the overall plan. Your

200

image is something to be considered carefully, because it can remain with you for the balance of your career. A thoughtful, high-tech type of image can be supplemented with some of the whimsy of a crazy inventor-type more readily than the opposite case.

The *product image* is the way a particular product is viewed by the public. The company and its inventor may have great images, but a product can have a tainted image for many reasons. This can, in time, reflect upon the company, but usually not upon the inventor. On the other hand, if a product is a fantastic success and is readily accepted by the public, you, as the inventor, can get even more personal acclaim and attention than your company. Various product images have specific overtones (i.e. children's play toys, high tech war machines), yet all can be produced by the same parent company and inventor. By manipulating the product image, a company and an inventor can dabble in several diversified fields with no problem.

The company image is probably the most important of the three images in the beginning of your career. It is something that can make or break a small inventor. Your public face can make the difference in matters such as investment and credibility with important resources not related to cash flow. A company image that has an air of prestige and stability is the best that can be accomplished by the small, independent inventor.

Creating Your Company Name and Logo

Selecting a good name and logo can be a hard task, even for the fertile mind of an inventor. The name is often the easy part. Many inventors will use part of their name in the title of the business. I chose this route with the creation of *GoldMind Associates*. Many others will look to descriptive words about their area of inventing or to the general genre of creativity. Names like *Creative _____*, *Inventive _____*, or *_____ Technologies* are common choices for inventors. Whatever name you choose, it should reflect your personal outlook on what you are doing with inventive talents.

A logo is a graphic symbol or words and graphic symbol that represent a company. We are all familiar with famous logos such as the Coca-Cola wave or the Playboy rabbit. A logo brings a certain image to mind. Companies work hard at creating that image via advertising and promotional efforts.

Your logo can be almost anything, but it should reflect the way you and your company want to be seen. Your product may have a logo all of its own or be directly connected to the logo of the company. Whatever the logo, it should be simple, very clean and visually specific.

I will use my company's image as an example of an invention company name and logo. When I started my consulting firm, its basic goal was to (a) develop my ideas for sale to other companies and (b) develop ideas under contract for outside firms. I chose *GoldMind* as the basic name because it linked my name *GOLD* with the company. *GOLD* also is a precious material, is extremely flexible, ageless and universally accepted as a form of wealth. I added MIND because all the creative talent for the company flowed from my mind. Also, the word mind has connotations of intellect and problem solving ability. The mind is the hub of the thought process, and it is a complex organ. The two work together to create subliminal projection of flexible and complex thought and universal and precious problem solving abilities. Not all company logos need to have significance past getting your company name across and remembered.

Your logo will appear on all letters and product information and because of this should be easy to recognize. It should definitely not offend or be confusing. The logo will have the responsibility of staying in the minds of the public.

The *GoldMind Associates* logo is simple. Three arrows moving upward with a single arrow breaking through all the lines and going off to the right. This is visually specific and confers the ability to break from the lines of conventional thought, to break from the crowd, to think and move in new and multiple dimensions.

When you, the newly established entrepreneurial inventor, consider your logo, you should make sure to take all the factors of your experience, field of endeavor and future direction for the company into consideration. Most of all, have fun. Creating a company image can be an exiting experience.

Image-Building Tips and Techniques

The following list is a compendium of ideas to keep in mind when establishing yourself as a credible, working inventor and establishing your company as a stable operating entity.

1. *Form affiliations with other small businesses in the inventing field.* This should include one or more:

a. *Model Makers.* Model makers are craftsmen who can fabricate models and prototypes from an inventor's conceptual writings and drawings.

b. *Patent Attorneys.* Patent attorneys are attorneys who represent inventors in the pursuit of patent protection for ideas.

c. *Graphic Artists.* Graphic artists are illustrators who can shape the image of an your ideas by creating realistic presentation art and brochures.

d. *Industrial Designers.* Industrial designers are designers and engineers who can help refine your concepts into the most precise prototype or production format.

e. *Electronic Engineers.* Electronic engineers are engineers who are capable of creating the electronic circuitry to make many electronic inventions come to life.

f. *Mold Makers.* Mold makers are craftsmen who create the precision molds that form the body and framework of modern, plastic-encased inventions.

g. *Attorneys and Accountants.* Attorneys and accountants are basic functional elements of any active business enterprise.

The idea behind these affiliations is twofold. First, to have a "network" of contacts to call upon for help in any given situation. Second, to be able to make presentations to investors, potential clients, and others, so that you can appear to be a "team" rather than a single individual. The "Associates" in GoldMind Associates is an independent, but structured group of professionals whom I can call upon to do contract work for my inventing enterprises. Sometimes they are a formal team who share part of the percentages in an idea. And sometimes they are piece workers who only do a small part of a task under contract. The arrangement works in a smooth fashion, because I organize it as needed on a project-by-project basis.

2. *Impress people and companies inexpensively by putting your image capital where it will do the most good.* The following is a list of image-making components that most small inventors can assemble to create a basic, overall "glow of prestige" that investors, media and manufacturers will notice. Even a good inventor and his company can look shabby without these elements. They include:

a. *Professional letterhead.* In this age of desktop publishing, this is a basic and inexpensive component of creating a company image. The company image and product image may be represented on the company stationery with a logo or motto. The inventor image should *not* be represented on the company letterhead. If you want to have your own personal letterhead, then the inventor's image may be represented with a picture or logo of your own, although this is not recommended.

b. *Raised-lettering business cards.* These are also a basic and inexpensive component of creating a company image. Business cards should indicate what field the company is in, who's card it is, and how he or she can be contacted, always include telephone and fax numbers. Business cards are paper introductions and should not be advertisements.

c. *A business address.* A post office box will suffice for a business address if you do not have an office or wish to keep your enterprise separate from other business you are conducting. You should list the box number as a "suite" number, if possible, to give the business more credibility. This can be done if the box is located at a commercial mail box company. You should never use your home address if at all possible, because it may come up later that the two addresses, home and business are the same. This looks less professional than having a business address. However, working out of the home is a common practice for full- and part-time independent inventors. There is nothing wrong with it, but it is not something that should be advertised. By having a separate business address, two things are achieved: the enterprise seems more solid to investors, the media, vendors and end users; and you are allowed to have a private home life without every person who has a business card or letter from the company knowing where to find you at any hour of the day or night.

d. *Company/personal history sheet.* The company/personal history sheet acts as your brochure. A sample is presented later in this chapter. A personal history sheet is an example of how an inventor can promote himself or herself with a simple, one-page sheet. It gives people the image of how he or she wants to be perceived. A company history sheet can be set up the same way. You may want to integrate a company and personal history sheet for maximum impact and effectiveness, but this depends upon its intended audience.

e. *Answering service or telephone answering machine.* The use of an answering machine is so commonplace in today's business world that every inventor must have one (unless there is sufficient cash flow to warrant a live answering service). If at all possible, use an answering service for the human touch. A machine can get people annoyed after a while. Also, an answering service will be able to: (a) get more information from people than they are willing to leave on a machine; and (b) provide important contacts with information that you have for them. The best situation is when you can afford a regular secretary or assistant to answer your telephone.

f. *Professional product drawings.* This is the artwork that you should have created by a professional graphic artist. This artwork will represent the product when you are doing dog-and-pony shows for investors, the media and end users. This same artwork is often used in product brochures and other advertisements.

g. *Product prototype.* You should strive to have some sort of product prototype available to show the public. A prototype is one of the most powerful tools available for convincing people that a product is viable. The use of mock-ups or other non-working display models is preferable to only having drawings available.

h. *Letters of reference.* These are letters from end users, potential end users, associates and contacts who have reviewed the invention. These letters should contain positive information about you, the product or the company. The information from these letters is used to help promote you or your product during all phases of development.

i. *Press releases/articles.* Press releases and articles that have been published about you, your invention or your company should be kept in a portfolio for promotional use during all levels of the product development. If the information is in the form of TV coverage, then a videotape portfolio should also be made.

j. *Industry or government statistics.* Industry or government statistics often prove the case for your product. All verifiable statistics and studies which prove the case for an invention should be kept in a single source report for presentation to end users, media and investors. This information forms the backbone for marketing at all levels of your product's development.

3. *Don't be afraid of projecting a powerful company image. Think big and act big.* General George Patton once wrote, "Nothing is impossible, provided you use audacity." The concept is more than valid in hundreds of cases where bold individuals have brazened their way to the top of their fields. You must have total confidence in your product and your course of action. When you behave confidently, it causes others to have the same feeling instilled in them. People will be willing to go a little further for what they perceive as a winning idea and a winning personality. It is said that "investors don't invest in ideas, they invest in people." By projecting an air of confidence in the invention and in a course of action, many inventors have gone far with only marginal ideas.

4. *A professional image that looks expensive doesn't always have to be expensive.* You can look good at meetings by having them at rented "executive suites" complete with audio-visual equipment and secretarial personnel. You may only own one good suit, but make sure it looks like it was tailor-made for you. People will assume it's just one of many in your closet. Don't be afraid to borrow or rent a luxury car to pick up that important contact at the airport. As long as you manage to create a lasting image, the short-term expenses will be well worth the effort.

5. *Connect yourself with the right associates.* Check out those people with whom you associate your business. If they have a good reputation, it can go a long way toward helping you establish the same. If they have reputations as scoundrels and con men, steer clear or the taint from the association could stay with your company for a long time. Cultivate business contacts with members of the local Chamber of Commerce, with civic groups and other professional organizations. You can create a great network this way, as well as being seen with a hard-working and upwardly mobile crowd. People will take notice of you and your inventions when you're seen with the right crowd.

6. *Don't let your professional image have a shy, backseat attitude.* If you don't toot your company horn, then few others, if any, will toot it for you. You must leverage your track record into as many opportunities as possible. Draw upon any success to get your venture off the ground. Anything from a steady work history to any achievement which has the slightest bearing on your ability to complete your inventive project should be highlighted and used to full advantage.

7. *Don't be shy about getting people to talk about you, or better yet, to write about you and your company.* Take full advantage of any opportunity for publicity and promotion. Remember, you're an inventor and you have an invention company! You're on the cutting edge of new ideas and new products. The rest of the world is waiting to hear what your company's next press release will unveil. So if you can't generate others' verbiage about you and your company, do it yourself with press releases, announcements, and other items. The basics of press releases are examined later in this chapter.

Basics of the Personal History Sheet

The *Personal History Sheet* (PHS) is a standard tool of self-promotion for inventors. The PHS is used to give the world at large an overview of who you are, what you have done, and what your invention is all about. A personal history sheet is different from a press release in that the information is not news, it is history. The PHS forms the basis on which many different people and companies will view you and your abilities.

Your personal history sheet should contain the following elements:

    a. *Opening line.* The opening line should tell people right away who you are today. This may include a professional title, such as engineer, or a descriptive title, such as entrepreneur. But the most important information to include is that you are an INVENTOR.

    b. *Personal background.* This should give the reader a glimpse of what made you who you are. This may include where you were born and raised, if you feel it is applicable, where you currently live, what schools you attended and what special honors were bestowed upon you. You may want to use information from press coverages to portray yourself via the quotes of others.

    c. *Business background.* This should show what areas of expertise you have attained through your business experiences. This information should also show your background as it pertains to your invention or creative abilities.

    d. *Creative capabilities.* This information is about any articles you've written or other pieces of energy that you have generated.

    e. *Where and what you are now.* The PHS should end with a summation of your life as it is today.

The PHS is a basic tool that can be used whenever you want to give a certain reader a look at who you are from your point of view. It can be used in the following ways for raising capital and leveraging your invention experience into other opportunities:

    1. When sending out proposals to investors, to give them a feel for who you are and what you have already accomplished.

    2. When sending out query letters to editors. When you are seeking writing assignments, it is always good to let the editor have a feel for who you are and what your experiences have been in relation to the article you want to write.

    3. When seeking consulting work, the company that hires you will want to know if your experience is compatible with the work they want you to do.

You should update this personal history sheet every time some important event happens that affects the course of your career. Minor changes should not be included unless they are crucial to understanding the greater overview of your background.

Remember, once a PHS is written, it establishes a certain background for you. New things may be added, but the basic facts as first sent out should never be altered. Take heed of this Turkish proverb: *Measure a thousand times and cut once.*

Think a thousand times about how you want the public to perceive you, then write it and send it out. A quick way to lose credibility is for investors, editors, manufacturers or any source for them to get hold of information conflicting with a PHS about an inventor's background.

When used correctly, the PHS can lay the groundwork for good media attention, good investor relations and enhanced credibility in the marketplace. A sample PHS is shown on the next page. It shows how to structure a quickly read and interesting personal profile.

Press Release Basics for the Entrepreneurial Inventor

 A press release is a one-page announcement of news that is sent out to the media. Use it when you have taken a concept to the point where you need to start generating publicity and promotional efforts to market the product. Press releases are also used to announce any newsworthy event in which you or your new product participate.

Ten Guidelines for Press Releases

There are ten basic guidelines for setting up a press release. If you follow these guidelines, the media will pay more attention to your information and will work with you toward your media goals. They are:

1. *Format.* The release should be on plain, 8.5-by-11 inch paper. Keep the length of the release to one page. Leave a three-inch margin at the top of the page. Place the source of the release in the upper left-hand corner of the page (within the 3-inch margin). This should contain the name, address and telephone number of the person to contact for further information (and a FAX number, if available). The contact person may be you or someone who is handling your public relations (PR) efforts. Place the release date, typed in capital letters, slightly below the source information, but on the opposite (right side) of the page.

2. *The recipient.* Keep your listing of news publications up to date, with the proper names of the editors. Media people like to get releases mailed to them, not the last person who had their job. To show them you are up-to-date and thorough in your release preparation, look on the masthead of the publication for the correct name and spelling. If that information is not available, call the paper or magazine and ask for the appropriate editor's name (make sure to verify spelling).

Robert J. Gold
Personal History Sheet
Updated Jan 1, 1994

Robert J. "Rob" Gold is an *Inventor, Writer, Speaker and Entrepreneur.* Born and raised in New York City, he moved to the Southwest in 1982. In 1983, the Arizona Republic called him "an inventive dynamo," and his inventions and work have been the topic of several newspaper columns, articles and television news spots around the country. Gold has been listed in four different editions of Who's Who since 1987.

From 1986 to 1988 Robert J. Gold was a contributing editor to Law Enforcement Technology magazine where he originated and authored his own column, "Less Than Lethal." He has also written various articles on topics ranging from nuclear security to counter-terrorist training for other major domestic and international law enforcement publications. Gold has been a featured speaker at several national conferences including The American Defense Preparedness Association, The North American Association of Wardens and The Tactical Response Association.

Robert J. Gold has been responsible for the creation of several major new concepts in law enforcement and counter-terrorist equipment. He is the inventor of the *Power Staf System,* a self-defense and riot-control device for security and corrections officers. Gold is also the founder of **FACTS, Inc.** (*First American Counter Terrorist Systems*) and the inventor of America's most advanced stun grenade, *The Shockwave.* He holds patents in numerous countries on less-than-lethal equipment and was a charter member of The American Society of Law Enforcement Trainers (ASLET).

Among the numerous product and business concepts that Gold has created and marketed was the national radio talk show publication, **TALKOUT** Magazine. Through the publicity of *TALKOUT,* Gold appeared as a guest on over 100 radio talk shows across the country. His advocacy of inventor's rights and protection from invention marketing scams earned him high praise from the media and the business community.

Gold currently operates several successful businesses from his Austin, Texas headquarters. Among his endeavors are **GoldMind Associates,** a consulting firm that works with the public and private sectors in the areas of new product research, development and marketing; and **RAD Ventures Inc.**, a research and marketing firm specializing in the development of entertainment media and interactive products.

Gold's latest venture is **Off World Laboratories, Inc.(OWL Inc.),** a research and marketing firm specializing in the development of **VTV**™(*Very Thin Video*™), a new technology in which Gold is a co-inventor. This project may revolutionize the world of video with micro thin screens that can be made into pocket sized personal units that play back digitally recorded videos, to wall sized screens playing high definition signals.

Robert J. Gold has been a professional inventor for more than twenty years. Currently, Gold uses that experience to teach a course on inventing, *"Practical Inventing Workshop,"* at the *University of Texas* at Austin. In 1990 he self published his first book, **Ideas Equal Income: The Entrepreneurial Inventing System**. The manuscript was purchased in 1991 by America's foremost business publisher, Prentice Hall. It will be published in spring 1994 under the title **EUREKA: The Entrepreneurial Inventor's Guide to Developing, Protecting and Profiting from Your Ideas**.

GoldMind Associates, 21407 Mopac N. 100, #191, Austin, TX 78758 (512) 837-9270
  Off World Laboratories, Inc., 8920 Business Park Dr. Austin, TX 78579

3. *The title.* Sum up the most important elements of the release in a headline. The headline should be all in capitals and centered on the page below the dateline. Underline for effect.

4. *The type.* All releases should be typed double-spaced with wide side margins for editor's notes. Doing the release on a computer and having it laser-printed will give the release a professional look.

5. *The content.* Make sure you cover all the most important journalistic elements in the first paragraph of the release. These elements are: who, what, where, when, how and why (not necessarily in that order). Place the most important and exciting element at the lead of the story. Avoid very technical language, unless the release is aimed at a highly technical market.

6. *The look.* Use a good grade of paper. It doesn't have to be white, but stay in the warm colors. A colored stock may help you stand out on an editor's desk. Don't ever send out a press release that has the look of a mass-produced COPY!

7. *The timing.* Find out in advance the lead time that your contact wants for information. Send it when they want it and can use it. Try to link your release to other timely news if possible. Only send out press releases when they are appropriate and advantageous to your marketing efforts. Sending out releases prematurely will not help you, and you will not get the media attention a second time when you do need it.

8. *The truth.* Don't try to pass off non-original material as exclusive. Lying in a press release can be the kiss of death for any future media coverage. The media is a small industry: word gets around.

9. *The news.* Don't try to make an advertisement of a press release. Editors will see through this in a minute and not give you any press coverage at all. The information must be fascinating for the readers. It must make the reader want to know more about the product, or you, the inventor. Try to make it as newsworthy as possible. Give the story a unique twist to get the editor to print the item. Give the reader an additional source to contact for more information. This can be another company involved with your product or an end user. Make sure you okay this with the second source person, in advance.

10. *The end.* After the release information, place "END" or "-30-" centered below the last line to indicate that this is the end of the release.

(See Appendix III for sample Press Release.)

Ensuring That Your Press Release Gets Attention

You can follow several simple rules to ensure that your press release gets the attention it deserves. These rules are:

    a. If the press release concerns a dog-and-pony show, be sure to include accurate information on where it will be held, when it will be held, and the nature of your demonstration. Make sure the information gets to the publication or news service in plenty of time for publication. Check with each media source to see what sort of lead time they need to make use of your information.

b. Editors usually cut a press release from the bottom and work upward, so make sure the most important information is spelled out clearly in the first paragraph of the press release.

c. Follow all rules of format. Editors are creatures of habit when it comes to accepting press release information. If your press release is out of format, it may be overlooked for what it is and not get you any media attention.

If you have done your homework, you should know the publication you are trying to get the press release into, you should have formatted the release correctly, and you should actually have news to offer. Then the press release is one of the best ways to generate usable publicity. Always remember that once something is news, it is never news again! Time press release information to do the greatest good, because it may be a one-time event for that particular news angle on a product or project.

Chapter 13

Marketing Your Invention and You All the Way to the Bank

There is no profit
to have learned well
if you neglect to do well.
—Publilius Syrus

 Entrepreneurial inventors of the 1990s are called upon, by the very nature of their chosen profession, to be multitalented individuals. As part of that cross-section of talents, you need to have a little showmanship within your makeup to realize your own potential. This chapter is devoted to equipping you with the basic information that allows you to let the world know who you are and what it is you have to offer.

This chapter is not meant to give you a definitive way to market and sell your invention. That would be self-defeating. Every invention is different, and every inventor's situation requires a unique approach to the overall question of publicity and market penetration.

Public and Private Marketing Resources

 There are many ways for you to market and sell your invention. The usual routes include direct mail, personal sales, agents, middlemen and distributors. Each one of these avenues has its benefits and pitfalls. The deciding factor in most cases is: Who is manufacturing the product?

If you are the manufacturer, then the options are open and depend upon the financial structure of your company and the type of product you are trying

211

to market. If the invention is a small, personal item, then direct mail and personal sales are viable options.

Personal sales are effective at the smallest level, but if you are trying to make a living doing this, you should consider that it will take almost all of your time. Therefore, plan to transform your career from that of inventing to that of sales. For this reason, I usually recommend that personal sales by inventors should be done only at the investment and dog-and-pony show levels. After that, let someone else do the selling of your product.

Marketing is another matter. I feel you can keep your hand in the marketing end of the project, if you are directly tied to the company selling the product. If you sell your invention to another company, your role in sales and marketing activities, however, may be limited or eliminated.

Direct Marketing

If you want to market your product directly (e.g., through printed ads in magazines and newspaper or by radio and TV ads), plenty of help is available. Open up the Yellow Pages, and you will find a number of direct marketing companies in your area. If you wish to direct market your product, here are some very simple resources.

The best source is the Direct Marketing Association (DMA). The DMA has almost 5,000 members and is made up of manufacturers, wholesalers, mail-order firms, publishers, advertising agencies and other entities with a vested interest in direct marketing. The DMA can offer you a host of information on getting started in the direct marketing of a product. Contact the Direct Marketing Association, 6 East 43rd Street, New York, NY 10017 or call 212-689-4977.

Another interesting direct marketing approach is the radio talk-show circuit. If you've created a product that has mass appeal, is interesting to talk about, and is fairly inexpensive to purchase, you may have the elements needed to do direct marketing over the radio. This is easier than it sounds. There are more than 5,000 radio stations in the United States. Radio talk shows are always looking for interesting guests to fill their air time.

One of the best ways to get a station's attention is through a unique magazine concept called *Radio-TV Interview Report* (RTIR). RTIR is targeted at all of the 5,000-plus stations across the country. It also goes to the hundreds of TV interview programs. Many of the radio talk shows will allow you to be interviewed over the telephone, which gives you the freedom of not leaving your home or office, yet still promoting your product. Thus, this type of marketing is very inexpensive. The interview acts as a free advertisement for your product, service, or book. You can capitalize on this exposure by having an 800 number set up to accept instant orders direct from the radio station listeners. I feel this is one of the best, least-expensive and most innovative direct marketing systems that anyone can use to promote a product. This system works best with books and items priced under $20. Contact RTIR in Lansdown, Pennsylvania, at 215-259-1070.

Manufacturers' Agents

You may want to get wider distribution and faster sales than direct sales options offer. Using agents and distributors is one way to do this, but first you must locate them. An important organization to contact for names of manufacturers' agents is the Manufacturers' Agents National Association (M.A.N.A., P.O. Box 3467, 23016 Mill Creek Rd., Laguna Hills, CA 92654; call 714-859-4040). This organization has almost 8,000 members who represent two or more manufacturers on a commission basis. The organization can direct a small business to local and national agents who might be interested in selling a new product. They can also help supply paperwork to get the business relationship set up between the business and the agent.

Trade Shows and Conventions

One of the most enjoyable and rewarding experiences that you can have as an inventor is direct feedback from end users in the marketplace. One way to get market exposure and feedback at the same time is to show an invention at a trade show or convention. Be forewarned: trade shows and conventions are expensive, even on a local level. You should expect to pay for booth space, all booth furniture, lighting costs, electric power (if needed) and a host of other miscellaneous charges that seem to come with every show. The cost of even a local, small show can top $1,000 for a two-day exhibit. Larger and longer shows can run into the thousands of dollars between the exhibit space, travel, and expenses.

Another expense is that you must print up and give away a large quantity of brochures on your product without the slightest guarantee of any financial return from any of the people at the show. Although some shows allow you to take orders on the convention floor, very few ever allow actual cash to change hands.

Also, be prepared to stand on your feet and talk for eight to twelve hours a day. Talking about your ideas is great when it's to a small group of friends or to a business associate, but at a trade show, you must be prepared to say the same thing over and over again...hundreds of times, to people who will ask the most inane questions about your product. If your patience wears thin easily, have someone else do your trade show presentations.

If trade shows don't scare you, then there are many types of conventions in which you might want to participate. The two most important are *invention shows* and *trade shows*.

The *invention show* is a convention put on exclusively for inventors to show their new products. Many inventor organizations produce these shows on a regular basis. Contact the various inventor organizations in your area for details. The Patent and Trademark Office holds a yearly Inventor's Conference and Exposition, as mentioned in Chapter 5. There is usually a charge for the booth space and other expenses related to participating in these shows. Many large and small companies come to these shows to get new products to market and sell. NOTE: Never show an unpatented device at any type of invention show. The idea may be pirated.

The largest and best invention convention is *The Invention Convention* produced by Invention Services International in Los Angeles. The convention is the brainchild of inventor champion Stephen Gnass. Held yearly since 1987, the convention brings inventors, investors, licensees, manufacturers, the media and the public together to form a fantastic synergy found nowhere else. Inventors can make deals, get publicity, test the market and generally promote their product or concept in a pro-invention atmosphere. *The Invention Convention* includes seminar programs featuring more than 50 experts covering all aspects of the invention process. For details, call 800-4589-5624 or 213-460-4408.

Trade shows are conventions held within a specific industry. Consult the Encyclopedia of Associations to locate the appropriate industry organization for your product. The information will list the trade shows and their yearly dates. Contact the association about requirements to get a booth at the convention. This is the best way to introduce a new product to end users in a specific industry. Working a trade show allows for instant feedback and sales leads. Some shows are geared toward the buyers for an industry, while others are geared toward the movers and shakers. Knowing who will be at a conference will allow you to gear your printed material and product talks toward the proper market end.

Another major source of information on trade shows is the *Trade Show and Professional Exhibits Directory* produced by Gale Research publications company of Detroit, Michigan.

Possibly the best source of up-to-the-minute information on trade and professional shows, however, is the organization called *Meeting Planners International* (MPI). MPI is an international trade organization that specializes in large-scale professional meetings and trade shows. Their members span the entire spectrum of industry. MPI can be contacted at 1950 North Stemmons Freeway, Dallas, TX 75207 or 214-712-7700.

Government Marketing Support

The Department of Commerce (DOC) is extremely helpful to all small businesses when it comes to getting a product marketed, both domestically and internationally.

One of the best ways to break into an international market is through the use of the DOC resource called *Commercial News USA*. This publication is distributed ten times a year through all U.S. embassies and commercial outlets. A quarter-page ad costs only $250 but will reach more than 100,000 agents, distributors and buyers in 140 countries. This is a fantastic value that works better than you can hope to expect. For example, I advertised my *POWER STAF* product in *Commercial News USA* once and received more than 400 international inquiries for sales representation, distribution and direct sales. Contact the DOC at Export Awareness Division, U.S. and Foreign

Commercial Service, ITA, Department of Commerce, Rm. 2106, Washington, DC 20230.

The DOC also provides catalog and video exhibitions at U.S. embassies on a regular basis. These events are shows where any company wishing for international exposure can have its brochures, catalogs, and videotapes distributed to potential foreign buyers. There is a fee for this service. Contact the Catalog and Video Catalog Exhibition Program, Department of Commerce, Rm. 2119, Washington, DC 20230.

The DOC conducts export seminars periodically around the US. These seminars cover a variety of topics ranging from one-day introductory export seminars to multi-session how-to programs. Contact the Office of Domestic Operations, U.S. and Foreign Commercial Service, ITA, Department of Commerce, Rm. 3810, Washington, DC 20230.

If you want to get aggressive about international marketing, the DOC has foreign importers lists of individuals and companies that want to buy goods manufactured in the U.S. These lists contain the names and addresses of manufacturers, agents, distributors and potential end users of American products or services. The lists span at least 130 countries and are available by industry classification. Contact the Export Services Branch, Office of Trade Information Services, ITA, Department of Commerce, Rm. 1312, Washington, DC 20230.

Every product will present its own unique set of marketing problems. You must remember two key concepts, however, to ensure the success of any project: (1) find expert advice at each step and (2) look at problems as opportunities. When these points are kept in mind, the marketing possibilities expand in every direction.

Also, always keep in mind that market is *everything* to a product. If you make sure the product is targeted at the correct market section, the market will reward your efforts. Remember, every idea can become income, if it is marketed correctly. So, get as many of your great ideas out on the market as you can and begin to enjoy the fruits of your labor.

Stepping Stones to New Careers as an Inventor

 During my years as an entrepreneurial inventor, I have had the opportunity to change directions many times. Each one of these new opportunities has arisen because of serendipity and what I call the "Stepping Stone Technique." I envision career opportunities as large and small stones that rise up through the river of life, which I am crossing. Some people never have the courage to step from one stone to the next and end up standing in the same place for years. Others lose their balance on their one small stone and get washed away down the river, toward an unknown future for which they have no abilities and have made no preparations.

By using the Stepping Stone Technique, you can take control of your life and make a future that has great potential. You also can create fallback positions which you can rely on for income and contacts if things go wrong.

There are five basic stepping stones that you can create to give you more maneuvering room in your career as an entrepreneurial inventor. These steps are: (1) consulting, (2) writing, (3) research and development, (4) self-promotion, and (5) networking. Each of these steps is a pursuit with its own set of rewards and opportunities. Each can be pursued individually or in conjunction with others. A truly successful entrepreneurial inventor may be able to incorporate all five. Let's look at the opportunities offered by each one.

 Consulting. Many of your inventor contacts will look to you for help in developing a new idea. Even if you are just starting out, you should look for opportunities to involve yourself in the crisis-management activities of your contacts. Offer to help them find unique solutions to their problems. This often can be done in the form of one of the other stepping-stone techniques, such as research and development or writing. Seek out businesses where you see that you can offer information or technology that will help them solve a problem. Make sure that any successful consulting work results in a letter of reference and a fee. Sometimes, a fee can be waived, in return for something else, such as free publicity for your business or services from a contact.

In the course of developing several law enforcement devices, I approached a number of companies with new ideas on how to develop their products into a better line of equipment. I didn't ask them to hire me or buy my ideas. I offered them my consulting expertise on the basis that if their product could be improved by my ideas, then increased sales would result and that would indicate my value to the company. Once this happened, I would then expect to receive a consulting fee equal to a predetermined percentage of the increased revenues.

My ideas were successful, and the companies did pay me. Very soon, they asked to start paying me a regular retainer to have access to other ideas I had.

Consulting usually doesn't occupy your full time on one project, so it is possible to generate several revenue streams simultaneously. You will also make a number of contacts who can help network your consulting talents to other companies.

Once you have established yourself as a new-product consultant in any specific field, you will be positioned to move on to the next—and possibly largest—stepping stone: writing.

 Writing. You will do considerable research in the areas where you are trying to invent, and this research often can be the basis for starting a writing career. You can start by writing free articles for newsletters and trade journals in the field of the invention. If that field also happens to be the field where you now work, then you have a head start on the process, because you already have some established credentials. If you don't yet have established credentials, getting some articles published is a quick way to gain them. Writing will expose you to many people and businesses. You never know who will read your work and contact you about what you have written. This can lead to consulting work and other writing assignments. You can get consulting work by approaching companies where your articles will create interest. You can offer to write articles about their products in return for a consulting fee. As you gain expertise in a field, you can start to write for money for the field's publications. The best of both worlds happens when a company pays you to write about their product, and a magazine is paying you for the articles you submit. Writing fees also can be bartered for publicity, products, and other perks.

Developing your writing talents can lead to ventures in other fields well outside the original field of your efforts. My writing efforts led me to create this book, which, in turn, has helped me get onto radio and TV programs. This chain of events started more than eight years ago, when I wrote an initial article for a trade magazine. Since then, I have written nonfiction articles that have been published in many countries around the world.

Research and Development. As an inventor, you can easily approach companies or individuals and ask to do research and development for them. This is especially so if you have established a track record through writing and consulting, as well as inventing. You may also be able to sell your own independent research efforts, if you have uncovered some documentation or created a database that has value to others. Independent research demonstrates initiative on your part, as well as insight into a given problem or field. You can use your findings to land a consultancy or convince a magazine to let you write an article.

Self-Promotion. As an entrepreneurial inventor, you must be in a self-promotion mode at all times. Self-promotion is especially useful when trying to find investors for a concept or when trying to promote your ideas, as well as yourself. Self-promotion can take the form of writing, consulting, or public speaking at any type of conference or gathering. Self-promotion can give you access to a variety of fields. Keep a professional scrapbook of all of your articles, speaking-engagement announcements, and any newspaper or magazine coverage on yourself or your products (see Chapter 11). Also keep videotapes of any air time that you or your products get. You can use these tools to convince prospective clients of your talents and worth to them.

Press releases, personal history sheets, and product brochures are all part of the inventor's self-promotion tool kit. Use them liberally to get your name and products known.

Using Publicity and Promotion to Your Advantage

Publicity and promotion are at the heart of making money with an invention, but you can use them only have you are well-prepared to take advantage of your possible market.

Everything you have learned up to this point are stepping-stones to the doorway of financial opportunity. Even if you just license your invention and walk away from it, you will have had to become involved in the process of promoting and marketing the concept. The brainstorming of the initial product, the dog-and-pony shows used to generate first investment, the creation of presentation artwork, the preparation of disclosure documents and patent applications are all elements that allow you to finally bring your product to the attention of the marketplace.

The methods for publicizing and promoting your product are relatively simple, yet sophisticated. They involve the development of promotional paperwork and the knowledge of how to use it. Publicity and promotion also involve knowing how to meet and deal with people in a vast cross-section of personal and business situations. In Chapter 10, you learned how to develop a network of contacts that will help you manage and manipulate the events surrounding your invention's progress in the marketplace. Now, you need to learn how to use that network to promote and publicize your product. The following is some basic information on many publicity, promotion, and marketing opportunities that are available in the public and private sectors.

Understanding the World of Publicity and Promotion

Getting publicity and promotion (P&P) is an important part of entrepreneurial inventing. Generating your own publicity and promotion is a continuous project that always requires new ideas. It can be one of the most enjoyable or frustrating things that you can undertake. When it works out right, it can be very satisfying and emotionally gratifying. You must constantly look for opportunities, however, because every day there are millions of other people looking for their moment in the spotlight. The best way to get a chance for good P&P is to create a new and newsworthy subject that has an angle, "a hook," to draw media attention. This can be done in several ways that extend beyond the basics of news releases discussed in the previous chapter.

The Power of Surveys

One of the best ways to generate press about your efforts is by conducting a survey. Your survey should relate to your product concept in a way that creates some sort of news angle in which people see the problem you are addressing or the excitement you are trying to generate. Send out the results of your survey in the form of a press release. Many news sources may want to follow up on the survey information by doing a story on you and your product. Try to aim the survey at the widest possible consumer group or special interest group. This will make the information stand out to an editor or news director. Make sure your product is key to them giving out the survey information, so they will mention your invention and its implications in connection with the survey.

Approaching Newspapers and Magazines

Sometimes even newsworthy items are overlooked, so it is important to take advantage of your contact network to get you as much press as possible. This may happen via a personal contact with a news person or it may be as simple as your call, or a friend's call about you, to the local media saying that you'd make a good feature story. I have generated articles in several newspapers including the Phoenix newspaper, *The Arizona Republic,* and the Austin newspaper, the *Austin American-Statesman,* using this technique. Call the Features desk or have a friend call and tell them about one of several different "hooks." The ones I have used successfully include: a "new and interesting person" has just moved to town; a "great new invention" is ready to be exposed to the public; and a new company with a "unique new business" has just opened up. One or more sections of a newspaper usually will jump at the chance to cover a new local story.

The reporter who covered the story from the Phoenix paper turned into a continuing media contact, a personal network connection and a friendship. The writer also did a column for the paper, and he mentioned me several times in his column while I lived in the Phoenix area.

Good publicity and promotion can also be achieved by using the stepping-stone technique of writing. Most small newspapers are always on the look out for new columns from creative people. If your area of expertise can be turned into a semi-regular feature, you are on your way to becoming a local celebrity via your appearance in the newspaper.

Magazine articles on your inventions or your views on topics related to your invention field are another excellent way to generate publicity. This will also begin to create impressive credentials that you can use when promoting your product and business efforts. Your best bet is to start with newsletters and trade publications in your invention field. Many of these publications (found through the *Encyclopedia of Associations*) are in need of fresh material for their readers. Most of these publications don't pay for articles, but the byline and publicity that you can get from the article is usually worth the effort involved. If your articles are good enough to draw attention from readers, the magazine or other publication may ask you back to write for future issues for a fee.

Specialized Placement Writing

Because of the unusual nature of their profession, entrepreneurial inventors usually can get special mentions in announcement columns of professional, trade and alumni journals. Sometimes, these announcements will extend into the business sections of newspapers. These announcements can be in connection with almost any activity that you want to promote. This includes the unveiling of a new product, the release of a new survey, or general news concerning your availability to consult for a particular section of the business community.

Product Publicity on Television and in the Movies

Getting products into movies and on television is a great way to generate publicity for your invention and yourself. There are several ways to accomplish this goal.

One route is to contact the large movie and TV prop houses in Hollywood. Anyone can do this with their product. Prop houses are always in need of the newest and best of all types of products. Don't expect to get paid for your product, or to get any screen credits for its inclusion in a movie or TV show. It is up to you to make the most of the publicity that is generated by such exposure, if it happens. I contacted a major prop house, Ellis Merchantile, about my product, the POWER STAF. I explained what I had and offered to let them have several working and nonfunctional models to keep on hand. I flew over to their location (at my expense) and introduced them to the product concept. Within a short period of time, they had made arrangements with a movie prop coordinator to use the product in a movie. That turned out to be the science-fiction movie, *The Running Man,* starring Arnold Schwartzenegger. Although most of the scenes where the product was used ended up on the cutting room floor, the product still appeared in the movie and I still got the chance to spend a day on a movie set with the prop and stunt men, getting them acquainted with the product. I also got to meet the stars of the film.

The same prop houses supply equipment for most major TV shows, so products at these locations have an equal chance for exposure in both mediums.

Your chances of getting on TV and radio are even better on the talk show circuit. One way to get onto radio and television talk shows, as well as be sought out by news and feature publications is to be listed in the *Directory of Experts, Authorities and Spokespersons.* This is published by Mitchell Davis, 2233 Wisconsin Ave. N.W., #406, Washington, DC 20007-4104. This publication reaches over 80 percent of the major media sources in this country.

Yet another way to advertise your expertise in any particular topic for the purpose of media attention is to take out an ad in one of the several magazines that specialize in promoting talk show guests. Or start your own magazine. At one point in my career I created a magazine called *Talk Out,* which reached over 1,000 radio and TV talk-show hosts, producers, and program directors. This was a reliable and inexpensive method I created to get my face and story in front of the people who were in a position to give me free air time to promote my invention or expertise.

NOTE: A word of caution to anyone seeking media publicity via these methods. **Know your topic!** The easiest way to ruin your media career is to overexpose yourself when you are not prepared for the attention. If you come across as a bumbling amateur who is just trying to get in print or on the airwaves, it may be your last time in the spotlight. Don't try to use the fact that you're an inventor as your hook to get interviews. Use your invention or expertise in a subject, instead. The reason for this is simple: inventors are seen as a dime a dozen, and worse, they already have a fairly poor public image. Everyone feels that their own ideas are great, but inventors have the responsibility of proving it via working products. Without the proof, why will you be any more interesting to put on the air than anyone else who says they're an inventor with an idea?

Get your products on TV and into the Movies; See page 246-247

THE RUNNING MAN

RM-8
Amber Mendez (MARIA CONCHITA ALONSO) tries to escape a
deadly pursuit in THE RUNNING MAN; a high-stakes, high-tech
televised game of survival.

221

Marketing Your Product with Brochures and New Product Releases

Another way to get publicity is to print it! An interesting brochure has a way of getting into circulation with very little help. You should have a good brochure made about your product. This is part of the leave-behind material that can be used at many types of presentations.

Press releases are another way to gain timely publicity and promote a product. Always call the print or broadcast medium that you are targeting for press exposure. Find out what their lead times are for receiving information, and if they require any special format. Many publications are very interested in new products and have special sections that do nothing but feature new technology. Send these publications a "new product release." A new product release is more than a press release. It is a combination brochure, press release and media event all rolled into one. Always include a good color or black-and-white photograph when submitting a new product release. When submitting it to a TV station, it is advisable to first see if they want to do a "spot" on the invention. If not, try to submit at least 30 seconds of video on the product in still shots and in action. This may find its way onto the air as a filler piece on a slow news night.

There are many other ways to gain publicity and recognition for you and your invention. Many books have been written on the topic of promoting products with a variety of specialized techniques. I suggest you investigate this type of information. The important thing to remember is to always be on the lookout for the opportunity to promote your concept. Never be shy about your invention! If you don't toot your own horn, few others will (unless you pay them!). The ultimate goal of publicity and promotion is to get people to know your product and feel comfortable with it. This, of course, leads them to purchase the product and use it, thus fulfilling your ultimate goal of creating something new and useful that people will buy.

Media Materials Checklist

The following checklist is designed to give you a quick and easy overview of your approach to getting media attention. The master checklist should be copied and a separate list should be kept for each project as it starts up.

The basic elements of the checklist are as follows:

1. *The personal history sheet.* This should be the latest version of your PHS. It should give the media people a feel for who you are and what your background is.

2. *The product brochure.* This is a basic product description or business concept outline that allows the media people to understand the basics of your invention or business.

3. *The press release.* Use the press release as a "hook" to interest the media in doing a feature or allowing you to come on their show as a

guest. Make sure the press release has all the proper elements and format to get the attention of the media professionals.

4. *The media contact list.* This is your list of the local and national media personalities and their contact information. It should include the local papers, TV and radio stations with news, talk show, and feature segments.

5. *Selective specialized writing list.* This is your researched list of associations and organizations that have publications to which you can submit articles about your product or venture.

6. *Letters of reference list.* This is your list of people whom you have already approached or will approach for letter of reference to support your product or venture.

7. *Prior news coverage list.* This is your list of existing news coverage materials that have been done on your product or venture. It is also a list of major national publications or media sources that you will target for coverage of your product or venture.

8. *Product photo/video.* This is your product photo or video that you will submit to the various media sources.

9. *Personal photo.* This is your personal photo that you will submit, in certain cases, to the various news media and publications.

10. *Miscellaneous information.* This is other information you may acquire that you feel belongs in your media kit, or can be made available to the media upon request.

MEDIA MATERIALS CHECKLIST

Inventor Name: _____ Date _____

Product/Project Name: _____

MEDIA GOALS:

Primary: _____

Secondary: _____

[1] The Personal History Sheet

Written [ ] Date _____ Edited [ ] Date _____

Printed [ ] Date _____ Copied [ ] Date _____

Notes: _____

_____

[2] The Product Brochure

Written [ ] Date _____ Edited [ ] Date _____

Photos Needed? Type: _____ Yes ____ No ____ Done [ ] Date_____

By: _____ Cost: _____ Paid: _____

Artwork Needed? Type: _____ Yes ____ No ____ Done [ ] Date _____

By: _____ Cost: _____ Paid: _____

Printed By: _____ Cost____ Per ____ Printed_____ Date_____

Notes: _____

_____

[3] The Press Release:

Written [ ] Date _____ Edited [ ] Date _____

Printed [ ] Date _____ Copied [ ] Date _____

Notes: _____

_____

[4] The Local Media Contact List:

TV Station: _____ Ch. _____ Show: _____

Contact: _____ Position: _____

Tele: _____ - _____ Ext: _____ Fax _____ - _____

Contact Date: _____ Reaction: _____

Booking to do a Segment: Date: _____ Time: _____ Length: _____

In Studio: _____ On Location: _____

Details of Arrangement: _____

_____

_____

TV Station: _____ Ch. _____ Show: _____

Contact: _____ Position: _____

Tele: _____ - _____ Ext: _____ Fax _____ - _____

Contact Date: _____ Reaction: _____

Booking to do a Segment: Date: _____ Time: _____ Length: _____

In Studio: _____ On Location: _____

Details of Arrangement: _____

_____

_____

Radio Station: _____ #. _____ AM/FM Show: _____
Contact: _____ Position: _____
Tele: _____ - _____ Ext: _____ Fax _____ - _____
Contact Date: _____ Reaction: _____
Booking to do a Segment: Date: _____ Time: _____ Length: _____
In Studio: _____ On Location: _____ Over Phone: _____
Details of Arrangement: _____
_____

Radio Station: _____ #. _____ AM/FM Show: _____
Contact: _____ Position: _____
Tele: _____ - _____ Ext: _____ Fax _____ - _____
Contact Date: _____ Reaction: _____
Booking to do a Segment: Date: _____ Time: _____ Length: _____
In Studio: _____ On Location: _____ Over Phone: _____
Details of Arrangement: _____
_____

Radio Station: _____ #. _____ AM/FM Show: _____
Contact: _____ Position: _____
Tele: _____ - _____ Ext: _____ Fax _____ - _____
Contact Date: _____ Reaction: _____
Booking to do a Segment: Date: _____ Time: _____ Length: _____
In Studio: _____ On Location: _____ Over Phone: _____
Details of Arrangement: _____
_____

Newspaper: _____
Contact: _____ Position: _____
Tele: _____ - _____ Ext: _____ Fax _____ - _____
Contact Date: _____ Reaction: _____
Details: _____
_____

Newspaper: _____
Contact: _____ Position: _____
Tele: _____ - _____ Ext: _____ Fax _____ - _____
Contact Date: _____ Reaction: _____
Details: _____
_____
_____

Newspaper: _____
Contact: _____ Position: _____
Tele: _____ - _____ Ext: _____ Fax _____ - _____
Contact Date: _____ Reaction: _____
Details: _____
_____
_____

[5] Selective Specialized Writing List

Publication: _____

Contact: _____ Position: _____

Tele: _____ - _____ Ext: _____ Fax _____ - _____

Contact Date: _____ Reaction: _____

Details: _____

_____

Publication: _____

Contact: _____ Position: _____

Tele: _____ - _____ Ext: _____ Fax _____ - _____

Contact Date: _____ Reaction: _____

Details: _____

_____

Publication: _____

Contact: _____ Position: _____

Tele: _____ - _____ Ext: _____ Fax _____ - _____

Contact Date: _____ Reaction: _____

Details: _____

_____

Publication: _____

Contact: _____ Position: _____

Tele: _____ - _____ Ext: _____ Fax _____ - _____

Contact Date: _____ Reaction: _____

Details: _____

_____

[6] Letters of Reference

Contact: _____ Date: _____

Relationship: _____

Agreed to Write Letter: Yes [ ] No [ ] Reason: _____

Letter Expected: _____ (date) Letter Received: _____ Date: _____

Comments: _____

_____

Contact: _____ Date: _____

Relationship: _____

Agreed to Write Letter: Yes [ ] No [ ] Reason: _____

Letter Expected: _____ (date) Letter Received: _____ Date: _____

Comments: _____

_____

Contact: _____ Date: _____

Relationship: _____

Agreed to Write Letter: Yes [ ] No [ ] Reason: _____

Letter Expected: _____ (date) Letter Received: _____ Date: _____

Comments: _____

_____

Contact: _____ Date: _____
Relationship: _____
Agreed to Write Letter: Yes [ ] No [ ] Reason: _____
Letter Expected: _____ (date) Letter Received: _____ Date: _____
Comments: _____
_____

Contact: _____ Date: _____
Relationship: _____
Agreed to Write Letter: Yes [ ] No [ ] Reason: _____
Letter Expected: _____ (date) Letter Received: _____ Date: _____
Comments: _____
_____

Contact: _____ Date: _____
Relationship: _____
Agreed to Write Letter: Yes [ ] No [ ] Reason: _____
Letter Expected: _____ (date) Letter Received: _____ Date: _____
Comments: _____
_____

Contact: _____ Date: _____
Relationship: _____
Agreed to Write Letter: Yes [ ] No [ ] Reason: _____
Letter Expected: _____ (date) Letter Received: _____ Date: _____
Comments: _____
_____

Contact: _____ Date: _____
Relationship: _____
Agreed to Write Letter: Yes [ ] No [ ] Reason: _____
Letter Expected: _____ (date) Letter Received: _____ Date: _____
Comments: _____
_____

Contact: _____ Date: _____
Relationship: _____
Agreed to Write Letter: Yes [ ] No [ ] Reason: _____
Letter Expected: _____ (date) Letter Received: _____ Date: _____
Comments: _____
_____

[7] Prior News Coverage
From: _____ Date: _____
TV Spot (Video Tape) [ ] Newspaper [ ] Magazine [ ] Radio (Audio Tape) [ ]
Copy Available: Yes [ ] No [ ] Reason: _____
Comments: _____
_____

From: _____ Date: _____
TV Spot (Video Tape) [ ] Newspaper [ ] Magazine [ ] Radio (Audio Tape) [ ]
Copy Available: Yes [ ] No [ ] Reason: _____
Comments: _____
_____

From: _____ Date: _____
TV Spot (Video Tape) [ ] Newspaper [ ] Magazine [ ] Radio (Audio Tape) [ ]
Copy Available: Yes [ ] No [ ] Reason: _____
Comments: _____
_____

From: _____ Date: _____
TV Spot (Video Tape) [ ] Newspaper [ ] Magazine [ ] Radio (Audio Tape) [ ]
Copy Available: Yes [ ] No [ ] Reason: _____
Comments: _____
_____

From: _____ Date: _____
TV Spot (Video Tape) [ ] Newspaper [ ] Magazine [ ] Radio (Audio Tape) [ ]
Copy Available: Yes [ ] No [ ] Reason: _____
Comments: _____

[8] Product Photo
Photos Needed? Type: _____ Yes _____ No _____ Done [ ] Date_____
By:_____ Cost: _____ Paid: _____
[9] Personal Photo
Photos Needed? Type: _____ Yes _____ No _____ Done [ ] Date_____
By:_____ Cost: _____ Paid: _____
[10] Misc. Information:_____
_____
_____
_____
_____
_____
_____
_____
_____
_____
_____
_____
_____
_____
_____
_____
_____
_____
_____
_____

Appendix I

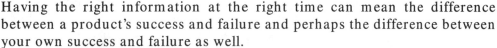

Government Agencies, Inventor Associations and University Resources

  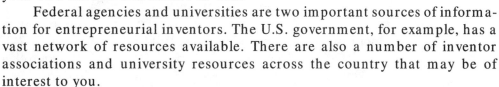 Having the right information at the right time can mean the difference between a product's success and failure and perhaps the difference between your own success and failure as well.

Federal agencies and universities are two important sources of information for entrepreneurial inventors. The U.S. government, for example, has a vast network of resources available. There are also a number of inventor associations and university resources across the country that may be of interest to you.

Most universities and some government agencies have information databases that can be accessed through Internet. Internet is an interactive computer database available to government, industry and the general public. The type and quantity of available resources changes too rapidly to list it in a book, since the information would be outdated before the type could be set and the book published. However, if you can conduct a "gopher" search you should be able to locate a wealth of useful information and download it to your home or office computer. Contact your local library, computer stores and computer clubs for details of use and subscription to the service.

When using these resources, try not to be totally businesslike and cold to the people to which you talk. Build a good rapport with your sources, and you will be building a bond that can be used as part of your personal network at another time. Later, you may get better information because of your good working relationships. If a government or university worker was helpful and friendly, send a thank-you note. Or, better yet, write a letter of appreciation to the worker's superior and send the worker a copy. You will be helping that person in their career. And, trust me, you will get fantastic service if you need their help again.

Congressional Resources

Every inventor should contact his or her local congressional representative and ask to be placed on the mailing list for the government publication *What's Next*. This is a free bimonthly newsletter that details technical, political, and social trends that may be of importance in the future. It is primarily written to help keep congressional representatives up to date on various events and technology so that they have a clear picture as they try to work on upcoming legislation which may be affected by that data. You will appreciate information that keeps them on the cutting edge of new trends which may spark business or product ideas.

The U.S. Congress, during the course of its business, holds hearings on almost every topic under the sun. During those hearings, industry experts on specific topics give testimony and evidence to prove a certain point of view. Additionally, all major information sources about a topic are brought to light by congressional investigators. The transcripts of these hearings are available to the general public. You will find important information on new technologies, markets, and other phases of a product's developmental life cycle within the available reports. A listing called *The Congressional Information Service Index* covers all publications of Congress, including hearing transcripts. It can be found at most public libraries, or it can be purchased from: Congressional Information Service, 4520 East-West Highway, Bethesda, MD 20814 or call 301-654-1550. You can also find out if a subject Congress is interested in has been the topic of congressional investigation by calling the Capitol Hill Operator at 202-224-3121 or the Bill Status Office at 202-225-1772. The Bill Status Office has a computerized database, which can tell you if any bills are pending or have been passed relating to a particular topic.

Department of Agriculture Resources

- The Department of Agriculture (USDA) maintains a large staff that administers various levels of research programs in all areas that fall under the Department of Agriculture's expertise. Inventors with ideas that pertain to farming, food production and distribution, insect control and veterinary sciences (to name a few areas) should contact The Agricultural Research Service, USDA, Room 302-A, Administration Building, Washington, DC 20250.

- Inventors with new food products who need marketing information on food purchases per household or per individual or other facts concerning nutritional data should contact the Human Nutrition Information Service, USDA, Hyattsville, MD 20782.

- The Food and Nutritional Information Center (FNIC) maintains a 24-hour message center for callers to leave messages that are answered by the FNIC specialists using their extensive database. The FNIC acquires data of all types on human nutrition, food services and food science. Photocopies of FNIC-generated articles are available upon request. Contact: The Food and Nutritional Information Center (FNIC, USDA, National Agricultural Library, 10301 Baltimore Blvd., Beltsville, MD 20705.

- Forest-related topics are researched and cataloged by the U.S. Forest Service division of the USDA. The Forest Service maintains data on topics that range from forest fires to wood chemistry and fiber products, as well as from atmospheric sciences to forest insects. For more information, contact: the Deputy of Research, Forest Service, USDA, Room 3007, South Building, Washington, DC 20250.

- The USDA issues grants to inventors and researchers to initiate and stimulate new or improved processes or services that will benefit the United States in the area of food production. The grant described here is only part of the USDA grant program for which inventors with agricultural inventions or concepts may be eligible. Title: *Agricultural Research-Competitive Research Grants*. Eligibility: *Individuals, non-profit organizations and state governments*. Objective: *To promote research in food, agriculture and related areas that will further the programs of the USDA*. Research grants are awarded on a competitive bases. The financial assistance range is $4,000 to $200,000. Contact: Director, Competitive Grants Office, Science and Education Administration, Department of Agriculture, 1300 Wilson Blvd., Suite 1300, Arlington, VA 22209.

- Inventors with new asexually reproducible seed variations are eligible for patents. Plant Patents information can be obtained by contacting the U.S. Patent Office or the Plant Variety Protection Office, Warehouse and See Division, USDA Agricultural Marketing Service (MS), NAL Room 500, Beltsville, MD 20705.

Department of Commerce Resources

- The Department of Commerce's Bureau of Industrial Economics (BIE) is a major source of statistical information and contacts for almost every industry in the United States. The BIE maintains a staff of more than 100 analysts who monitor specific industries. The BIE is one of the best places an entrepreneurial inventor can start to gather basic research and marketing data on an industry. The analysts are more than happy to provide you with insights into any phase of a particular industry, as well as give you leads on where to go and who to talk to for further information in that field. Contact the BIE by writing to: Director, Bureau of Industrial Economics, Dept. of Commerce, Room 4878, Washington, DC 20230.

- The Department of Commerce publishes a daily newspaper called *Commerce Business Daily,* which carries information on all federal procurement invitations. This is the way the government lets private industries know when and what the feds want to buy. This newspaper is an excellent source of leads for any entrepreneurial inventor looking for product markets. *The Daily* can be located at any public library or is available by subscription. The price is $160 per year by first class mail or $81 by regular mail. Contact the Superintendent of Documents, Government Printing Office, Washington, DC 20402.

- The National Technical Information Service (NTIS) has a service that allows citizens to access its vast "Government Research and Development Data Base" and other basic data listings. This combined data base and report storage has over one million abstracts and full reports generated by government-sponsored research and development projects and other government research. The information covers a wide range, from scientific data through marketing and business procedures. The National Technical Information Service will run a free initial search to let you know how many abstracts exist under a certain topic heading. To run an actual search, there is a minimum charge that varies with the material requested. Contact the TIS, Information Analysis Branch, 5285 Port Royal Road, Springfield, VA 22161.

Another important NTIS program for entrepreneurial inventors is the Center for the Utilization of Federal Technology (CUFT). The CUFT is a free service specifically set up to help businesses locate and use federal technology. The CUFT will place any business name on their mailing list and will often forward the company information to other government agencies which might be able to offer additional assistance in specific areas. To get on the CUFT mailing list, send your name, company name, company size, mailing address and any specific areas of technological interest to TIS. Center for the Utilization of Federal Technology, 5285 Port Royal Road, Room 8R, Springfield, VA 22161.

The largest of the NTIS goodies for you may be the *Directory of Federal Technology Resources.* This is a huge, detailed compendium of over 800 resource summaries, arranged in thirty categories for easy reading and data location. The purpose of the directory is to lead large and small businesses to any and all scientific resources available from the federal government. The directory lists contact names and phone numbers along with detailed descriptions of resources available at each location. The directory costs $25 and is listed as publication number PB84-100015. To preview the directory, you can order a free descriptive brochure, number PR 746. Contact the NTIS, 5285 Port Royal Road, Springfield, VA 22161.

The NTIS seems to exist for the advancement of entrepreneurial inventors! It proves this by publishing a monthly newsletter called *NTIS Tech Notes* that informs readers of new federal technology that may have potential for commercial development. The newsletter contains one- to two-page fact sheets on newly developed technologies in twelve different areas. These sheets are often illustrated and are packed with vital information for integrating the technologies into new product concepts. To get more information on the *Tech Notes,* contact the NTIS at the above address and order their free brochure number PB 365, or order the newsletter by category at $60 per year or $250 for all twelve areas (a real bargain).

The Guide to Innovation Resources and Planning for the Smaller Business is an 85-page publication available from the National Technical Information Service (NTIS). The guide specifies more than fifty federal and state government offices that assist small businesses in bringing new technologies to the marketplace. The guide is broken down into two parts, the first section gives advice on various steps in the innovation process, while the second section gives agency listing and resource information. The guide may be purchased from the NTIS for $13.50. Contact the National Technical Information Service, Dept. of Commerce, 5285 Port Royal Road, Springfield, VA 22161.

More information on government and private resources, copies of the guide (listed above) and assistance in developing and marketing technology may also be obtained from The Small Business Technology Liaison Division, Office of Productivity, Technology and Innovation, U.S. Dept. of Commerce, Room 4816, Washington, DC 20230.

- The National Bureau of Standards (NBS) conducts research into many areas affecting government agencies and equipment. One of these areas is fire prevention. The NBS has information available in reports and through database on all aspects of fire, ranging from equipment specifications to the physics of fire to the motivational characteristics of arsonists. This and other information on subjects researched by the NBS can be invaluable to anyone in search of hard statistics to support product research and marketing efforts. Contact the National Bureau of Standards at the Center for Fire Research, NBS, Building 224, Room A247, Washington, DC 20234 or call 301-921-3143. For additional publications and information by the NBS, contact Technical Information and Publications division, National Bureau of Standards, U.S. Dept. of Commerce, Route 270, Gaithersburg, MD 20234.

- The Patent and Trademark Office is an important part of the Department of Commerce. (For information on patents, see Chapter 5). For additional patent information via the Patent and Trademark Data Base files, contact Patent Data Base, U.S. Department of Commerce, Patent and Trademark Office, Washington, DC 20231.

A service called "Technology Assessment with Patents" is provided by the Office of Technology Assessment and Forecast of the Patent and Trademark Office. It is comprised of both off-the-shelf and customized information on domestic and international patent activity in selected categories. This service is an excellent indicator used to forecast future technology. For more details about this service, contact the Office of Technology Assessment and Forecast, Patent and Trademark Office, Dept. of Commerce, CP6 Room 1225, Washington, DC 20231.

Department of Defense

- The armed forces are a storehouse of information that inventors can use. Among that information is a large database of ergonomic information on how humans interface with machines. The Army calls it "human engineering." For information on human factors, their capabilities and limitations, as well as human factors applications, contact the Army. They have developed general reference information that can be used in the engineering of products for all markets. Contact the Director, Army Human Engineering Laboratories, Army Material Command, Department of Defense, Aberdeen Proving Ground, MD 21005.

- You may come up with ideas (from the mundane to the earthshaking) that can be of benefit to our nation's military. When this happens, there are several agencies to contact that accept unsolicited proposals. For proposals in the natural sciences (i.e., aeromechanics, electronics, and solid state sciences; mathematics, physics, informational sciences, etc.), contact the Office of Scientific Research Opportunities, Directorate of Contracts Air Force, Department of the Air Force, Dept. of Defense, Bolling Air Force Base, Washington, DC 20332. Industrial organizations and individuals can participate in research and development programs with the military by submitting unsolicited proposals that contain new ideas. These proposals should have nothing to do with any specific materials already being solicited by the Department of Defense. To find out who and where to contact, write for a free booklet, the *Guide for Voluntary Unsolicited Proposals*. It is available from the Army Material Development and Readiness Command, Attention DRCDER-LU, Dept. of Defense, 5001 Eisenhower Ave., Alexandria, VA 22333.

Department of Energy Resources

- The Department of Energy (DOE) is seriously looking to the entrepreneurial inventors of America to create new energy-related technologies that involve conservation or alternative sources of energy. The DOE has set up an "Energy Related Inventions" program which is aimed at encouraging innovations in non-nuclear energy technology. They do this by providing assistance to individual inventors and entrepreneurs with small research and development businesses involved in developing promising energy-related inventions. The DOE will provide financial assistance up to $70,000 to help you attain your goals. Contact the DOE to get information on the application process: Energy Related Invention Program, Office of Inventions and Small Scale Technology, Conservation and Renewable Energy, Dept. of Energy, MS 6A116 Forrestal Building, 1000 Independence Ave., W1, M5C-24, Washington, DC 20585.

- The DOE publishes an annual index with abstracts of all energy-related research and development literature based upon U.S. government-oriented projects. The index is called *Energy Research Abstracts* and is priced at $165 per year. It is available from the Government Printing Office, Superintendent of Documents, Washington, DC 20402.

- The Technical Information Center (TIC) is the central hub for all energy-related information generated, used, obtained or disseminated by the DOE. It has access to over 1.8 million abstracts, reports and on-line data sources via the DOE data base. For more information on obtaining data from the TIC, contact the Technical Information Center, U.S. Dept. of Energy, P.O. Box 62, Oak Ridge, TN 37830.

- Grants are available from the Department of Energy for what it considers "Appropriate Energy Technology." The objective of the Appropriate Energy Technology program is to encourage research and development of energy-related, small-scale technologies. The program is open to anyone interested in applying for the $350 to $50,000 grants that are available. Contact: Appropriate Energy Technology, Dept. of Energy, Forrestal Building, 1000 Independence Ave. S.W., Washington, DC 20585.

- The DOE is open to the submission of unsolicited proposals for energy-related inventions and systems. They will provide you with a free pamphlet that describes the types of inventions sought and the types of research they will fund. The material will also tell how to submit a proposal to the DOE that will get serious consideration. To get the free pamphlet, contact: Business Liaison Division, Office of Small and Disadvantaged Business Utilization, Procurement and Contracts Management Directorate, Dept. of Energy, 1000 Independence Ave. S.W. 1E-061, Washington, DC 20585.

Department of Health and Human Services Resources

- The Department of Health and Human Services has experts on every disease and condition known to man. If you have an idea for a new device, treatment, or therapy for a condition and wish to get information to further your research, the Department of Health and Human Services has the person to whom to talk. Contact them at The Health Information Clearinghouse, 1555 Wilson Blvd., Suite 600, Rosslyn, VA 22209.

- One of the largest opportunities for future inventions is in the area of the elderly. In twenty years almost half of our population will be considered geriatric. The Department of Health and Human Services prints *Aging Magazine,* a bimonthly publication that is geared to health professionals in the field of aging. It is a good source of data in an area that does not have extensive material available to you. The subscription is $13 per year and is available by contacting *Aging Magazine,* Administration on Aging, Department of Health and Human Services, Room 4243, Washington, DC 20201.

- The Department of Health and Human Services publishes a free directory of all the biotechnology resources available in the U.S. today. The directory lists biotechnology-related research projects with a description of the application of the technology under investigation. This is a prime source of information for you, if you're looking to get in on the cutting edge of biotechnology before it hits the marketplace. Contact the Research Resources Information Center, 1776 East Jefferson Street, Rockville, MD 20852.

- The BioTechnology Research Program of the Department of Health and Human Services concentrates on the application of the physical sciences and engineering as they relate to medicine. This program is operated from the same address as the free directory above and may be able to help direct your efforts in obtaining useful technology from the appropriate source. Contact them at The BioTechnology Research program, 1776 East Jefferson Street, Rockville, MD 20852.

- The Department of Health and Human Services maintains scientific projects data base called CRISP. This is an acronym for Computer Retrieval of Information on Science Projects. CRISP contains in-depth information about all research projects carried out by or supported with grants from the Public Health Service. It also has information relating to projects undertaken by the National Institutes of Health and the National Institute of Mental Health. CRISP data is free to the general public and is available by contacting Research Documentation Section, Statistics and Analysis Branch, Division of Research Grants, Westwood Room, Building 148, National Institutes of Health, Bethesda, MD 20205.

Department of Justice Resources

- The National Criminal Justice Reference Service (NCJRS) is an international clearinghouse and reference center that is open to the justice field professional and the general public. The National Criminal Justice Reference Service publishes a bimonthly journal, *JIJ Reports,* which has news of criminal justice research, abstracts of related publications and new product announcements. This is the main reference service for anyone wishing to locate information about the nation's law enforcement efforts and agencies. Contact the NCJRS at the National Criminal Justice Reference Service, National Institute of Justice, Department of Justice, Box 6000, Rockville, MD 20850.

- A massive Justice Library is maintained by the Department of Justice. It includes information, abstracts and a reference service on topics relating to the Department of Justice. It is available by contacting the Justice Library, Department of Justice, 10th and Pennsylvania Ave. N.W., Room 5400, Washington, DC 20530.

- The Justice Department maintains various Law Enforcement Standards Laboratories which do research and evaluation of the standards of performance for law enforcement equipment. Entrepreneurial inventors wishing to develop products in this area should contact this division of the Department of Justice for the reports and other data generated by the NIJ (National Institute of Justice). These are available as Law Enforcement Research Publications. Contact the Reference and Dissemination Division, Office of Development, Testing and Dissemination, National Institute of Justice, Department of Justice, 633 Indiana Ave., N.W., Room 810, Washington, DC 20531.

Department of Labor Resources

- The Bureau of Labor Statistics (BLS) compiles vast amounts of data on all phases of the American labor force, from the consumer price index to productivity data for government and industry. There is a wealth of information that you may be able to use in compiling anything from a business plan to a product use profile. For referral to the appropriate BLS office or specific data, contact the Bureau of Labor Statistics, BLS Inquiries and Correspondence, U.S. Department of Labor, 44 "G" Street N.W., Washington, DC 20212.

- The Occupational Safety and Health Administration (OSHA) is the government watchdog for safety in the work place. Yearly, OSHA requires industry to employ extensive safety precautions to ensure workers a safer work environment. This is a prime area for creative thinking by entrepreneurial inventors. Industry is constantly in need of better safety equipment and better devices to replace older, unsafe tools and machines. OSHA keeps technical data on all of their projects and requirements, and this information can be accessed by contacting the Technical Data Center, Directorate of Technical Support, Occupational Safety and Health Administration, Dept. of Labor, 200 Constitution Ave., N.W., Room N2439 Rear, Washington, DC 20210.

- Forecasting how technological trends will impact the future is an important tool for every entrepreneurial inventor. The Department of Labor maintains the Division of Industry Productivity and Technological Studies to do just that: predict how current technologies will impact jobs and entire industries in the next five to ten years. Contact the Division of Industry Productivity and Technological Studies, Bureau of Labor Statistics, Dept. of Labor, 200 Constitution Ave. N.W., Room S4325, Washington, DC 20210.

Department of State Resources

- The Department of State maintains experts on every country in the world. These experts or "desk officers" are available to you for any information that may be required about a particular country. This may include patent protection, international sales of various types of products or other miscellaneous information that may be needed. Contact these experts at "Country Desk Officer for _____," U.S. Department of State, 2201 "C" Street N.W., Washington, DC 20520 or call the Department of State at 202-634-3600 and ask to be connected to the appropriate "Country Desk."

- The Department of State's Office of Business Practices deals with the protection of industrial and intellectual property in foreign countries. They can also help with various problems relating to international licensing agreements. Contact the Office of Business Practices, U.S. Department of State, 2201 "C" Street N.W., Room 3531A, Washington, DC 20520.

Department of Transportation Resources

- The Advanced Marine Vehicle Technology Branch of the Department of Transportation reviews and researches new and existing boat designs. They are a good source of data and reference if you are interested in new watercraft technology. With two-thirds of the planet covered in water, this is a market opportunity that many inventors should consider. Contact the Advanced Marine Vehicle Technology Branch, Technology Division, Office of Research and Development, Coast Guard, Dept. of Transportation, 2100 2nd Street S.W., Washington, DC 20593.

- It seems like the other third of the planet is covered by roads, cars driving on them, and people waiting to cross those roads. Because of this, many entrepreneurial inventors should be interested in the Office of Driver and Pedestrian Research. This division of the Department of Transportation conducts R&D into the interaction of people and machines. They cover eight basic areas of research as they relate to drivers and pedestrians. Some of the topics that they investigate include motorcycles and helmet use, teen driving, alcohol, drugs, unsafe driving, standards for driver licenses and driver safety systems. Contact the Office of Driver and Pedestrian Research, Research and Development, National Highway Traffic Safety Administration, Dept. of Transportation, 400 7th Street S.W., Room 6226, Washington, DC 20290.

Miscellaneous Government Resources

- The Consumer Product Safety Commission conducts evaluations of consumer products to determine the items' relative safety. The Human Factors Division prepares periodic reports on how man and machine interface to cause accidents. This division is a fine source of information if you are looking to define specific parameters for a new product in relation to how it will interact with man. The division is comprised of multidisciplinary professionals who can answer most questions about man-machine interfaces. Contact them at the Consumer Product Safety Commission, Human Factors Division, 5401 Westbard Ave., Bethesda, MD 20207.

- The Environmental Protection Agency (EPA) offers assistance to companies and individual entrepreneurs in the quest to keep our environment safe and sound. The EPA has hundreds of resident experts who can tell you what's in and what's out when it comes to chemical use, emissions standards, energy conservation, and so forth. The EPA publishes a free directory of the offices within the agency and the experts who can answer your questions. The directory has handy items such as agency organizational chart, a map of the regional offices and a complete subject index to guide you through the maze of this important government resource. Contact them at the Public Information Center, EPA, 820 Quincy Street N.W., Washington, DC 20021.

- If your invention has anything to do with remote control devices, radio frequencies or other broadcast or channeled electromagnetic emissions, then you should talk with the folks at the Federal Communications Commission (FCC). The allocation of domestic and international radio frequencies (radio, television, remote control equipment, etc.) is administered through their office. Contact them at the Spectrum Management Division, Office of Science and Technology, Federal Communications Commission, Room 7218, 2025 "M" Street N.W., Washington, DC 20554.

- The National Aeronautics and Space Administration (NASA) maintains a division that researches, organizes and disseminates information developed by NASA, its contractors and grantees. This office also is charged with responsibility for gathering important information from outside the NASA group that may be of interest to the space program. They have a wide variety of abstracts and publications from which to choose. Contact the Scientific and Technical Information Facility, Information Systems Division, National Aeronautics and Space Administration, P.O. Box 8758, Baltimore/Washington International Airport, MD 21240.

NASA also publishes a quarterly journal called *Tech Briefs*. It contains abstracts of technical innovations developed by NASA which might have commercial applications. Each issue provides information about the NASA patent licensing procedures for the technology. This can be a prime source of basic technology for you. Contact the Technology Utilization and Industry Division, National Aeronautics and Space Administration, 600 Independence Ave. S.W., Room 5113, Washington, DC 20546.

- The National Archives and Records Administration has a set of elaborate patent and trademark drawings from the ninteenth century as part of their archival collection of patents and trademarks. These drawings could have some promotional value to those inventors with an artistic flair. Copies of the original artwork can be purchased for a nominal fee. Contact the Cartographic and Architectural Branch, National Archives and Records Administration, 8th and Pennsylvania Ave. N.W., Washington, DC 20408.

- The National Science Foundation (NSF) has a vast number of divisions that can be of service to you. Their mission is to promote the progress of science through the support of research. For specific information on what they can do for you in any particular field, contact Public Affairs, National Science Foundation, 1800 "G" Street N.W., Washington, DC 20550.

- The National Science Foundation maintains a program aimed at helping small firms with an orientation toward science and technology. This program called Small Business Innovation Research (SBIR), is designed to let these small companies perform innovative research on high-risk scientific and technical problems that could have significant public benefit. If you have concepts worthy of this type of program, you should contact the Industrial Program, Directorate for Scientific, Technological and International Affairs, Division of Industry, Science and Technological Innovation, National Science Foundation, 1800 "G" Street N.W., Room 1250, Washington, DC 20550.

- If the two listings above for The National Science Foundation sound like there may be a maze of calls and paperwork ahead for any small business or entrepreneur wanting to get involved, then the Office of Small Business Research and Development is your answer. The Office of Small Business Research and Development is specifically set up to provide information and guidance to anyone wishing to know more about NSF programs and research opportunities. Contact the Office of Small Business Research and Development, National Science Foundation, 1800 "G" Street N.W., Room 517, Washington, DC 20550.

- The Small Business Administration (SBA) has a number of programs set up to help finance small business and to lead them to capital resources and business opportunities. Like the NSF, the SBA is part of the SBIR program. The Small Business Innovation Research (SBIR) program is set up to stimulate technological innovation by helping small companies get involved with government funding for new research projects. The SBIR program also provides incentives for the commercialization of the newly developed technology. The SBA is one of 12 government agencies that are required by law to participate in the program. The other agencies are the Departments of Agriculture, Defense, Energy, Health and Human Services, Interior, Transportation and Regulatory Agency. The Small Business Administration can help put you in touch with their part of the program or any of the other 11 agencies. Contact them at the SBA, Office of Innovation, Research and Technology, 1441 "L" Street N.W., Room 500-A, Washington, DC 20416.

- The Library of Congress (LOC) maintains a vast Science, Technology and Social Sciences data base which can be accessed by the general public. The National Referral Center (NRC) of the LOC maintains a directory of more than 12,000 individuals and organizations who are qualified and ready to provide information to the general public on topics in the areas of science, technology and social science. A typical referral from the NRC contains the name of the resource, a mailing address, telephone number, area of special interest, available publications, data bases and special services that may be available to the person making the request. This service is available free of charge by contacting the National Referral Center, Library of Congress, Washington, DC 20540.

Inventor's Associations

The following is a list of inventor associations across the country that may be of interest to you. This list may be incomplete, but does contain the majority of known inventor organization. Contact your local associations for information on what they can do for you. Organizations that have multi-state or national affiliations will have an asterisk (*) next to their name in this listing.

ALABAMA

Alabama Inventors Association
3409 Fountain Circle
Montgomery, AL 36116

ARKANSAS

Arkansas Inventors Congress Inc.
One State Capital Mall
Little Rock, AR 72201

CALIFORNIA

Inventors Workshop International*
3537 Old Conejo Rd., Suite 120
Newbury, CA 91320

Inventors of California
215 Rheem Blvd.
Moraga, CA 94705

National Inventors Foundation
345 West Cypress Street
Glendale, CA 91204

Inventors' Resource Center
P.O. Box 5105
Berkeley, CA 94705

California Inventor's Council
P.O. Box 2036
Sunnyvale, CA 94087

Inventors Council of California
250 Vernon Street
Oakland, CA 94610

National Congress of Inventor Organizations*
214 Rheem Blvd.
Moraga, CA 94556

Technology Transfer Society
11720 West Peco Blvd.
Los Angeles, CA 90064

COLORADO

Affiliated Inventors Foundation Inc.*
501 Iowa Ave.
Colorado Springs, CO 80909

National Inventors Cooperative Assoc.
P.O. Box 6585
Denver, CO 80206

FLORIDA

Palm Beach Society of American Inventors
P.O. Box 26
Palm Beach, FL 33480

Society of American Inventors
505 East Jackson St., Suite 204
Tampa, FL 33602

Tampa Bay Inventor's Council
805 West 118 St.
Tampa, FL 33612

Central Florida Inventors Club
4849 Victory Drive
Orlando, FL 32808

Society for Inventors and Entrepreneurs
306 Georgetown Drive
Casselberry, FL 32707

The Inventors Club
Route 11, Box 379
Pensacola, FL 32514

GEORGIA

Inventors Association of Georgia
241 Freyer Drive NE
Marietta, GA 30060

Inventors Club of America
P.O. Box 450261
Atlanta, GA 30345

Inventor Associates of Georgia
637 Linwood Avenue, NE
Atlanta, GA 30306

HAWAII

Inventors Council of Hawaii
P.O. Box 27844
Honolulu, HI 96827

ILLINOIS

Inventors' Council of Chicago
53 West Jackson, Suite 1041
Chicago, IL 60604

Chicago High Tech Association
20 N. Wacker Dr., Suite 1929
Chicago, IL 60606

INDIANA

Indiana Inventors Association Inc.
612 Ironwood Drive
Plainfield, IN 46168

International Association of Professional Inventors
Route 1, Box 1074
Shirley, IN 47384

The Inventors and Entrepreneurs Society of Indiana Inc.
P.O. Box 2224
Hammond, IN 46323

International Association of New England Professional Inventors
818 Westminster
Kokomo, IN 46901

MASSACHUSETTS

Innovation Invention Network
132 Sterling Street
West Boylston, MA 01583

Inventors Association of New England
P.O. Box 325
Lexington, MA 02173

MICHIGAN

Inventors Council of Michigan
2200 Bonisteel Blvd.
Ann Arbor, MI 48109

MINNESOTA

Midwest Inventors Society
P.O. Box 335
St. Cloud, MN 56301

Minnesota Inventors Congress
P.O. Box 71
Redwood Falls, MN 56283

Society of Minnesota Inventors
20231 Basalt Street, NW
Anoka, MN 55303

Inventors and Technology Transfer Society
P.O. Box 14775
Minneapolis, MN 55414

MISSOURI

Inventors Association of St. Louis
P.O. Box 16544
St. Louis, MO 63105

MISSISSIPPI

Mississippi Society of Scientists and Inventors
P.O. Box 2244
Jackson, MS 39205

Confederacy of Mississippi Inventors
4759 Nailor Road
Vicksburg, MS 39180

Mississippi Inventors Workshop
4729 Kings Highway
Jackson, MS 39206

NEBRASKA

Omaha Inventors Club c/o SBA
11145 Mill Valley Road
Omaha, NE 681145

Lincoln Inventors Association
P.O. Box 94666
Lincoln, NE 68509

Kearney Inventors Association
2001 Ave. A, Box 607
Kearney, NE 68847

NEW JERSEY

National Society of Inventors
539 Laurel Place
South Orange, NJ 07079

American Society of Inventors
402 Cynwyd Drive
Absecon, NJ 08201

NEW YORK

NY Society of Professional Inventors
SUNY at Farmingdale, Lupton Hall
Farmingdale, NY 11735

OHIO

Inventors Council of Dayton
140 E. Monument Avenue
Dayton, OH 45402

Inventors Club of Greater Cincinnati
18 Gambier Circle
Cincinnati, OH 45218

Columbus Inventors Association
2480 East Avenue
Columbus, OH 43202

OKLAHOMA

Oklahoma Inventors Congress
P.O. Box 75635
Oklahoma City, OK 73147

Invention Development Society
8502A SW 8th Street
Oklahoma City, OK 73128

OREGON

Western Inventors Council
P.O. Box 3288
Eugene, OR 97403

PENNSYLVANIA

American Society of Inventors
P.O. Box 58426
Philadelphia, PA 19102

TENNESSEE

Tennessee Inventors Association
P.O. Box 11225
Knoxville, TN 37939

Appalachian Inventors Group
P.O. Box 388
Oak Ridge, TN 37830

Tennessee Inventors Association
1116 Weisgarber
Knoxville, TN 37919

TEXAS

Texas Inventors Association
4000 Rock Creek Drive, Suite 100
Dallas, TX 75204

UTAH

Intermountain Society of Inventors & Designers
P.O. Box 1056
Tooele, UT 84074

WASHINGTON

Northwest Inventors Association
723 East Highland Drive
Arlington, WA 98223

Inventors' Association of Washington, Inc.
P.O. Box 1725
Bellevue, WA 98009

WISCONSIN

Midwest Inventors Group
P.O. Box 1
Chippewa Falls, WI 54729

University Resources

Many universities have programs geared toward helping inventors evaluate, protect, develop and market their ideas. Each university program is different in its approach and capabilities. Some are free, and others charge to help defray their costs. Some of these programs are affiliated with inventor organizations, while others are not. Keep in mind that these institutions are not bound by any laws or restrictions concerning the secrecy of your ideas. It is always wise to have them sign secrecy agreements prior to revealing your concept to their personnel. This will also keep the concept from becoming "public domain" by keeping it secret. Once an idea is disclosed publicly, remember, you only have one year to apply for a patent or the idea slips into the area of public knowledge, and patent protection is lost forever.

The following is a list of universities with programs of interest to you as an entrepreneurial inventor. Contact each university to get complete details of their capabilities and fees.

CALIFORNIA

California State University at Fresno
Bureau of Business Research and Service
Fresno, CA 93740

Stanford University
Innovation Center
Stanford, CA 94305

DISTRICT OF COLUMBIA

George Washington University
Innovation Information Center
2130 H Street NW
Washington, DC 20052

GEORGIA

Georgia Institute of Technology
Patent Assistance Program
Atlanta, GA 30332

ILLINOIS

Illinois State University
Technology Commercialization Center
Hovey Hall-401L
Normal, IL 61761

University of Illinois at Chicago
Technology Commercialization Program
815 West Van Buren Street
Chicago, IL 60607

KANSAS

The University of Kansas
Center for Research Inc.

2291 Irving Hill Road Campus
West Lawrence, KS 66045

KENTUCKY

University of Louisville
Center for Entrepreneurship, School of Business
Louisville, KY 40292

MASSACHUSETTS

Massachusetts Institute of Technology
Innovation Center, Rm. 33-111
Cambridge, MA 02139

NEW MEXICO

University of New Mexico
Technical Applications Center
Albuquerque, NM 87131

OREGON

University of Oregon
Innovation Center, College of Business
131 Gilbert Hall
Eugene, OR 97403

PENNSYLVANIA

Carnegie-Mellon University
Center for Entrepreneurial Development
4516 Henry Street
Pittsburgh, PA 15213

TEXAS

Texas A&M University
Technology Business Development
310 Wisenbaker Engineering Research Center
College Station, TX 77843

Baylor University
Hankamer School of Business, Suite 308
Center for Private Enterprise and Entrepreneurship
Waco, TX 76703

UTAH

University of Utah
Utah Innovation Center
417 Wakara Way
Salt Lake City, UT 84112

University of Wisconsin
Wisconsin Innovation Service Center
402 Mc Cutchan
Whitewater, WI 53190

Appendix II

Glossary

 Inventing, like any other specialized field, has a language of its own. Most of the terms presented here are drawn from the basic elements of inventing. The definitions I have given these terms often reflect my own feelings about inventing and about the people who devote part, or all, of their lives to the pursuit of an idea.

ADHESIVES (Types): Adhesives are glues, substances which can adhere on material or to another section of glue. There are many types of adhesives manufactured today. Each has a special purpose. Some, like white glues (Elmer's™ wood and fabric type) are designed to work with porous surfaces, because they bond into the pore. Others like Super Glue™ bond by the displacement of air thus creating a powerful vacuum for adhesion. Many adhesives can be combined with other structural elements to form composite structures of great strength.

ARTIST RENDERING: Artist renderings are professional color, two-and three-dimensional drawings of a product concept. Artist renderings usually show the product in one of several ways (e.g., in use by the end user to illustrate its size and function; as a cut-away to reveal its inner workings, etc.). These drawings are usually expensive and time-consuming to produce. They are often used in sales, marketing and technical development of the product.

BRAINSTORMING: The simultaneous art and science of generating ideas via sustained amorphous and/or straightline thinking. Brainstorming is one of the most enjoyable methods of creative thinking. It can lead to unexpected lines of thought and open new vistas for the imagination. Brainstorming can be done individually or in groups.

BUSINESS PLAN: A Business Plan is a formal business proposal complete with all background and data needed to understand the proposed business. Business plans are complex projections of what a company is expected to do from its inception through a point three-to-five years in the future. A good business plan can make or break an inventor's chance to obtain working capital through most established financial sources. Consult your attorney and accountant before releasing any business plan to investors. If incorrectly structured, the business plan can hurt you and your invention. There are many good books on preparing business plans. Consult one before beginning one.

COMPANY IDENTITY: The face that your company puts on for the world at large is your company's identity. It doesn't matter if it's just you and your answering machine. You must have some sort of company identity. It will be reflected in your business cards, stationery and the way you conduct business. Part physical, part psychological and totally the production of the inventor, a company identity is put in place long before the invention ever sees the light of day. The DBA (Doing Business As) is your first step toward creating a company identity. Getting a DBA is a simple filing with the county in which you are conducting business. It allows you to conduct business under the name of the company. This allows you to open a bank account and cash checks made out to the company as well as open a post office box under your company name. It is an important first step to establishing a company identity.

COMPANY IMAGE: This is the "face" you put on your company for all the world to see. Everything that your company sells, produces, prints or distributes, either in product or promotional material, contributes to the overall company image. Good company images take on a life of their own and can help market and sell almost any type of product.

COMPUTER ARTWORK: Computer artwork is any artwork generated by a computer. Many new computer systems can be used to create very precise technical artwork as well as freehand line art for product representation. The best of the new machines are capable of producing color renderings that rival the best work of many conventional artists and photographers.

CONCEPT: A concept is an idea whose parameters have been fleshed out. A concept may be one idea, or it may consist of several ideas that make up a product, service, or business. A concept always contains the elements of product and market. Concepts rarely are sold to anyone at this stage of development, except investors who know and trust the inventor.

CONCEPT DRAWINGS: Concept drawings are usually the original, basic drawings done by the inventor. They may be very crude or they may be of professional quality depending upon individual talents. The concept drawing is the general name given to artwork that does not represent a true final product, only the concept for the product in its earliest stage of conception. Inventors often use them during dog and pony shows for the raising of initial capital during the very early phases of the product's development.

DEALS: As Donald Trump put it, The Art of the Deal is the essence of business negotiations. Deals are nebulous things until they firm up and become real. As the inventor, you are at the center of the entire process, and must learn to see the deal as a physical structure that benefits everyone involved. Deals are totally without structure until one side or the other puts limits, goals or expectations on paper. Then the deal is something to be played like a hand of poker. You must use your skills to protect your interests, while giving up enough to keep backers interested in doing business. Make "drop dead" points or benchmarks (on paper for your own use) beyond which you won't negotiate any further on a given point (without concession on other important points). This definite mindset and plan will help you attain a positive business position and create deals that work for everyone involved.

DESIGN PATENT: Design patent is a patent on any new, original and ornamental design for an article of manufacture. The design patent protects only the appearance of an article, not its structure or function. A design patent has a life of 14 years.

DESTRUCTIVE TESTING: Destructive testing is a variety of tests used to determine the expected life of a product when exposed to various external destructive elements. It is a process of determining the operational envelope of a product. This is the chance that the inventor has been waiting for, to take a sample of his product and beat the.... out of it, for all the grief it's caused him! Get all your frustrations out during the destructive testing phase. It's good for your inner peace to be able to blow off steam at your product for a good cause. The testing process is also important to document the ability of the product to operate under various conditions.

DISCLOSURE DOCUMENT: A disclosure document is (1) the set of papers describing your idea that is sent to the Patent Office for registration with the Disclosure Document Program, and (2) a document that is used to disclose your idea to anyone in particular when you first invent it. This document should have a witness stamp on it to verify its date.

DISCLOSURE DOCUMENT PROGRAM: This is a program offered by the Patent Office, it allows inventors (in total confidence) to disclose and register ideas with the Patent Office. It has a limited time frame of two years until the ideas are discarded (destroyed). It is not a patent application, nor is it any sort of patent protection. It is solely to help inventors establish credible date of conception for dealing with the many aspects of the inventing process. The program has value in setting up meetings under proper secrecy protocol.

DISCLOSURE DOCUMENT STAMP: This is the official stamp put on the documents by the Patent Office when they register your idea with the Disclosure Document Program. It contains your registration number and date the document was received by the Patent and Trademark Office.

DOG & PONY SHOW: A "Dog & Pony Show" (D&P) is any presentation that you use to promote your idea. D&Ps can be used to raise money or get publicity for your product. Any time you present an idea to anyone, you are doing a form of D&P.

DREAMERS: Often confused with inventors and visionaries, dreamers are people who only dream about a product or venture. Dreamers are rarely doers. Inventors, by contrast, are dreamers who act on their ideas.

DREMEL TOOL™: A Dremel Tool is a motorized, multipurpose tool that has interchangeable heads for drilling, shaping and cutting a variety of materials. It can work on woods, plastics, foams and some metals. No inventor worth his salt should be without this most basic prototyping tool. Once you have one, you'll never understand how you got along without one up until that point. Several companies make this type of tool, but Dremel is the top on the line and has a wide variety of adapters that increase its abilities.

ENTREPRENEURIAL INVENTOR: An entrepreneurial inventor is a rare breed of individual who has the courage and drive to pursue dreams. Without entrepreneurial inventors, there would be no future, no progress, only a continuation of today. Entrepreneurial inventors are thinkers, tinkerers, promoters, project managers, and leaders—rolled into one.

ESTIMATES & PROJECTIONS: Estimates and projections are various areas of accounting that must be presented to investors to create a comfort level regarding your project. Your projections must substantiate your claim that the product will make money for an investor with minimum risk to his capital. This doesn't mean you should distort the facts in any way. Instead, you have a goal to work toward in preparing your numbers. You can reach this goal through proper, detailed research of your concept. Almost any project can be structured to attract one type of investor or another. Simple estimates and projections can usually be prepared by an inventor and his team (if one exists). Otherwise the inventor may have to call on accounting and finance expertise in preparing his business plan. The most important thing to remember while preparing your projection is that you may have to live with exactly the funding you have said the project requires. So, be sure to include contingency cash in your estimates to cover a worse-case scenario.

FIDUCIARY RESPONSIBILITY: Fiduciary responsibility is the responsibility that an attorney has to safeguard your confidential information.

Attorneys normally take this responsibility very seriously. If yours doesn't, get a new attorney!

FIELD TESTING: Field testing is a way of determining the actual elements that must be modified or changed to make the final product function effectively. Field testing should always be done by end users who will not go lightly on the product. Most field tests are conducted using pre-production prototypes.

FOAM CORE: Foam Core is a prototype material made of a thin layer of open-cell Styrofoam sandwiched between two pieces of paper. It is rigid, workable material that is ideal for making models and mock-ups. It can be painted, cut, glued and sanded.

FOAMS (Types): There are many different types of foams. Foams are man-made (artificial) substances. Foams come in rods, sheets, tubes, blocks, etc. Foams come in various densities and hardness. Foams are also available in mixable configurations that "set up" in a matter of moments. These foams (mostly of the urethane type) are ideal for prototyping because they are moldable around other objects. They can be sanded, sawed, shaved and generally worked to any surface texture and shape. Each type of foam has different qualities that make them suited for different uses. Foam is a versatile material for many prototype and production applications.

FOREIGN PATENTS: Almost all countries have patent systems. There is no such thing as an "international patent." Each country has different rules and requirements to get a patent. However, several groups of countries will allow you to patent your device in one and get a patent in the others with little or no paperwork. Among these are the EEC (European Economic Community) Common Market countries (EEC Patent application) and the Nordic Patent which includes Denmark, Finland, Norway and Sweden. Most foreign patents require a periodic payment (yearly in most cases) to maintain your patent. If you intend to market your device in any particular country and want protection there, make sure to apply for a patent in that specific country. Be forewarned, it is very expensive to obtain and maintain foreign patents.

FUTURISTS: Futurists are individuals (or groups) whose concern for the future is shown in their action today. They may be forecasters, inventors, designers, environmentalists, etc. Their bond is an awareness of the future and a desire to participate in the shaping of the future. Their concerns touch every field of human experience and endeavor. Many futurists are members of The World Future Society. Their ranks include many famous thinkers and scientists.

GESTALT: The dictionary defines it as a system or pattern of psychological events that act as a functional unit. I believe that an inventor's gestalt exists, almost as a subliminal hive mind on a planet-wide scale. This is the reason behind the simultaneous parallel development of many inventions. Although I do not address this concept within this book, I believe it and, I discuss it within the context of my university course.

HEAT SHRINK MATERIAL: Heat shrink materials are thin plastic sheets and tubes that shrink when exposed to hot air or direct heat. These can be used to adhere parts together, secure tubing with a flexible joint or cover large or small surfaces with a strong, tightly stretched surface.

IDEA: An idea is just that, an idea. In inventing, it is a moment of thought with no real substance, except that granted to it by the inventor. An idea may occur for a product, service, or business. An idea is the first step from which a concept is built. Ideas are the basis of all inventions. Ideas can come to you in various ways and at the strangest of times. Keep them to yourself until you have a chance to document them with a witness. Ideas are extremely fragile creatures that need to be nourished and supported or else they will wither and die. Never assume an idea is not original until you are proven wrong by evidence of its prior existence. Even then, ideas can be reconfigured to modify existing concepts and products. Many great ideas were spurred on by deficiencies found in similar existing technologies.

IDEA/CONCEPT PADS: Idea/Concept Pads are single sheets of paper used to work on ideas at odd times and places. I have developed the BIDS (Basic Idea Development Sheet) System for just this purpose. These sheets can be witnessed and notarized to help prove "Reduction to Practice" of an invention. I find these sheets helpful in developing an idea from several angles at once (i.e., technical, promotional, manufacturing, etc.). You can keep the sheets in loose leafs to make a comprehensive overview of the idea as a project. Any information that you develop that you consider "bedrock information" about your idea should be transferred from your loose leaf into a safe or into a hardbound idea log book specific to that concept.

IDEA DEVELOPMENT: Taking a raw idea and fleshing out the parameters of its reality. This includes taking a realistic look at what it takes to turn the idea into a working and profitable product or business system. There are about twenty-four basic areas that must be looked at in order to see the real truth about any new idea. These areas are discussed in the Idea Development Check List.

INVENTION: An invention is the physical reality of an idea or concept. Inventions are real products, services, or business ventures that can be touched, seen, or used. An invention in the new business sense is at least a written business plan that outlines in detail the proposed business operation and market.

INVENTION MARKETING COMPANIES: Most of the companies that advertise to help inventors are a RIP OFF! Anything that an invention marketing company can do for you, you can do better for yourself with a little forethought and the facts from this book. Beware of any company that asks you for money in advance to work on developing little more than brochures or literature for your ideas. Find out, in writing, exactly what the company plans to do, how long it will take and what the costs. Some companies do exist that actually can help inventors. Ask for their credentials, references and past clients. Talk with several members of the company to get a concise overview of who they are and what they do. Be thorough in your investigation. If they are frauds, they may have had plenty of practice duping inventors! Check with the Attorney General's office for complaints or violations. Remember, this is your baby, you're entrusting them with. If they can't impress you with actual success stories, forget them!

INVENTOR IMAGE: This is the "face" an inventor develops to show the world at large. It includes your credentials package, your background and your visible personality, as you show it at trade shows, during media events and in general business. An inventor's image can blend with your company's image or it can be unique and radical. Think carefully about what type of image you want to project; once done, it is hard to change.

INVENTORS: Inventors are a rare breed without whom there would be no progress, no future, only a continuance of today. Inventors come from all walks of life, and, for many reasons, turn their time and talents to the pursuit of creating new technologies, both great and mundane. Inventors, especially independent inventors, often have an obsession to create combined with a single-minded resolve to be no man's employee. Albert Einstein said, "I am a horse for single harness." Inventors vary in education and earnings, yet their brotherhood is as strong as any dues-paying union. Inventors invent for many reasons, including necessity, war and greed. But the reasons why an inventor invents usually have nothing to do with their personal situation. Most inventors, to paraphrase the words of Alexander Graham Bell, "can no more help inventing than they can help thinking or breathing." Inventors are seen in many different lights. To some, inventors are godlike people with a gift for creation and thought on a higher plane. To others, inventors are con men who don't deserve the time of day, because they're little more than daydreamers. Most inventors are a little of both. Today, inventors must be promoters of their ideas, because they are the original true believers. They must be public speakers and sales people to get others to believe in their ideas. They must be technocrats and project managers capable of organizing skills on multiple and complex levels. They must be financial managers and estimators capable of developing business plans. Lastly, they must be leaders, capable of instilling confidence in their actions and the future of their ideas.

INVENTOR'S LOGBOOK: The inventor's logbook is a book, preferably hardbound, where an inventor logs all his new ideas. Updated information on an idea should be put into the same book. Each entry should be witnessed and dated. Multiple ideas can be put in one logbook, or it can be specific to a single idea. This book should be kept in a safe place.

LETTERS OF RECOMMENDATION: Letters of recommendation are letters received from contracts, end users, supporters, etc., who sing your praise or the praise of your invention. These are a very important part of the overall credentials package that you can develop. These letters should be sought at every opportunity. They should be collected in a master display book for use when interfacing with anyone who has an interest in your activities.

LINE DRAWINGS: Line drawings are black and white two and three-dimensional drawings that represent a product. Line drawings are used extensively in product development because they are less expensive than renderings, while still being very concise. Line drawings are used on product specifications sheets. Line drawings include cut-aways, exploded views, cross sections, diagrams and schematics. Most inventors produce original line drawings as their first conceptual art of a product idea.

MANUFACTURERS: Manufacturers are companies that produce any item or component part. Manufacturers are the best place to prototype parts because they are the original source. They will be able to quote the lowest production costs. Many manufacturers have research divisions that can help you to develop an idea if your idea will use a large number of manufactured parts. Manufacturers are usually in touch with the latest technology in an industry. They are often a prime source of research data while developing an invention from the conceptual to the prototype stage. If you can interest a manufacturer in the invention, a marketing deal or outright purchase of the invention may be in the future if the manufacturer can be made to realize the potential of the invention.

MANUFACTURING PROCESSES (Types): There are many manufacturing processes available to construct parts. A manufacturing process is any process that changes the form or structure of a material to create a new product part. These processes include machining, stamping, coating, molding, chemical application and heat treatments to change or enhance properties, forging, plating, parts assembly via bonding, laminating or welding, etc. You should become familiar with processes that are involved in the production of your product concepts. Almost every type of process has a job specialty and association linked with its function. Contact these associations for basic information on the specialized processes or talk with a design engineer to find out what processes you should look into.

MARKET: The Edison Philosophy of Invention states that "Market is EVERY-THING!" A market is composed of the places where your product will be sold and the people to whom it will be offered. Without a market, you are inventing for yourself. This is known as creating a "vanity invention," a project that has no real market except your own enjoyment or edification.

MARKETING: Marketing is the efforts undertaken to sell your product image to the end user. This is different than sales, where the actual product is sold directly to a customer. Marketing is winning the hearts and minds of the end users before they get to the point of sale. Marketing is setting up distribution and service so the customer has a good comfort level with your product. Marketing is the hype of and excitement for the product.

MEETING DISCLOSURE AGREEMENT (MDA): The MDA (Meeting Disclosure Agreement) is a document that establishes that a formal meeting took place and who was present at the meeting. The MDA also establishes what each party's rights were in respect to the idea at the end of the meeting. This documentation allows an inventor the chance to lock in a manufacturer on a specific idea when it is shown to them. The MDA should only be used at meetings taking place at the headquarters of the individual, or company, you are dealing with. This is due to the "put up or shut up" nature of the demands of the MDA. MDAs are explained under the secrecy protocol outlined in chapter six.

MOLDS (Types): Molds are used to create parts for prototypes and production products. There are many types of molds (e.g., vacuum form molds, casting molds, injection molds, etc.) for the production of parts made from varied materials including urethane, plastics, etc. The molds can be constructed out of various materials (e.g., foam molds, clay molds, wood molds, steel or aluminum molds), depending upon their intended purpose and the material to be pumped into the mold. RTV (Room Temperature Vulcanized) Rubber Compound is a common and versatile molding material for the inventor. Once a mold is constructed from RTV, it can be filled with epoxy or polyester resins, with or without fillers, to produce high-quality prototype parts. Mold production can range from very simple techniques to very expensive, time-consuming CAD/CAM processes. A professional mold-maker is the best source for information on the type of mold needed for any particular job.

MONEY BROKERS: Money brokers are middlemen who have contacts and take a percentage or fee for getting you together with money people. Some money brokers are legitimate and others are complete frauds. Beware anyone who wants you to pay them for services in advance. Almost all real brokers will take a percentage of capital raised. It should not be more than 5 to 10 percent of the total. Make the financial people with whom you are dealing aware of this aspect of the deal. It must be figured into your costs so that you don't get shortchanged on the development capital. Also, many investors will talk the brokers into stock options or other deferred payments to try to lower their upfront spending to the bare essentials, while making sure the invention project receives the maximum amount of capital sought.

NETWORKING: Networking is an art and a science. It is the ability to make contacts in many fields and cultivate those contacts into a useful resource for business and pleasure. Networking is as old as business itself, but has not been recognized as an important business resource until recent years. Anyone can develop a good network, but using it effectively and keeping it going requires a lot of time and effort.

NON-DISCLOSURE AGREEMENT (NDA): This is an agreement that you can use with any person you show an idea concept. The NDA or secrecy agreement as it is commonly known states that the person signing will not disclose the information to anyone else without your permission. This type of agreement does not always fully protect you against piracy of your idea, but it gives you something to work with in a legal sense that will establish the fact that the idea was pirated. It also acts to document the people to whom the invention was shown. You should be wary of any person who is reluctant to sign a secrecy agreement before viewing an idea. The secrecy agreement works well in conjunction with the meeting disclosure agreement.

OPM: OPM stands for Other People's Money. You should use OPM whenever possible. OPM is the only money that will get you past most of the financial hurdles that you will face as an inventor. If you use YOM (Your Own Money) when you should be using OPM, you may find yourself in considerable financial jeopardy.

OVERVIEW: The overview, or pre-proposal is a document of any size that generically outlines a business or product for investment purposes. The purpose of the overview is to open lines of communication with investors without giving away the product concept or business idea. As a pre-proposal it can give as many details as the inventor sees fit to reveal to gather investor interest. The pre-proposal approach is most often used when a patent has not been applied for yet or the idea is unpatentable and very easily pirated.

PATENT: A patent is a license from the government that allows the holder to prevent others from making, selling, or using his invention without compensation. The law calls patents "Intellectual Property" belonging to the inventor. A patent may be sold for profit or licensed to others for payments called royalties.

PATENT AGENTS: Patent agents must have all the same qualifications as patent attorneys, except they are not licensed to litigate any formal court proceedings in the event the patent is disputed in court or hand other legal remedies that may be called upon by the patent process.

PATENT APPLICATION: A patent application is the basic paperwork sent to the Patent and Trademark office to start a patent file with your name and invention. This should be done with and by a patent attorney! Doing it by yourself is foolish in my opinion, unless you happen to be a patent attorney.

PATENT ARTWORK: Patent artwork is a very specific set of drawing parameters under which every patent's artwork must be prepared. These are usually done by special patent draftsmen who do nothing but patent applications for a living. Patents are regularly rejected for unacceptable artwork, so it pays to have a pro do the art for your concept. Most patent attorneys have a patent artist that they regularly use.

PATENTS: Stacy V. Jones, patent columnist for The New York Times, once said, "A patent is society's reward for ingenuity." The patent system, created in 1790 by our first president, George Washington, is a concept borrowed from Europe and refined to allow the common man a chance to take advantage of his moment of inspiration. For the first time in history, the patent bill gave the inventor the intrinsic right to profit from his invention. The law calls patents "Intellectual Property" that can be sold in whole or in part, or can be licensed for use by others in return for payments called royalties.

PATENT SEARCH: The patent search is a systematic search of the records of the U.S. Patent Office to determine what other patents exist that may interfere with your ability to patent your idea. It is advisable to conduct a search through your patent attorney prior to actually paying for a full-blown application. A search usually costs about twenty percent of the patent fee you will have to pay for an actual patent to be issued. You can do your own preliminary patent search at most good public libraries.

PLANT PATENT: A plant patent is a patent that can be gotten for any newly invented, asexually reproduced plant. Various other new plant and animal life that is created in the lab is also capable of being patented. The bounds of patent law are continually being stretched to cover the advances in science.

PLASTIC (Types): There are many different types of plastics. Plastics are man-made (artificial) substances. Plastic comes in rods, sheets, tubes, blocks, etc. Each plastic has different qualities that make it well-suited for different uses. Plastic is a versatile material for many prototype and production applications. I suggest that a basic assortment of plastics be kept on hand in the workshop to help develop new ideas. Many "finds" are plastic (i.e., containers from many household items). These parts can often become the basic framework for many simple prototypes.

PRESENTATION ARTWORK: Presentation artwork is artwork of various types that you use to illustrate your concept. Presentation art should be professionally done. It can range from cut-away art of the guts of an invention to picture the invention in its final form being used by the end consumer.

PRESS COVERAGE: Press Coverage is any time your name or associated information (company name, product name, etc.) appears in any type of media. This includes newspapers, magazines, radio interviews, TV, etc. The press can play games with you or they can be your greatest asset, depending upon many factors. Always play it straight with the press and they can't hurt you. If you mislead them, you may find you'll regret it in the future. Making friends with the media is the best path to follow.

PRODUCT: A product is something you actually sell to the end users. It is the final stage in the development of an idea into an invention. If you sell your idea or invention at another stage of its development, then it can be considered your final product.

PRODUCT IMAGE: Product image is the "face" the actual invention has for its end users. The product image must portray the product in a specific light that the manufacturer wants the end user to perceive. If the product is a toy, it should be seen as fun. If it is a weapon, it should be seen as menacing and effective. If it is a household item, it should be seen as useful, labor-saving and easy to use. Developing a good product image can be hard, but once accomplished it can last forever, barring any radical bad press.

PROMOTION: Promotion is the effort undertaken to attain publicity and to get the name of the product and inventor known to as wide an audience as possible. Promotion can be very specific to a select group of end users or can be very general. Promotion often involves events that are structured to gain media attention. You will want to take every opportunity to promote yourself and your invention.

PROTOTYPE: A prototype is any form of an invention, any physical manifestation of the idea that is not the final product. Some prototypes that are prepared for presentations look like the final product but don't work worth a damn. Other prototypes that have been prepared for research and development don't look at all like the final product, but function like it. Inventions often are sold to manufacturers at the prototype stage.

PROTOTYPE PARTS COLLECTION: This is an inventor's grab bag of parts and data relating to those parts. This is a prime source of new product ideas. By having samples of various products and materials to experiment with, you can often build new product ideas with off-the-shelf parts. These parts will inspire different combinations and ideas for further combinations or custom parts made from the materials. Use the Request for Parts/Info letter included in chapter x to start a major prototype parts collection.

PUBLICITY: Publicity is the media activity that brings you, your company or your product to the attention of the public. Publicity can be good or bad, depending upon what is said or written. Bad verbal publicity is better than bad printed publicity, because people tend to forget the content and remember the product or inventor. Favorable printed publicity is the best to be hoped for because it is easy to circulate and will stay the same forever. You can get publicity in many ways, such as by accident, by planned press releases, by paid advertising, etc. In today's video society, you should try to get some televised exposure to promote your name and product.

RAISING CAPITAL: An art form that encompasses every phase of contact and communication with the overall effort directed at having an investment source put money into your project. You can raise capital from friends, family, strangers and institution. It can be done on an individual level and on a group level.

REDUCTION TO PRACTICE: Reduction to practice is a term used by the Patent Office to mean the inventor's continuing efforts to take his idea from a concept to a working, saleable invention. The ability to prove "reduction to practice" efforts is the main reason for complete and accurate documentation of an inventor's efforts in the development of his concept/device.

RESEARCH GRANTS: Money is available to inventors from various sources for the purpose of developing your product. These monies don't have to be repaid (in most cases), but if your research results are lousy and your product doesn't pan out, you may have some tough questions to answer.

RESOURCES: Resources are any physical material, person or piece of information that can help an inventor. Development of an individual resource data bank is crucial. I find the best method is to clip or photocopy articles from their source. Then put each article or piece of data in its own clear plastic page protector. These are then kept in looseleaf binders. This system is easy to reference and update as needed. Reading through your data resource book on a regular basis will help stimulate ideas from the vast cross-referencing your will do with the information in the book.

ROYALTIES: Royalties are the monies paid to an inventor for the sale, license or assignment of the patent rights to another individual or company.

SBA: See Small Business Administration.

SEED MONEY: Seed money is the initial capital that is generated to get a project off the ground. Most seed capital comes from the inventor and a close circle of family and friends.

SELF-PROMOTION: Self-promotion is your efforts in promoting yourself and your invention. Self-promotion is a never-ending process that is not for the shy or meek at heart. Self-promotion can make you a celebrity, if you're good at it. More importantly, it may sell lots of your products to investors, manufacturers and the general public. People believe in people, not products. The personal touch is what self-promotion is all about. Self-promotion includes writing articles, creating video spots, creating press events and generally getting your face and product out in front of the general public.

SERENDIPITY: The word was coined in 1754 by Horace Walpole to denote the faculty of findings things not sought for, the art of being able to profit from the unexpected. In a letter to a friend, Walpole explained that he had formed the word from the title of a fairy story, "The Three Princes of Serendip." It seems that the princes of the title were always making discoveries of things they were not in quest of. This realization by accident has played an important part of many of history's most important inventions. Other terms have been coined to express the same concept. One of the most recent and expressive is "synergy," or the mixing of unrelated forces to create a new direction for action. Whatever it is called, inventors have always used, and always will use, this powerful creative force to shape the future.

SMALL BUSINESS ADMINISTRATION (SBA): The Small Business Administration is part of the U.S. Department of Commerce. This agency was designed to help small business get finances and give them guidance. In reality, it can do very little for your financial needs. Sometimes an SBA loan can be arranged, but it is rare in the case of an invention.

STEPPING-STONE TECHNIQUES: Stepping-stone techniques are the actions that you can take to move from one level of your career to the next. These techniques involve the use of one current situation or ability to act as a stepping-stone to the next situation or ability. You can use many different phases of your project's development to step into other areas that are income producing careers. See chapter x for more about Stepping-Stone techniques.

THE THOMAS REGISTER™: The Thomas Register is a set of 23 books that is a major data resource for inventors. It is a compendium of the nation's industrial resources. Almost every material or service that is available from industrial America is listed in the Thomas Register. I recommend that you buy a set (about $280) or locate a set at the public library. Most people find that just leafing through the books inspire ideas for new inventions based upon the incredibly diverse technologies that can be found within the covers. The Register is also a basic resource for getting printed information on any industrial process. Many manufacturers have extensive printed information on their area of expertise available at no charge. And most of these companies have toll-free 800 numbers to facilitate inquiries. Many manufacturers will supply, upon request, samples of many of their products. The Thomas Register is a great resource for collecting sample parts for a prototype parts collection.

TIME LINES: Time lines are linear diagrams of the time flow in relation to how a project will be accomplished. They can be graphic or be a simple spreadsheet. They can be of several configurations and complexities. Investors appreciate time lines, because they indicate when their money will be spent in relation to when profits are estimated. Time lines are the easiest of estimates and projections to do, but are rarely as accurate as you might wish they were. Basic time lines should reflect worst-case scenario. This gives a project leeway and insures a realistic time frame.

TRACK RECORD: A track record is simply your credentials that you have attained, which includes your background as it relates to your present endeavor, prior inventions, current work on an invention, a resume, any letters of reference, published articles, accomplishments and experience.

UTILITY PATENT: A utility patent is a patent on any device based upon the function of the device, not its shape or appearance. The Utility Patent has a life of 17 years from its date of issue. A utility patent is the basic patent that everyone thinks of when using the term patent.

VENDORS: Vendors are sources for manufactured parts. Sometimes vendors are manufacturers, but this doesn't necessarily have to be the case. A vendor may be a middleman or distributor for a product that is not available through any other source. Some vendors are exclusive representatives of companies that do not deal with the public or are located in other countries.

WITNESS STAMP: A witness stamp is a stamp that goes on all documentation of your ideas for the purpose of having someone date and witness your idea for maximum protection.

Appendix III

Other Forms and Items of Interest to the Inventor

BASIC INVENTOR'S DISCLOSURE STAMP DESIGN

Copyright 1989 Robert J. Gold and GoldMind Associates

The two basic designs for inventor disclosure stamps are illustrated on this page. The first design is for a disclosure to a witness. The second design is for a disclosure to a witness and a notory. Every idea / concept should be written down on paper. Each page of an idea disclosure should have one of these stamps on the front or rear of the page. The stamp should then be filled in and signed by the inventor and his witness. The witness should be someone the inventor knows will be available in the future if the inventor needs in-person verification of the witness procedure.

Basic Inventor's Disclosure Stamp (Sample Design)

I, (INVENTOR'S NAME), SS# 123-45-6789, do hereby declare that the invention described on this page is solely my creation, conceived on_____19_____.

Signed_____ Date_____

I, _____(PRINT IN WITNESS NAME)_____, do hereby declare that (INVENTOR'S NAME) showed me this invention disclosure document on _____19_____. I have reviewed the invention and fully understand its operation, function and purpose. I have signed my name below as witness to the creation of this invention concept.

Signed_____ Date_____

Notorized Inventor's Disclosure Stamp (Sample Design)

I, (INVENTOR'S NAME), SS# 123-45-6789, do hereby declare that the invention described on this page is solely my creation, conceived on_____19_____.

Signed_____ Date_____

I, _____(PRINT IN WITNESS NAME)_____, do hereby declare that (INVENTOR'S NAME) showed me this invention disclosure document on _____19_____. I have reviewed the invention and fully understand its operation, function and purpose. I have signed my name below as witness to the creation of this invention concept.

Signed_____ Date_____

I, __(PRINT IN NOTORY'S NAME)_____, a sworn and active Notory Public for the State of ____(PRINT IN STATE NAME)_____, do hereby swear that on _____19_____ ____(PRINT IN WITNESS or INVENTOR NAME)_____ appeared before me and signed this invention disclosure form. My commission expires on_____19_____.

Signed_____ Date_____

PRODUCT MEETING DISCLOSURE FORM

MEETING DATE:_____ TIME:_____PAGE ___OF____ CODE:_____

DISCLOSURE TO(Company):_____

ADDRESS: _____Zip_____
INDIVIDUALS PRESENT AT MEETING:

_____

SIGN NAME   PRINT NAME & TITLE   COMPANY

_____

SIGN NAME   PRINT NAME & TITLE   COMPANY

_____

SIGN NAME   PRINT NAME & TITLE   COMPANY

I,_____, do hereby acknowledge that the product concept known as:

(name and short description of product concept/application)

which was revealed to me today by_____ (hereinafter known as the Inventor) is **not** a product concept currently under any stage of development by my firm. I acknowledge that a full product description with technical and marketing information was revealed to me and the members of my firm (listed above)under the terms of a secrecy agreement signed prior to the information being revealed. I further acknowledge that the reason the product concept was revealed to me and my firm was for the purpose of our evaluation of the idea in respect to possible Investment, Purchase or License for commerical use and profit. My signature on the line below indicates my acceptance of all terms of the secrecy agreement and acknowledgement of the idea as an original concept of The Inventor.

signature _____ Drivers Lic. Number or S.S. #_____ Date _____

Witness signature _____ Drivers Lic. Number or S.S. #_____ Date _____

=== OR ===

I, _____(hereinafter known as the Inventor), do hereby acknowledge that the product concept known as:

(name and short description of Invention / product concept and application)

which I revealed today to: _____

is a product concept already under development by his/her firm. This has been demonstrated to me by the immediate presentation of materials and/or documentation that validates the existance of prior work on a concept or product that is similiar in application and capability to my product concept. The Inventor acknowledges that the above mentioned individual/Company is not bound by the secrecy agreement signed in connection with this product concept and that no remuneration or compensation is due to the Inventor from the above mentioned person or company in respect to this product idea.

_____   _____
The Inventor   **Date**

POWER STAF

"IT IS HIGH TECHNOLOGY APPLIED TO REAL WORLD PROBLEMS."
— *Survival Guide Magazine*

"THE POWER STAF IS A NEW WEAPON FOR USE IN CROWD CONTROL SITUATIONS, AND FOR THE EFFECTIVE SUBJUGATION OF VIOLENT CRIMINALS IN SITUATIONS WHERE THE USE OF FIREARMS WOULD BE INAPPROPRIATE."
— *Law Enforcement Technology International Magazine*

"...IT PACKS MORE PUNCH THAN MOHAMMAD ALI IN HIS PRIME, HAS A LONGER REACH, AND CAN JAB FOUR TIMES PER SECOND."
— *The Atlanta Constitution*

"...EQUIPPED WITH POWER STAF, OFFICERS ARE LESS VULNERABLE, MULTIPLE ADVERSARIES LESS FORMIDABLE, AND SITUATIONS MORE CONTROLLABLE."
— *International Law Enforcement Magazine*

KINETIC ARMAMENT-1 (KA-1)

The **POWER STAF**® **KA-1**™ is a multiple discharge pneumatic piston impact weapon™ designed for close range confrontations. This means it fires a piston shaft driven by high pressure compressed air. The air can be supplied by an integral **Mini-Tank**™ or shoulder carried **Riot Pac**™.

When the trigger is pulled, a burst of air drives the **KA-1**™ piston shaft forward. The shaft extends out to 18 inches and retracts back into the barrel in .250 of a second. When the shaft strikes a target it delivers the full kinetic energy of its moving mass and the high pressure air behind it. That translates into an incredibly swift, hard hitting linear blow that can be delivered with pin point accuracy against an aggressor.

The **POWER STAF**® **KA-1**™ can release single shots or full auto bursts as the operator deems necessary. With proper training the operator can defend against offenders up to 6 feet away from his body. This gives the user a 12-foot diameter of control. A full training course is

available that teaches officers to use the unit effectively in offensive, defensive, arrest and crowd control situations.

Amazingly, the **POWER STAF**® **KA-1**™ doesn't have to strike an offender to prove itself effective. The sight of its flashing piston shaft, coupled with its abrupt noise in a **"Deterrent Burst"** will make even the most determined opponent reluctant to engage in a physical confrontation with an officer equipped with the **POWER STAF**® **KA-1**™.

When physical force is needed, the impact that is delivered to the target is humane, controllable and precise. The Fluid Shock Wave™ Impact Head delivers two separate impacts micro seconds apart. This induces momentary localized muscle dysfunction that is characterized by weakness in the area and loss of motor coordination. It allows an officer to control an offender without electrical shock, chemicals or random physical violence.

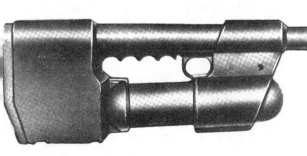

When the situation calls for an effective, professional response to a wide range of law enforcement situations...reach for the Power Staf System.

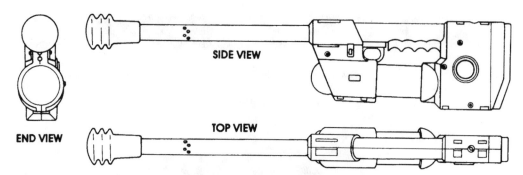

SIDE VIEW

TOP VIEW

END VIEW

SPECS: POWER STAF KA-1

- SIZE: 34 INCHES • WEIGHT: 6.8 LBS.
- SHAFT EXTENSION: 18 INCHES
- SHAFT SPEED: APPROX. 30 FT/SEC.
- SHAFT ENERGY: APPROX. 25 FT/LB. FOR .5 SECONDS AT IMPACT
- IMPACT HEAD: MULTI-TIER FLUID SHOCK WAVE DESIGN
- BARREL TYPE: PNEUMATIC PISTON IMPACT WEAPON
- BARREL CONSTRUCTION: HIGH STRENGTH FIBER WRAPPED COMPOSITE

- POWER SOURCE: COMPRESSED AIR MINI-TANK (2000 PSI)
- MINI-TANK CONSTRUCTION: NON-SHATTERABLE SPUN STEEL
- NUMBER OF ACTIVATIONS ON A SINGLE CHARGE: 30
- RECHARGE CAPABILITY: FROM SCUBA TANK, COMPRESSOR, SCOTT AIR PACK
- MINI-TANK RECHARGE TIME: 15 SECONDS (OFF SCUBA ADAPTOR)

All specifications subject to change without notice

THE POWER STAF SYSTEM

- The POWER STAF Basic Unit comes standard with the KA-1 barrel. The Basic Unit can accept all other barrels in the POWER STAF SYSTEM.

- Other barrels in the POWER STAF SYSTEM that will be available soon:
  (A) LG-1 (Launchable Stun Grenade-1) Counter Terrorism/Hostage Rescue
  (B) PX-1 (Power Axe-1) Emergency Access Tool for Police & Firefighters
  (C) MOB-1 (Multiple Ordnance Barrel-1) Counter Terrorism/Hostage Rescue
  (D) CS-1 (Chem-Shell-1) Riot Control for Police, Corrections and Military

- POWER STAF RS-II Recharge Stations house built in 3000 psi compressors with full recharging capability for Mini-Tanks, Scuba Tanks, Scott Air Packs and Riot Pacs. The RS-II has storage capacity for 12 POWER STAF KA-1 units and spare parts.

- The Power Staf is virtually maintenance free and comes with a one-year warranty on parts and labor.

- A full Training Program is available via on-site instructors, video tape and in manual format. All techniques and tactics are easy to learn, safe to use and court defensible.

- POWER STAF, Inc. maintains an Advisory Board of Law Enforcement, Legal and Medical Professionals that are always available to any purchaser for information and referral.

ADVANTAGES OF THE POWER STAF KA-1

- The KA-1 works on simple, safe compressed air. No munitions, chemicals or electricity.

- The KA-1 is capable of delivering a stunning force independent of the physical capability of the user.

- Its "Deterrent Burst" capability gives an officer a non-contact, low liability alternative in situations where there is a need to show total command of a situation.

- The POWER STAF KA-1 can be used in any climate conditions. Its state-of-the-art construction will give many years of service even under tough street conditions.

- The POWER STAF KA-1 has the instant response of a gun combined with the less than lethal effectiveness of a night stick impact.

DISTRIBUTED BY

POWER STAF ®

U.S. & Foreign
Patents Pending

© 1987 POWER STAF INC.

NETWORKING CONTACT SHEET

Property of_____

Date:_____

Page_____ of _____   Date 1st Started:_____   Contact Code:_____

NAME:_____TITLE:_____

COMPANY AGENCY:_____

WORK ADDRESS:_____

CITY, STATE &ZIP:_____

TELEPHONE: (_____)_____EXT.:_____

FAX: (_____)_____AUX. No._____

TELEX: _____COMPUTER LINK UP INFO:_____

HOME ADDRESS:_____

CITY, STATE & ZIP:_____

TELEPHONE: (_____)_____EXT.:_____

FAX: (_____)_____AUX. No.:_____

1st CONTACT:

DATE:_____EVENT:_____

INTRODUCED VIA:_____

LOCATION OF 1st CONTACT:_____

1st CONTACT: [ ] IN PERSON [ ] MAIL [ ] PHONE [ ] TELEX [ ] FAX
[ ] OTHER:_____

1st MEETING OVERVIEW: [ ] EXCELLENT [ ] GOOD [ ] FAIR [ ] BAD

REASON FOR 1st CONTACT RAPPORT:_____
_____

DESCRIPTION : [ ] MALE [ ] FEMALE AGE:_____ HAIR:____EYES:____ WT:_____

ADDITIONAL PHYSICAL DESCRIPTION:_____

BUSINESS INFO: TYPE OF BUSINESS OR JOB:_____

SPECIAL CONTACTS:_____
_____

DISCOUNTS, PERKS OR INFO AVAILABLE THRU CONTACT: _____
_____

FEATURES OF 1st CONTACT/MEETING: _____
_____

STATUS OF PERSON: [ ] SINGLE [ ] MARRIED [ ] DIVORCED [ ] WIDOWED
[ ] SINGLE PARENT [ ] OTHER:_____

CHILDREN: No._____ AGES_____ NAMES:_____

CONTACT BIRTHDAY:_____ FAVORITE PASTTIMES:_____

NICKNAME:_____SPOUSE NAME:_____

CONTACT NAME:_____

Page_____ of _____   Date 1st Started:_____   Contact Code:_____

DATE   NOTES

____   _____
____   _____
____   _____
____   _____
____   _____
____   _____
____   _____
____   _____
____   _____
____   _____
____   _____
____   _____
____   _____
____   _____
____   _____
____   _____
____   _____
____   _____
____   _____
____   _____
____   _____
____   _____
____   _____
____   _____
____   _____
____   _____
____   _____
____   _____
____   _____
____   _____
____   _____
____   _____
____   _____
____   _____

CONTACT: R.J. Gold or Mona Zimmerman   IMMEDIATE
         Author's National Service Bureau   RELEASE
         PO Box 201601, Austin, TX 7820-1601
         (512) 345-7531   FAX (512) 467-9403   MAY 1, 1991

NEW AUTHOR'S PROMOTION SERVICE: NATIONAL BOOK MARKETING WITHOUT LEAVING HOME!

New and self-published authors can now promote, market and sell their books from the comfort of their home or office. Author's National Service Bureau (ANSB) announces the opening of it's unique service that takes the majority of work out of marketing and selling a new or self-published book. ANSB is the first service company that publicizes, promotes and actively schedules authors on radio talk shows that allow guest interviews by telephone.

Most of the 50001 radio stations across the U.S. require guests to appear in person for talk show interviews. The time, travel and expense involved with in-person interviews has always been a problem for publishers and authors with limited budgets. To solve this problem, ANSB works with the 9001 stations nationwide which allow guests to appear on their programs via telephone. ANSB's service is unique because it is unlike other promotional methods which simply advertise talk show guests to stations. ANSB uses full page ads in their monthly magazine *TALK OUT* combined with active telephone contact of 500 of the 9001 stations each month. ANSB personnel aggressively promote authors to these key stations and helps coordinate booking arrangements leaving more time free for authors to pursue their normal schedules.

Author's National Service Bureau also offers order fulfillment services, including major credit card acceptance using its inhouse 800 number. This allows authors to book radio appearances, promote their books and fill orders through one convenient, low priced service. For additional information on Author's National Service Bureau, contact them on their toll free number 1-800-TALK OUT (1-800-825-5688).

-30-

Practical Inventing Workshop

Presented by GoldMind Associates

at the

UNIVERSITY OF TEXAS, INFORMAL CLASSES

CERTIFICATE OF COMPLETION

THIS IS TO CERTIFY THAT FROM

19 ___ TO ___ 19 ___

ATTENDED THE PRACTICAL INVENTING WORKSHOP.
THE ABOVE NAMED STUDENT RECEIVED INSTRUCTION IN ALL MAIN
AREAS OF THE PRACTICAL INVENTING DICIPLINES INCLUDING:
* INVENTOR PSYCHOLOGY & MINDSET * MULTI-LEVEL BRAINSTORMING *
*NETWORKING, RAISING CAPITAL, MARKETING & PROMOTION *
* CONCEPT DEVELOPMENT, PROTECTION AND DOCUMENTATION *
* THE BASIC PATENT SYSTEM AND PATENT ATTORNEYS *
* PROTOTYPE TOOLS AND DEVELOPMENT TECHNIQUES *

_____
Robert J. Gold,   Instructor

Index